Miraculous Simplicity

Miraculous Simplicity

Essays on R. S. Thomas

Edited by

William V. Davis

The University of Arkansas Press
Fayetteville 1993

97 96 95 94 93   5 4 3 2 1

This book was designed by Gail Carter using Lilith and Bembo typefaces.

The paper used in this publication meets the minimum requirements of the
American National Standard for Permanence of Paper for Printed Library
Materials Z39.48-1984. ⊚

Library of Congress Cataloging-in-Publication Data

Miraculous simplicity: essays on R. S. Thomas / [compiled by] William V. Davis.
    p.   cm.
    Includes bibliographical references.
    ISBN 1-55728-265-X (cloth)
        1. Thomas, R. S. (Ronald Stuart), 1913-   —Criticism and interpretation.
I. Thomas, R. S. (Ronald Stuart), 1913-   II. Davis, William Virgil, 1940-
PR6039.H618Z77   1993
832'.914—dc20

                                                        92-24609
                                                        CIP

For Carol and Bill

Acknowledgments

For permission to reprint essays included in this collection I would like to thank the following:

R. S. Thomas for the line from "Autumn on the Land" (*Song at the Year's Turning: Poems 1942–1954* [London: Rupert Hart-Davis, 1955]) and the sentence from "Words and the Poet," *R. S. Thomas: Selected Prose,* Sandra Anstey, editor [Bridgend: Poetry Wales Press, 1986] used as epigraphs; for his autobiographical essay from *Contemporary Authors;* and for his interview from *Planet* with Ned Thomas and John Barnie.

John McKernan, editor of *The Little Review,* for the essay by Brian Morris.

R. George Thomas and Greg Hill, editor of *The Anglo-Welsh Review,* for the essay by R. George Thomas.

Critical Quarterly for the essay by J. D. Vicary.

Planet and Robert Nisbet for his essay.

South Central Review for the essay by William V. Davis.

Religion and Literature and Donald Davie for his essay.

ELH and The Johns Hopkins University Press for the essay by Vimala Herman.

Belinda Humfrey for her essay from the *Anglo-Welsh Review.*

Julian Gitzen for his essay from *Contemporary Poetry.*

Tony Brown and *The Powys Review* for his essay.

Renascence for the essay by Patrick Deane.

"A man, a field, silence—what is there to say?"

"Art is not simple, and yet about so much of the best,
whether in painting, poetry or music,
there is a kind of miraculous simplicity."

—R. S. Thomas

Contents

Preface

In the summer of 1983, at the beginning of a sabbatical, my family and I moved to Wales. We had six months before I was to take up a Fulbright Lectureship at the University of Copenhagen, and we planned to spend this time in Wales seeing something of this native land of our name. I planned to work on my own poetry. With the help of a friend, we rented a semidetached house called Sŵn y Môr, "Sound of the Sea," at the end of a rocky-roaded lane in Southgate, near Swansea, on the Gower peninsula. From our front gate it was only a short walk over the moors to Pobbles beach and Three Cliffs Bay, where the windswept ruins of Pennard Castle still guarded the silt-filled estuary. Equidistant in the other direction, along the high cliffs above the Bristol Channel, was "The Garth," Vernon Watkins's house, where Dylan Thomas often visited.

I had hardly heard of R. S. Thomas, knew only a few of his poems from anthologies. But everyone in Wales, it seemed, knew him, or of him, and knew his work. Everywhere we went, at the slightest mention of any interest in poetry, immediately, his name came up. I began to read Thomas systematically, and quickly abandoned everything else to write on him.

Back home in late 1984, I began to seek out the few readers here who had heard of Thomas or knew his work. Miller Williams, director of the University of Arkansas Press, was interested in Thomas and had acquired the rights to reprint his poems in this country. We discussed the possibility of a conference devoted to Thomas (which never materialized); and then, finally, the possibility of a collection of essays on him. Such a book would complement the American edition of the *Poems of R. S. Thomas* published by Arkansas in 1985 and provide a critical base for the rapidly growing interest in Thomas, both in this country and abroad. Thus, this book was born.

For the successful completion of this project I am indebted, first and foremost, to R. S. Thomas himself: for his poems which have so haunted the minds and imaginations of readers; for his kind support; and for giving me permission to reprint his autobiographical essay and the recent interview with him. I also want to thank each of my contributors, as well as the journals in which their essays first appeared, for permitting me to reprint these essays. And, in particular, I specifically want to thank Wynn Thomas and Jim Davies, who have written new essays especially for this collection; and Tony Brown, who revised and updated his essay and supplied me with photocopies of several essays hard to find here. Finally, without Miller Williams's encouragement and support none of this would have been possible. In short, many have worked together to make this book a reality. I am honored to have been one of them.

In editing these essays I have restricted myself to regularizing the spelling, punctuation, and the use of quotation marks to conform to American customs; regularizing the transliterations of Welsh names and places (primarily Prytherch and Llŷn); adding (or removing) commas for the sake of sense, or, in sequences, to follow American convention; and revising obvious misprints. In essays that contain footnotes, I have reproduced them as they appear in the original; however, when full bibliographical information was not included in the original, I have added it.

WVD

December 31, 1991

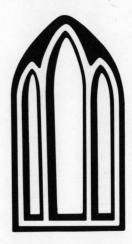

R. S. Thomas

Autobiographical Essay

*Reprinted from Contemporary Authors: Autobiographical Series, 4 (1986): 301–13.

Cardiff, 1913. Pain, and a woman bearing it; the child, too, but only half-aware. A difficult birth; the child too large. Then meningitis; the photographs show one only half-sane. All forgotten. How far back can one remember? I am on the floor by a door. The nursemaid opens or closes it too suddenly. Next I am on someone's lap with adults fussing about me. "It's ridiculous. You can't possibly remember as far back as that." But why shouldn't one remember a dislocation? In any case childhood is composed of memories. My father was a sailor. We followed him from port to port. We were in Liverpool for most of the first World War. There was gas in the bedroom. One night it sank to the size of a maggot. We learned next day that a zeppelin had approached. Liverpool was smells and ships' sirens and parks, the one escape from streets and houses into something like country. I bent to smell a flower and an insect went up my nose. Panic. The park resounded to my bellowing, as I sought my mother. There were ferries over the Mersey to the Wirral. As we disembarked at New Brighton, there would be a one-legged man climbing to a platform from which to plummet into the water for the coins thrown to him.

One day on the sands at Hoylake my father pointed southwest to where some blue-green hills loomed. "That's Wales," he said. Prophetic words. Sometimes when his boat was in, my mother would go down to the quay to dine with the other officers, and I would be taken and put to bed in my father's cabin. Occasional faces would appear at the door, inquiring whether I was all right. In between, to my horror, a cockroach or two would run across the floor. How can grown-ups realize what such things mean to a child?

At the end of the war my father found employment on the cross-channel boats between Caergybi (Holyhead) and Ireland. The day we arrived it was raining. I stared without interest through the taxi window upon the bleak, wet streets. But on the morrow, ah! The sun shone, the sky was blue, the sea bluer. I ventured out into a world whose like I had not seen before. I was supposed to be delicate. I had a reprieve from school on condition that I was taught at home. I learned to copy marks which was supposed to be a lesson in writing. Such tasks over, I was free to explore our new surroundings. I linked up with other children who taught me to go bird-nesting. The pale, china-like eggs lying in the mud's cup fascinated me.

When school could no longer be avoided, I went to a "refined" kindergarten, where I met, among others, two boys who lived with an elder sister and their widowed mother on the west coast about two miles out of town. Their house, Bryn Awel, became the place I loved most to go to with the sea wind blowing around it, secret tunnels through the gorse bushes and a view of the Welsh mountains from the upstairs windows. Sometimes I would stay the night there, and in the morning, before anybody was up, I would steal to the window and stare out over the fields at the sea, gray and cold in the dawn light. It was this family who taught me the joys of Guy Fawkes' night. Len, a year older than I, and Colin, the same age, would spend much time beforehand dragging in dead gorse to make a bonfire, and on the evening of the fifth I would arrive to help to put the finishing touches to the guy. My parents would arrive before dark with their fireworks to put with the others. After letting off a few we would light the fire and off it would go belching thousands of sparks into the air. The guy would ignite and collapse, and after the last and biggest rocket had gone hissing into the darkness, we would go indoors to play at bob-apple and ducking apple, until it was time to walk home with the gorse bushes in the hedges squeaking and fidgeting in the night wind.

When it came time for us to leave the kindergarten for the secondary school, none of us was up to standard, so two teachers had to be engaged to coach us. The one who taught us English was surprised at my vocabulary. Is it fair to criticize one's school in retrospect? Think what a Philistine I was, my head full of games and the open air. But I would opine that it was not a very good school. Caergybi was famous ornithologically for its cliff-nesting birds; but no one ever drew our attention to the fact, much less took us to see them. There was little interest in games and no coaching. It was also very un-Welsh in accordance with the climate of the day.

Once a year on St. David's Day there was a concert, and in the evening a Welsh play, when, to our surprise, we discovered that quite a few of the staff could speak Welsh. The number of Welsh speakers in Wales has declined disastrously since then; and yet there is more Welsh and Welsh history in the schools now. And there are secondary schools where Welsh is the medium of instruction, a thing unheard of, when I was a boy.

The school was coeducational. I was conscious of the girls and their attractions, but shy. The idea that I should walk out with one would have been dismissed by my mother anyway, and she was the boss. My father being much of the time at sea, it was to her I was answerable. As I reached the top-form, there were background debates as to what I was to do. My father, a former sailing-ship apprentice in the bad old days, was against the sea. My mother, early orphaned and brought up by a half brother who was a vicar, fancied the Church. Shy as I was, I offered no resistance. Is this also how God calls? The only change in my curriculum was the introduction of Greek into my course. I had already been reading Latin for years. I have suggested that it was a poor school; but in one thing I was fortunate. The headmaster, Derry Evans, was an excellent Latin teacher. It was surely to him I was indebted for passing the senior examination and proceeding to University to take a not very good degree in Classics. Little ability and a poor memory were responsible for the latter, not he. But the occupation with words and their meanings, and the translating from one language into another were surely laying the foundations of the practice of poetry that was ahead.

Before I was ready for University my father had had to give up the sea as a career owing to deafness. This deprived him of becoming captain of a ship and led to subsequent stomach trouble because of worry. Money was scarce at home, and I was entered for a Welsh Church scholarship, which I secured. (No one ever failed!) When the time to go up to college arrived, my mother accompanied me to Bangor, ostensibly to see that my lodgings were all right, but really loath to relax her hold until the last moment. Mercifully being a nonentity, I was unnoticed, and by evening she had departed, leaving me really on my own for the first time. The following day I registered, and late in the week found myself standing undanced with at the Freshman's Ball. This was actually the beginning of a series of unsuccessful flirtations. I knew little of girls, less of the so-called facts of life. Whoever agreed to consort with me very soon dropped me. But the heartbreaks were short-lived. There were other excitements: the first breath of freedom; the managing of my small allowance—those were the days when sixpence mattered; the attempt to get into the Rugby teams, although I never made it beyond the Second Fifteen, and I was in and out of that. But above all there was new territory to explore. One moonlight night I slipped out after supper down through the town and out along a track beside the stream that came from Felin Esgob. The way led beneath the trees. Tawny owls called; the water flashed and rippled under the full moon; a feeling of exhilaration at being out in the country at night, young and free, possessed me. Not that my mother had ever prevented me from going where I would by day. She only expressed occasional doubts about the advisability of my being so much alone. On this night I returned late to my lodgings to be let in by the landlady. If she thought about it at all, she, no doubt, took it for granted that I had been out with a girl.

I discovered the mountains. The peaks which had been visible thirty miles to the southeast of Caergybi were now within reach. I would catch a bus to a certain point, then, leaving the road, climb the nearest of them and walk along the ridges of Carnedd Llywelyn and Carnedd Dafydd and down into Bethesda to catch another bus back. The first time I did this and was confronted by the whole sweep of the mountains, I stood on a hillock and shouted "Mae hen wlad fy nhadau," the Welsh national anthem, for no reason I knew.

The second year the Church Hostel had been enlarged and there was room for twenty-one of us, so I left my lodgings and became a boarder. There was a pleasant little modern chapel with a sanctuary light burning. As the Warden was a high churchman, there was generally a smell of incense there. From the window of my bed-sitter I could look out over the Menai Strait to Ynys Môn, Anglesey. My approach to my course was quite wrong, but knowing that my parents would have difficulty in supporting me until I was twenty-three, my one thought was to pass my degree examination, so apart from much unintelligent swotting, I took such time off as I could to go my unproductive way. One sacrifice I made; I did not play cricket. I was moderately good at it, but it is a slow game and would have taken too much out of the summer term. But that worry about passing left its mark. For many years I had a recurring dream that I was about to face an examination and was not ready.

It was reported that a faith healer was to visit Bangor. With a mixture of vocational trust and youthful enthusiasm I persuaded my father to attend a session. Never had I prayed so hard. Kneeling in the Hostel chapel, I lifted my eyes time and again to the large wooden crucifix that hung before the altar. The evening arrived. The large marquee was full. My father's turn to go up came. The healer put his fingers in his ears, said something and dismissed him. Outside afterward my father declared that he could hear a bird singing, something he had not done for years. There was a feeling of well-being and gratitude. Later I saw him and my mother to the train. Alas, within a week or so his newly recovered hearing had ebbed away. My mother was foolish enough to accuse him of having lost his faith.

There were holidays spent away from Caergybi. My parents would choose some place and off we would go, ostensibly for my father to fish for trout, but as my mother was unwilling to go in the spring, we rarely caught much. The first time, we changed trains at Llandudno and went up Dyffryn Conwy. As the glorious scenery of hill and stream and woodland unfolded, I rushed from side to side of the carriage to admire it. It was so different from the flat, rocky bareness of Caergybi. Another time we went to Llanwrtyd, a village in South Wales. One morning I set off on my own to discover the cave of Twm Siôn Cati, an eighteenth-century outcast, who had a hideaway in the hills. On the top of one of these a little man with a black beard rode toward me on a mountain pony. "From this spot here," he said, "you can toss a stone into three counties."

· · ·

Having, after a lot of worry and hard work, graduated, I prepared to attend the theological college at Llandâf outside Cardiff. There were four terms a year here, which meant leaving Caergybi in July to go down to the stickiness and dust of a city. I was unhappy there. The students, being mostly South Walians were, of course, friendly, but the atmosphere was constricting. Worse still, there was nowhere to go for a walk. To reach such country as there was meant walking along a busy main road. There were two parts of a General Ordination Examination to pass, entailing a stay of two years. But a certain Canon Lloyd of Chirk, near Wrexham, wanted a curate, and being a man of influence he persuaded the Bishop to ordain me at the end of my first year at theological college, having passed only Part One of the examination. So to my relief and the disgust of the staff I was spared Part Two, and left Llandâf with no tears shed. Two pleasant memories of that year remained. I saw Wales defeat New Zealand at rugby in 1935, and heard Kreisler give a recital in the city.

In the autumn of 1936 I entered upon my first post as curate of Chirk, a mining village right on the Welsh border, and adult life began. I had to preach sermons, which I had shirked doing until then, and I had to begin visiting a fairly stratified parish from two earls at the top through a residential class down to the miners at the bottom, as it were. I soon realized that I was under an obligation to read outside my course to equip myself better for my responsibilities. The first thing was to begin building a small library, for I had nothing in the way of books but a few left over from my terms at college. There was a book firm in London, which ran a hire-purchase system, and from them I ordered some fifty books, which, having arrived, made me feel I was both a scholar and well on the way to being a man of letters, too.

It was October. I went for a long walk up the Ceiriog valley, following the river of that name. The sun shone, the leaves glowed. I wrote a lyrical description home, which made my father say that I must be going to be a poet. It was exciting to be on my own and receiving a small salary, although rent took half of it. It took my mind temporarily off what I had done. But with November the weather changed to the damp, sunless cold so characteristic of the border country, and I realized how far I was from the sea, where, if it rained one day, the sun broke through the next and piled the clouds in white masses above the hills of Eryri, Snowdonia. Still, there was work to do. I had to get to know the parishioners. The miners had to be visited; the residential class invited me to a meal. One day two of the girls from a neighboring house on their way to play golf stopped the car and invited me to join them. I was off to catch a train to the neighboring town. The daughter of the house was driving, but my eyes were on her passenger. I gave her that look which a man gives to the woman of his choice. As we got to know one another, I discovered that she was a recognized painter, and this made me wish to become recognized as a poet.

I had been writing verse since school days, conventional, sentimental stanzas about nature based on Palgrave's *Golden Treasury*. Even after reaching Chirk, Yeats, Hopkins, Eliot did not exist for me. What had we been taught in school? The Georgians mainly, but hardly Edward Thomas. Discovering him, I tried to write about the hills about Chirk, as he had written about the English downs. I discovered Fiona Macleod, and lost my head completely. His re-creation of the Gaelic scene reminded me vividly of my island home. I became sick for the sea and the west coast, even transferring my longing to the Hebrides. My painter friend, Elsi, abetted me. She shared my inner dissatisfaction with modern society. We dreamed of breaking away, and going to live in a cottage "on water and a crust." Yeats, too, had now entered my life; the Yeats of the Celtic twilight, of course, as I was too immature to be aware of the significance of his later work.

Elsi had an Austin Seven, which was ready for anything. Early one morning in August we set out for Scotland with vague plans in our minds. By half-past two we were crossing the border and stayed that night well up in the Highlands. We had decided to catch the MacBrayne steamer for the outer isles, but the road to Mallaig was under reconstruction and by the time we came in sight of the quay the boat was fast drawing away. We wandered the dockside rather at a loss. I saw a fishing boat moored there. "Are you going to the islands?" I asked a rough-looking man in an old sailor's jersey.

"Which islands?" he asked, somewhat dauntingly.

I took breath. "Barra," I said hopefully.

"Nay; I come from Soay," he answered. Then with a canny look he said:

"I'll take you there, if you like."

And so it was. Bidding Elsi "good-bye" and leaving her rather ungallantly to her resources, I went aboard, and presently we were on our way to the island of Soay by Skye. After an hour or so a small island under the Cuillins began to draw near. There was a beach with four or five crofts lining it, and a few dinghies drawn up on the shore. Two or three children were playing by the water.

The boatman took me to his cabin, where I was given a meal by his wife, who was none too pleased at what her husband had brought from the mainland. The upshot was that I was billeted with a family a few doors away. Their cabin contained a husband, wife, two large sons, and a daughter. I was treated as a guest and put in the parlor, from where I could hear the soft swish of their Gaelic in the kitchen. I was put to sleep in a feather bed over which the ceiling sagged. As one by one the family climbed to their beds, wherever those were, the whole house creaked and swayed. Unfortunately, it rained most of the time and I had no suitable clothes. The reality of a Hebridean island began to dilute my dream. As soon as the next MacBrayne appeared off-shore, I left my kind hosts and returned to Mallaig, where I learned that Elsi had gone to Canna. Selfishly, I telegraphed for her, begging her to return with me to Wales for the rest of our holiday. So ended my infatuation with the Hebrides.

I was more fortunate with the west of Ireland. Having heard that Seamus O'Sullivan, the editor of the *Dublin Magazine,* was sympathetic to young writers, I had already had a poem or two accepted by him as well as meeting him while he was visiting his brother in North Wales. One Christmas Day after morning service the Vicar told me that I was free for a week or so, if I wished. I jumped on my bicycle, made for Caergybi, and within a day or so was visiting O'Sullivan in Dublin. Armed with an introduction to a professor at Galway University, I caught an early morning train from Dublin and before mid-day presented myself at the house of Liam O'Briain, Professor of Celtic and former Irish rebel imprisoned in Wales after the 1916 rising. He had a great love for and knowledge of Connemara, and insisted on accompanying me a few miles on my walk west, talking all the time. Presently he turned back, and I walked on through the dying light with the smell of peat heavy and sweet about me. It was now that the kelp carts, which I had seen in the square in Galway, began overtaking me with the drivers calling out in Irish, as they passed. That night I stayed at a house recommended by O'Briain, and in the morning found that I was looking over the sea to the Aran Islands. I continued my walk through an increasingly beautiful and wild landscape of blue loughs and small, white cabins, each with its stack of turf as large as itself, until I came to the other house recommended to me, that of the painter, Charles Lamb. Here I was kindly entertained for a night or two, by which time it was New Year's Eve. There was a girl staying with the Lambs, and after supper we went out to see the hundreds of candles shining from the windows of the cabins around the loughs and beaches. This was the crofters' way of seeing the New Year in and of indicating to whatever spirits were abroad that there was a welcome within. The next day, it being time to return, I caught a bus back to Galway. Everyone in the bus was speaking Irish.

Alas, unheeded by me the European situation was deteriorating fast. After settling down in Chirk I was approached by one of the members of Toc H, who informed me that my predecessor had been their chaplain, and they hoped that I would follow suit. This entailed among other things giving them an occasional talk. As the threat of war increased, I had been reading a booklet by Hewlett Johnson, the "red" Dean of Canterbury, about the evils of capitalism and its wars. Fired by this, I gave Toc H a talk based mainly on this booklet, which was enthusiastically received. A day or two later happening to mention to my vicar how much I agreed with Johnson, I was met with the curt command: "Don't you preach that stuff here." This was my awakening to the general attitude of the Church to war between states, an attitude completely contrary to the teaching of Christ, who was that most unpopular creature in most circles, a pacifist.

The war came, and in 1940 Elsi and I decided to marry. I now learned that the Vicar did not want a married curate, so I had to look for a curacy with a house attached. I became Curate in Charge of Tallarn Green in the parish of Hanmer, and woke up one morning to see the Welsh hills fifteen miles away over the flat country of Flintshire. I was now farther away from the real Wales than ever.

It was while we were in this house that the Luftwaffe attacks on British cities began. Every evening after dark on suitable nights the droning of approaching aircraft would be heard, to be followed later by the sound of bombs being dropped on Merseyside, some fifteen to twenty miles away. I'm afraid I didn't set my new wife a fine example of male steadfastness. Apart from the physical apprehension of having these killers overhead, the thought that they were going to drop their loads on defenseless people in the towns and the senselessness of it all worried me. Standing in the doorway with Elsi one night, looking toward the red glow over Merseyside, I felt the wind from the bomb blast move through my hair and saw her skirt stir. Another night, unwilling to face the barrage to the Mersey approaches, the planes began circling overhead, and some released their bombs and land mines. Happening to look out of an upstairs window, I heard a bomb whistling down quite close, but there was no explosion. The next day it was discovered that it had plunged into the ground within a couple of yards of a corrugated iron cabin, where two old people were asleep, without going off or so much as waking them.

Partly from a cowardly wish to get away from this in a place where I did not belong, but more from a desire to have the whole of Wales open to me, I began to take Welsh lessons. I discovered a teacher in Llangollen, and used to go over once a week, while Elsi was holding an art class nearby. Still progress was slow, and I was quite unready to take over a Welsh parish. Presently, however, a benefice in the Montgomeryshire hill country fell vacant, and through the influence of my former vicar, I was appointed Rector of Manafon at the age of twenty-nine.

• • •

During my return by train from theological college to Caergybi I used to pass through the Welsh border country. Since it was an evening train, I used to see the Welsh hills outlined darkly against the afterglow in the west. My imagination was stirred, and I thought of lonely farms and dark-faced people, and a past of strife and bloodshed. Although it was no longer Welsh speaking, Manafon was situated among such hills. It was in a river valley, with a church, a school, a pub, and a post office, and farms scattered along the hillsides. The rectory was on the banks of the stream, the Rhiw, which rose in the moorland about ten miles to the west. It was thick with trout, which gladdened my father's heart, when I told him. Seeing the clouds at dusk scudding along the edge of the hill made me feel that at least I was back within reach of where I wanted to be. The farms nearly all had Welsh names, as did the parishioners, but the language had not been used in church since the first World War.

The harsh simplicity of the life fascinated me. In 1942 it was still largely unmechanized. One gray autumn afternoon, coming away from a hilltop farm I had been visiting, I saw the farmer's brother in the fields, docking swedes. I came back home and wrote "A Peasant," the first of my poems about Iago Prytherch, my symbol of the hill farmer. During the war Keidrych Rhys had revived his magazine *Wales*. The Anglo-Welsh movement had come to life again as a result of Welsh people's experiences in the forces. Thrown together with English and other servicemen, some of the Welsh became very conscious of their difference, and the writers among them articulated these feelings. Under the stimulus of this movement I wrote several poems, deliberately choosing Welsh names and places to emphasize the fact that, although I wrote in English, I was really Welsh.

The parishioners had more to teach me than I them. They were hard, hard-working and narrow, with the crude wisdom of workers on the land. Theirs was mixed farming, so they had little time for cultural pursuits. The Vicar of Chirk had warned me against preaching at them about cruelty to animals and such like. Any of my enthusiastic expressions about the beauty of the surrounding country were met with faint smiles, half-amused, half-cynical. Yet they loved the land in their way, and were prepared to talk about it for hours, when I visited them of an evening. One of the subjects to avoid was religion! They liked to entertain the Rector and his wife to supper, and after a farm meal and a talk by a wood fire, it was an adventure to walk back down over the fields to the Rectory below, where the river glittered under the moon or stars, and murmured of other things, or surged wildly by in full spate. "I wonder if it comes into the cellar?" I asked one day during flood water. I opened the cellar door, as I spoke, and there it was almost to the top of the steps. I shut the door quickly on it, as though it were a wild beast.

March was the time for lambing, and from the house at night I could see lights in the fields, as the farmers moved about with their lanterns among the ewes. Sometimes, visiting them, I would find an orphan lamb in a box by the kitchen fire, white as fresh snow. The war was far away, and being farmers the men had not been called up. I preached about farming as an innocent vocation, and of nature as part of the economy of God. I became obsessed with the importance of small communities and the worth of the individual, however insignificant; that is, with the small farmer in his few acres. They listened to me or half nodded off to sleep.

Llangollen was too far away for me to continue my Welsh lessons. I discovered there was a Welsh chapel on the hill between Manafon and the next valley to the north. I began visiting the minister, H. D. Owen, and his wife Megan. They were kind and put up with my stumbling efforts to speak Welsh. Gradually I improved, but progress was still slow. I attended meetings and concerts and preaching festivals to gain practice, but it meant that I always had to leave the parish to do so, and as petrol was rationed, it meant many journeys on foot. No wonder it took years.

As the end of the war came in sight, Elsi expressed her desire to bear a child. I had never really given the possibility much thought, but so it was, and in 1945 a son Gwydion, was born. "Now Gwydion was the best storyteller in all the world," as the Mabinogion has it. In order that I should go on writing and Elsi painting, a nurse-help was obtained, and Elsi started art classes in the neighboring towns to help pay her. But Gwydion proved to be a poor sleeper; so, unable to expect the nurse to be with him day and night, Elsi and I took it in turns to sleep with him. By the time he was three he had improved, and the nurse departed. But she had been a help, more so through her little boy, who though somewhat older than Gwydion, often minded him and played with him. The proximity of the unfenced river was a worry, and when it was running high, carrying all manner of debris by like goods trains, we had many anxious moments.

Manafon was a cold place. Five hundred feet up and yet down in a valley bottom, it incurred severe frosts. Most memorable was the bad winter of 1946–47. It began suddenly on 23 January 1947. The wind changed and it began to snow. The east wind drove up the valley, and since the drive to the Rectory ran north and south, it was soon full of six feet of snow. When the snow stopped, I began digging my way to the village, while some of the villagers dug from their end, so that I had a narrow passage to the main road. But for nine weeks I was unable to take the car out. The east wind blew tirelessly, and the poor farm women had to battle into it over the fields to give the hens their food. There came tales of the moorland farmers walking miles down to the nearest village to buy bread. At night, out visiting some of my own farmers, I nearly got lost sometimes on my way home owing to the uniform whiteness and absence of landmarks. Sometimes on clear nights with the stars sharp as glass, the temperature fell dramatically, one night reaching −10° Fahrenheit, 42 degrees of frost, which was as cold as anywhere in Britain. That night I was aware of the house cracking and grieving as the frost tightened its grip. Gwydion was still not two, and much time was spent entertaining him, since it was too cold for him to go out. The arrival of Roy, the nurse's little boy home from school, signaled by a snowball thrown at the window, was always a welcome event. Needless to say the river froze pretty well solid, and when the thaw came there were loud cracks as large sheets of ice reared up before being carried away like large pieces of masonry on the surging brown flood.

Being far from the sea, Manafon was not affected by salt winds, so the leaves often stayed long on the trees in autumn. With the red of the cherries, the russet of the birches, and the yellow of the ash, the valley could be very colorful in late October, provided no severe frosts occurred prematurely, as they could do. At the entrance to the Rectory drive there was an enormous ash. One year the leaves stayed longer than usual; but at last a sharp frost came during the night. Next morning, as the sun reached them the leaves began to fall. This they did for about two hours, so that it was like a huge golden fountain continually playing.

The years passed. I kept an eye on the Church in Wales papers to see what Welsh-speaking parishes were vacant. Some vacancies happened from time to time, of course, but somehow they were never quite what suited both of us. Then in 1953 I saw a notice in a daily paper to the effect that a bird observatory was being opened on Ynys Enlli, Bardsey Island. The name of the secretary was given as William Condry of Eglwysfach. We went over to visit him and his wife, Penny, and a friendship began. We arranged to visit the observatory the following August. We were warmly advised to call on the Keatings on our way to Aberdaron. These were three unmarried sisters, who lived in Rhiw in the Llŷn peninsula. This we eventually did, and made new friends.

After our stay on Bardsey, we had not been long back, when Bill Condry wrote to say that their vicar was retiring, and why not be the new one? I wrote to the Bishop, indicating my interest in the parish, and somewhat to my surprise received a letter back offering me the benefice. So in October 1954 after twelve and a half years among the Montgomeryshire farmers, we moved over to Eglwysfach, a small roadside parish just inside the Ceredigion border. This was rather inconvenient for Elsi, who was halfway through an extensive mural painting for the Orthopaedic Hospital in Gobowen. But she coped in her usual competent way. Although I had not known beforehand, Eglwysfach was a very different parish from Manafon. It was rural and had farms, but there were also a number of residential houses containing retired tea planters, ex-army officers, a small preparatory school as well as a village school, and the villagers themselves, mostly Welsh, but many of them married to English women. There were Welsh services every Sunday and Welsh was spoken in the parish, but the emphasis was on the English Sunday morning service, which was far better attended. The River Dyfi flowed down the northern boundary of the parish and was tidal, bringing salt water in daily from the sea about five miles to the west. All this, I felt, had been a step in the right direction. The country was very beautiful. The hills came close to the main road, and valleys ran up into them down which clear torrents poured over the boulders. The whole district was excellent for birds, and because of the estuary and its salt marsh provided species which there had been no hope of seeing in Manafon.

The different congregation called for different approaches. Many of them, especially parents visiting their children at preparatory school, were better educated than the Manafon farmers. But as at the English services I always had thirty or so young boys, I had to make myself interesting and intelligible to them, too. So twelve years in Manafon and twelve and a half in Eglwysfach trying to make myself clear had its effect on my poetry. That also was straightforward; rarely clever or obscure; perhaps overexplicit at times.

Before leaving Manafon I had met James Hanley, the novelist, who was living in the north of the county. Finding that I had not yet been published in London, he undertook to correct this and introduced my work to Rupert Hart-Davis. By the time we moved, Rupert had accepted a collection of verse, got John Betjeman to write an introduction to his new poet, and invited me up to London to meet John, that engaging man-about-town, who invited me to breakfast at his flat in Cloth Fair.

One of the attractions in prospect at Eglwysfach had been its proximity to the National Library of Wales and the University at Aberystwyth. But after one or two perfunctory visits to the former, and a dull lecture at the latter, I reverted to my old habits of preferring to be out-of-doors rather than in the stale air of library or lecture room. Bill Condry was a naturalist and a member of the Kite Protection Committee. After a while I, too, became a member, which meant going out and about the lower end of the county in April to find as many nests as possible, and keep a record of their progress. It was a real joy to explore the small oak woods in spring, with tree pipits, redstarts, and pied flycatchers singing in them, and to discover a large, fork-tailed raptor sailing in the sky above. Through the activities of the Kite Committee the birds built up from only two or three pairs after the first World War to over a hundred birds on the wing by the 1970s. There was for me the added attraction that Wales was their only breeding area in Britain.

Eglwysfach was a parish of factions, and I had to be careful to keep a balance. There were two landowners, dividing the parish between them, Hubert Mappin and a retired major general, Lewis Pugh. Then there was the preparatory school. All employed parishioners, and all had their following. They were self-interested, but Mappin was generous and a good friend of the Church. But they tended to be jealous of each other, and there was always the possibility of friction, especially at meetings. Pugh, like many of his kind, could never forget his rank, and made a nuisance of himself. In Manafon I had grown tired of the crudity and narrowness of farmers, but at least they were extenuated by their lack of education. They had also provided me with material for poems. Some of the Eglwysfach people had had the advantage of education and travel, so there was less excuse for their jealousy and small-mindedness. They were material for slight novels rather than poetry, so I tended to revert to the Montgomeryshire background for poetic inspiration. The only variation was a period of Welsh political unrest, which induced me to write several more explicitly patriotic poems.

Hubert Mappin's estate, Ynyshir, contained many interesting bird habitats including the Dyfi salt marsh, so Bill Condry and I persuaded him to declare it a sanctuary with no permission for shooting over it. His wife was my churchwarden, which was a help. Unfortunately, he became terminally ill and our plans for getting him to covenant his estate with the National Trust were endangered. With the help of a kind friend, David Ormond, we were able to expedite matters, and Hubert signed the document within a day or two of his death. Bill and I had also been trying to interest the RSPB (Royal Society for the Protection of Birds) in the estate, and later Mrs. Mappin sold it to that society as Ynyshir Nature Reserve. Bill Condry, now well known for his books on natural history, became its first warden.

In 1966 Bill and I went to Spain. I had been reading Guy Mountfort's *Portrait of a Wilderness,* a description of the Coto de Doñana in south Spain, and fascinated by the numbers of birds to be seen there, I persuaded Bill to accompany me. One morning in late April we said farewell to our wives and set off in my Mini Estate van bulging mainly with Bill's equipment; he was a photographer. We had decided to skip culture by avoiding the towns and camping out in the country. I was fascinated by Spain, which had great atmosphere. Bill had already been to Africa and had seen many of the birds which were new to me. But southern Spain reminded him of that country. There was still no proper road to the Coto, so it was, indeed, a wilderness with its myriads of birds and mosquitos, wild cattle and wild boars, and sand gradually encroaching from the Atlantic coast. The time went all too quickly, and it hardly seemed that nearly a month had passed when we arrived back safely in Eglwysfach, having luckily experienced no trouble with the Mini after a journey of nearly three thousand miles.

• • •

We had been in the habit of spending holidays in the Llŷn peninsula in one of the cottages on the Keatings' estate, and eventually they gave us a long life-tenancy of one of them. They were enthusiastic supporters of the National Trust and had already bequeathed this cottage, so that actually we became tenants of that body. When I heard that the parish of Aberdaron at the end of Llŷn had become vacant, it seemed a good idea to move there, if we could. But by now it was clear that Hubert Mappin was seriously ill, and I did not feel it would be right to leave. Luckily for me no candidate for the parish offered himself, so after Mappin's death, I intimated my desire to the Bishop of Bangor, a different diocese, and again had my wish granted. I was offered the benefice, and in May 1967 moved into the vicarage, a large house on the slope above Aberdaron and only four miles from the cottage at Y Rhiw. The house was in the sun from morning till evening, but was consequently exposed to every wind that blew. The sea was visible half a mile away, and the summit of Bardsey Island could be seen from my study window. With the wind and the sea and the strong sun and the herring gulls calling from the chimney pots, it was like a return home.

This move more or less coincided with a new direction for me in poetry. The last of my books from Hart-Davis's old firm came out the year following my move to Aberdaron. Rupert had retired and sold his firm, which had changed hands more than once since. I became dissatisfied with the new publishers, and was advised by Rupert to offer my next book to Macmillan, to whom several of the Hart-Davis staff had repaired. So my next book in 1972 came from that firm. In Eglwysfach I had continued to write about the Montgomeryshire hill country and its farmers, but having moved to Aberdaron I did not then write about Eglwysfach.

I began writing many different poems. I had said more or less all I had to say about hill farms, as well as about the Welsh situation. Manafon was un-Welsh. Eglwysfach, although more Welsh, was very much dominated by the English people who lived there. As a member of the so-called Anglo-Welsh school I had indulged in a certain amount of attitudinizing, a kind of beating the breast and declaring: "I'm Welsh, see." But after reaching Aberdaron I found myself among a simple but kindly people, who had never spoken anything but Welsh, until the English visitors began arriving. In moving among them and speaking Welsh daily, I gradually lost any need to emphasize my Welshness, but settled down to be what I had always wished to be: a Welsh-speaking Welshman in a thoroughly Welsh environment. True, as a seaside parish Aberdaron was visited by an increasing number of English visitors, some of whom had cottages there. English services had long been provided for these, and unfortunately several of the Welsh came to these morning services and neglected their own evening service, as was the case in so many of the churches throughout Wales. The nonconformists were more loyal to their language. However, my Sunday School was Welsh as was the primary school, and my two other churches in the district were monoglot Welsh.

Aberdaron was a twelfth-century church, situated uniquely on the seashore, with a sea wall to protect it from the high tides. In the period of Celtic Christianity it had been one of the mother churches of Wales, and had connections with the abbey on Bardsey, which was a place of pilgrimage in medieval times, three visits there being considered equal to one to Rome. At the Holy Communion service in the early morning the sea could be heard breaking on the sand outside, as it had done long before there was any church.

This was the atmosphere of the place, then: an area pervaded by memories of Celtic Christianity and pilgrims and still inhabited by Welsh speakers. But as if to introduce a tension there were the English tourists with their ice cream and newspapers and transistors, and as another emphasis of the twentieth century there was the roar of planes overhead as the Royal Air Force practiced for the next war. But beyond this I became aware of a much older time scale. It was, of course, satisfying to think of those early Christians, and to look at the Romanesque arch over the church door and the Pre-Reformation water stoup. But out at the end of the peninsula opposite Bardsey there were Pre-Cambrian rocks, which were anything up to a thousand million years old. The mind reeled. As I stood in the sun and the sea wind, with my shadow falling upon those rocks, I certainly was reminded of the transience of human existence, and my own in particular. As Pindar put it: "A dream about a shadow is man." I began to ponder more the being and nature of God and his relation to the late twentieth-century situation, which science and technology had created in the western world. Where did the ancient world of rock and ocean fit into an environment in which nuclear physics and the computer were playing an increasingly prominent part? Or how did the traditional world of Llŷn harmonize with the latest in technology?

Corresponding to the above subject matter, my poetry underwent a change of style. I broke up the lines and introduced more scientific or technological terms into my verse. It appeared that many of my readers, accustomed to thinking of me as a Welsh country poet, were unable to adjust to the new work, and, for all I know, still are. There was, of course, the occasional poem that reverted to former themes, but this was a tendency which could lead only to repetition and an appearance of exhaustion, so I found myself throwing the poem away, when I saw myself going back over old ground.

As long as I was a priest of the Church, I felt an obligation to try to present the Bible message in a more or less orthodox way. I never felt that I was employed by the Church to preach my own beliefs and doubts and questionings. Some people were curious to know whether I did not feel some conflict between my two vocations. But I always replied that Christ was a poet, that the New Testament was poetry, and that I had no difficulty in preaching the New Testament in its poetic context. The puzzlement comes in viewing what the so-called Christian makes of the message. In my first two parishes I felt a certain bitterness at the failure of the people to be worthy either of the beauty of their surroundings or of the Bible insights. In Aberdaron, with the growth of nuclear rivalry between the major powers and the increasing power of the multinationals, there was a growing feeling that the few inhabitants of the peninsula could hardly be blamed for the world situation. Apart from the need to preach Sunday sermons, therefore, the tendency was for me to become more absorbed with my own spiritual and intellectual problems and to see what poetry could be made from them. And the ever-present background was the sea. Beneath that smiling surface, what horrors! And as if conscious of the grotesques within it, the sea would sometimes become wildly agitated. With the wind west-nor-west often the spray would be whipped up higher than the summit of Bardsey, which was 548 feet. I became obsessed with the mirror image, comparing the sea now to a window, now to a looking glass. Several poems were on this theme.

Elsi became seriously ill in 1969, and there followed a long convalescence, never back to full health unfortunately. In an effort to give her something to look forward to after a spell in a hospital in 1972, I arranged for us to visit Mallorca in the autumn. I had never seen the Mediterranean before, and looking at its blue waters against the honey-colored rocks, I was reminded that this was the sea that Aeneas and Odysseus had sailed, and my years of not very successful study of the Classics came back to me. I was impressed with a feeling of being back near the cradle of Western culture.

In 1973 my mother died. Since my father's death in the Sailors' Hospital in Caergybi, she had lived alone, although surrounded by kind neighbors. I knew that she had hoped after my father's death to come and live with us. But I knew also that it would never work, so it was a case of being cruel to be kind. I used to go over to see her fairly regularly. Sometimes on the way back I would call on Charles Tunnicliffe, the bird painter, always to find him hard at work in his bungalow at Malldraeth on the Cefni estuary. Friends told me that although he had become blind before he died, he kept painting right up to the end without knowing what he was doing.

We had a large, roomy, if drafty, house at Aberdaron, and I loved the feeling of being right at the end of the peninsula, where I could slip out to the headland and watch the sea birds migrating in spring and autumn, and sometimes the cetaceans, too. I was conscious that the cottage at Rhiw would be very confining after the vicarage, and made inquiries about future plans for the parish, but nobody seemed to have any. There were other movements afoot in the Church in Wales at this time. The services were being revised and there were vague plans for reunion with the Nonconformists. Neither of these did I like, but would have been prepared to cope with them reluctantly in return for staying on in the vicarage. So with my sixty-fifth birthday in sight, I wrote to the Bishop to say that, if he did not intend appointing a successor, I would be prepared to stay on and do voluntary duty for the sake of the house. Receiving only an inconclusive reply, I wrote back giving the necessary six-months' notice of resignation, and immediately after Easter 1978 we retired to the cottage at Rhiw.

I had, of course, been making some sort of contingency plans, and with the consent of the National Trust had added a room to the original cottage to act as a bed-sitting study for myself, leaving Elsi in her small room at the other end of the house. But we had to get rid of most of our things. The walls of the vicarage had been covered with Elsi's paintings; but the cottage walls, consisting mainly of boulders, made this impossible. Of our three-thousand-plus books, we gave over half to Gwydion, keeping what we hoped would be most needed by us. The Rhiw stone is a dolerite outcrop and very heavy. Some of the boulders in the walls of the cottage are enormous and must weigh about a ton. One wonders how the original builders got them into place. The cottage itself is approaching four hundred years old, and stands on a slope overlooking Porth Neigwl, or Hell's Mouth, as the English maps have it because of its bad reputation in the last century. Once running in before a southwesterly gale, sailing ships found it very difficult to get out again. It was out over this bay I now found myself gazing day and night. Sometimes, when it was calm, there would be a sudden crackling, followed by a long rush of water, as the swell from the far-off Atlantic came in and spent itself on the sand. On clear days to the southeast Cadair Idris could be seen, and from a few paces down the garden, Yr Wyddfa, Snowdon, was visible forty miles to the northeast.

There was now more time than ever to read and to ponder some of the themes of my later poetry: the being and nature of God as presented to the twentieth century; the mystery of time; and the assault of contemporary lifestyles on the beauty and peace of the natural world. Apart from the overindustrialized south, Wales, though small, is of a beauty to bring tears to the eyes, and I am familiar with most of her special places, her moorlands and mountains and rushing torrents. I have always claimed that, if someone blindfolded me in some other country and brought me back by night and removed the bandage, I would know I was in Wales by the dark shape of a hill looming up before me and the sound of running water. But if pressed to name the pick of Welsh scenery, I think I would always choose the country between Beddgelert and Maentwrog for its hills and rocks, its birch trees and hurrying streams.

. . .

The problem I have always had difficulty in coming to terms with is the majesty and mystery of the universe and the natural world as a kind of symbol of God over against the domesticating urge in man. To kneel in my furnished room with its chairs and books, and then to look out and see Orion and Sirius rising above the bay makes it difficult to hold the two in proportion. I know that mind in the case of exceptional human beings is capable of a range beyond Orion. I know also that my experience of human nature has been restricted both intellectually and emotionally, so that it is man's urge to domesticate and exploit nature that I have been most conscious of. I acknowledge the validity of the mystics' claim to know God immediately; but it would seem that the deity has chosen to mediate himself to me via the world, or even the universe, of nature. I realize, therefore, that, because I have chosen the love of created things, I may not have reached the highest state possible to a human here on earth, but must be content with the fact that that is the sort of poet I am.

Although I live in a secluded and beautiful part of Wales, the peace is shattered most days by jet aircraft practicing overhead. But it is not just they that disturb my peace. They are a reminder of the uneasy peace that exists between east and west, and of the fact that if war were to break out, it would inevitably deteriorate into nuclear holocaust, which really makes it impossible to sit back and contemplate one's navel. This is not just from fear for my own skin, but I have a son and a grandson, like most other people. And there is the thought of all the wonderful and innocent forms of life that would be charred to ashes, if the worst should happen.

Soon after I retired, a branch of the Campaign for Nuclear Disarmament was started in Pwllheli to embrace the peninsula and beyond. I joined and soon became a committee member and representative to the county movement. With Wales as a supposedly nuclear-free country, this has involved me in considerable activity, and much ground has been covered with, alas, too little fruit. But once in, one can scarcely withdraw from a cause which seems so categorically sane and just. We seem to be winning the argument and losing the struggle.

This has been a dull autobiography. To have dealt more with the Welsh side of my life would not have been possible through the medium of English. It is kitchen talk. I have moved in unimportant circles, avoiding, or being excluded from the busier and more imposing walks of life. I was rarely happy in numerous company, and kept out of literary circles. I have always had a bad memory for what I have read, and in the presence of better and more knowledgeable talkers would have had to remain silent. It appears that some people are always anxious to meet poets, but in most cases they will be disappointed by the contrast between the man and his work. If I remember rightly it was Keats who warned that a poet is the most unpoetic of men. Was it a slight gift of Keats's negative capability that made it often so difficult for me to believe in my separate, individual existence? Certainly it has come to me many times with a catch in the breath that I don't know who I am. I do know, however, more from intuition than experience, that there are countless more intelligent, more able, better traveled people in the world than I, whose autobiographies would be a thousand times more interesting. It is just that I developed a small talent for turning my limited thoughts and experience and meditation upon them into verse that caused me to be asked to tell you something about my life.

Probings

An Interview with R. S. Thomas

Ned Thomas and John Barnie

*Reprinted from Planet, 80 (April/May 1990): 28–52.

Ned Thomas.   You have written in Neb, *and indeed in some of your poems, about your parents and your immediate relationship to them. I'd like to work beyond this to your grandparents' generation, in an attempt to place you within a wider Welsh social history. Could you say a little about that older generation and your relation to it? We talked a little about this when I was trying vainly to compile a* Bro a Bywyd *volume about you, and I was struck then by the way you spoke of your father's father as representing a "Welshness" associated with prosperity, from which your family had slipped away. This is rather different from the many Anglo-Welsh writers of your generation and earlier who emerged from Welsh poverty into English Literature.*

What I know of my forebears is almost entirely hearsay. My mother's parents died young leaving her an orphan, so she had no pictures of them to hand on to me save ones garbled by childish memories. As far as I know her father was a cashier in a colliery in what the South Welsh call Merthyr Vale. My father's father also died young, leaving eleven children. I have a boy's memory of his mother as we sometimes stayed with her in Wandsworth Common, London, with two daughters and, I think, a son, although the sons are vaguer figures, coming and going. The story was that she had possessed a fine soprano voice, when young, and there were attempts to get her to Italy to be trained with the prospect of becoming a talent comparable with Tetrazzini. Many of my mother's memories reflected the musical atmosphere of the Morgannwg of her youth. My father's mother was Welsh speaking and was a Miles. I became aware of this only as a student at Bangor. During a dance at an inter-college week a young man approached me informing me that he was a cousin. This was Dafydd Miles. A woman and her son called at my digs, informing me, if I remember rightly, that she also was a Miles, but married to Tom Evans, former headmaster at Llanelwy. His son Gwyn, got a Blue for cricket at Oxford, and bowled out Bradman in the Varsity match against Australia. I stayed with them while I was being made a priest at the cathedral. I was already toying with learning Welsh and Tom Evans was full of encouragement. I realized that my mother had never made much of the Miles connection, mainly, I fancy, because they were Welsh speaking! My knowledge of my father's father is insecure. The story was that he had gone through a fortune, died, moderately young, and left his widow to bring up eleven children on nothing. I know there was talk of houses they had lived in: Mwyndy in Llantrisant and Crofftau (toward Llanilltud Fawr) and he had also owned the Porth Hotel at Llandysul, of which my father had happy boyhood memories. It is probable that my father had some Welsh at that time which was erased by his being sent to sea as an apprentice at sixteen to help to support his mother. There was evidently money on that side as his father, if I have my dates right, had with David Davies, Llandinam, sunk the first pit in south Wales. Certainly a brother of my father's father lived at Lanelay Hall to give it its English name. So there was an air of the Thomas's as having come down in the world for what that is worth. It was as I learned the Welsh language that I became more interested in the Miles connection and less so in the Anglicized Thomases.

NT.   In your autobiography you pass rather quickly over the years at university in Bangor and subsequently at theological college in Cardiff, perhaps because you feel they were uneventful. But I should be interested to know what exactly your studies consisted of, particularly perhaps in philosophy; whether any authors read then (or lectures even) were particularly influential in the sense of directing your later reading. I ask about philosophy rather than poetry since you have mentioned Yeats as an early model in the field; but I'd be interested to know how much time you gave to the reading and writing of poetry when a student. It presumably formed no part of your formal studies.

Because my father was often at sea and because my mother was of a domineering nature I was ruled mainly by her. And being an only child I was the center of her attention for good and ill. Consequently, going to university was something of an escape. Not that I was restricted in every way. Strangely enough I had been allowed to run free from very early days in Caergybi. But because of the long period in school, by the age of nineteen I needed more than physical freedom. But coupled with this was the knowledge that there was financial stringency at home. My father had become deaf which meant he had had to abandon his prospects of becoming master of a ship for a lesser job ashore. As I was also in receipt of a Welsh Church Scholarship, I was obsessed with the idea that my main task was to gain a degree and so pass into the paid ministry via theological college. My approach to college life was, therefore, completely misguided.

I studied the stipulated subjects of Latin and Greek and spent the rest of my time mostly fooling about and going for long walks. I don't remember reading a book or magazine outside the set subjects. I had had spells at home of trying to write lyrics, based entirely on my reading of Palgrave's *Golden Treasury*. Some time after reaching Bangor I became aware that there was an English-medium college magazine called *Omnibus*. I contributed a lyric or two to that; I can't remember how many. Few, I hope. What has always astonished me was the pseudonym I adopted: Curtis Langdon. And yet it was revelatory of my home background. My mother often used to ask the Boots librarian if she had anything nice for her to read. So coming from an atmosphere of Ethel M. Dell and Warwick Deeping it was not unlikely that I should choose the pen name I did. A new editor took over and I happened to overhear him saying in the common room that there would be no more poems by that bloody Curtis Langdon as long as he was editor. My *amour propre* must have been pricked, because I wrote an equally weak poem, got a fellow student to copy it out in longhand, and submitted it under the pseudonym "Figaro." It duly appeared. Was this my first experience of literary prejudice? Mercifully, I cannot remember a line of the poem or certainly my triumph would be disastrously qualified. No, I don't remember my days at University with any satisfaction. My background was culturally *borné*. School did not instil a thirst for true learning, but I myself must take my share of the blame for being unable or unwilling to avail myself of services which must have been there.

NT.   I think you have said that you entered the Church in Wales because your mother thought it would be a nice job and because there was some family tradition. You have never given the impression of having been very comfortable within that Church, yet English publishers often turned to you as the bucolic vicar-poet who would introduce George Herbert's work, for example. You have found much to criticize in Welsh Nonconformity yet have acknowledged it as a fuller manifestation of Welsh religious feeling than the Church. Some critics have read The Minister *as a laying bare of your own lonely predicament; others as a critique of Nonconformity. After all, you had a great deal more independence than your Nonconformist colleagues. Then there is the aesthetic question. Could you try to unravel some of the contradictions which perhaps by now seem overtaken by an overwhelming secularism?*

Who can deny the finger of God? It may have been a disaster for other people, but it was a blessing for me that I entered the Church. Talk about the parson's freehold! It has given me time, which is the most necessary of all to a poet. I soon realized that to be able to stand up and deliver a sermon, I must read. So books entered my life. I realized, too, that a priest was expected to be studious, so had no qualms about time spent in my room. I discovered also that the ambition of most of the country clergy was to obtain a cure in a town. I loved the country, was not ambitious, and thus had no feelings of guilt about remaining there. I realized that a town parish would make severe demands on my time in the fulfilment of routine duties, thus leaving less of it for study and poetry. Here the Anglican custom of putting such a man in a country cure and leaving him to pursue his studies was also congenial to me in my effort to see things in perspective. So perhaps it was Anglicanism as demonstrated in George Herbert's life rather than in his writing that appealed to me. Of course, all this has turned into a hotch-potch of ecumenism and revisionism by now, but mercifully I am out of it. I don't know where I acknowledged Welsh Nonconformity as "a fuller manifestation of Welsh religious feeling," as you put it. What I admired was its independence of the Englishness of Anglicanism and its opposition, as far as it could, to the English State. I admired its greater awareness of and sympathy with Welsh identity over the last two centuries. *The Minister* was not about myself at all. It was written out of my sympathy with the lot of many a Welsh country minister at the hands of materially minded deacons. One of the great weaknesses of later Nonconformity.

You mention the aesthetic question, which is central. You know that I am a romantic and a *laudator temporis acti.* Aesthetically, the history of the Church is a long decline. The music, the architecture are not what they were, to put it mildly. Like many people I have a dislike for what is neither fish, flesh, fowl, nor good red herring. Let us have a great Gothic cathedral with the music of Palestrina and Monteverdi or later of Bach and Mozart soaring to the clerestories, or let us have the simplicity of a small stone church in the country with plain glass windows and the cadences of the Bible and Prayer Book in classical Welsh or English, but oh, none of the tasteless hybrids between. For anyone who saw Maes yr Onnen as I once saw it, what a falling off there took place in Welsh Nonconformist architecture. How can anyone come into contact with God in the varnished, pitch-pine mothball-smelling chapels of Wales with the worshipers, so-called, wiping a prayer off their faces before turning to take stock of who is there?

And only a little better are so many of the churches, especially after generations of patrons with little taste have foisted their family memorials upon them. To me one of the great disasters of the latter-day churches is the organ. When one thinks of plainsong, unaccompanied polyphony, or even the accompaniment of oboe and bassoon, what a catastrophe are the storms of sound created by an organist let loose on a large organ with a respectable congregation trying to put in its Vicar of Bray accompaniment. My wife is a painter; I should have been a musician so that we could have designed a church and made music in it that would have been a little nearer the way in which God worships himself in mountains, flowers, and bird-song.

NT. I think you have made it quite clear that your first contact with political nationalism in Wales came after the end of the war, when you were in Manafon and learning Welsh. Were you not in some degree aware of a movement before that, though not involved with it? I mean, as a student in Bangor, or as a young curate at the time of Penyberth and the subsequent trial of the three? And, to take a more literary dimension to the same question, when did you first come across Keidrych Rhys's Wales? *Was it the postwar revived* Wales, *or had you seen it before the war?*

Leading on from this, did you see yourself as contributing through the postwar Wales *to some kind of Welsh renaissance? Keidrych Rhys took quite a strong Parliament for Wales line in those years, and reading the magazine there is a sense of a movement. I seem to remember a rather angry outburst of a letter from you when the* Welsh Review *was re-started, as if something was being undermined. Can you help illuminate the literary politics of that period in Wales?*

I have indicated the sort of home I came from. My mother also loved the country and many of my afternoons were spent walking with her. Otherwise I roamed the fields and coast by myself or played games. So I really lived in a world of my own, in which politics and the business of the wider world had no part. I am ashamed to say that news of "the three" never reached me at all in the month before I was to leave home for good and become curate of Eglwys y Waun (Chirk). Munich was my first awakening to politics and it is indicative of my attitude that I should become aware of the threat of war in its English context. It is here, of course, that

I am personally indebted to the Church for affording me immunity to "National" Service. It is doubtful whether my pacifist and conscientious objections to war would have matured sufficiently to have resisted as a layman in 1939.

I had seen one or two copies of the pre-war magazine *Wales* edited by Keidrych Rhys with their white and red cover and names like Vernon Watkins and Dylan Thomas on them. Then in Manafon the later *Wales* came to my notice and I contributed poems like "A Peasant" to it as being akin to it in flavor and intention. I had wanted to go to Manafon as a return to the Welsh hill country, which I had seen nostalgically far to the west from Tallarn Green in Hanmer parish, Maelor Saesneg, a curacy I moved to on marrying. This was the time when I began seriously to study Welsh and to come in contact with Welsh Nonconformity. I was full of romantic ideas about the moorlands to the west and the Welsh speakers who lived there. My wanderings in those moors among the ruins of a peasantry who had been forced to migrate by the depression of the Thirties awakened me to Welsh social problems, so one way and another I was fallow ground for the ideas which Keidrych was circulating in his attempt at a revival of Welsh writing in English. My poems were beginning to receive attention and I was invited after the war by Douglas Young to visit various societies in Scotland to talk about Wales. I also attended the first postwar meeting of the Celtic Congress in Bangor in which Ambrose Bebb asked me to chair an address given by the Scots Gaelic poet Sorley Maclean. It must have been about this time that I first went to call on Saunders Lewis in Llanfarian. Having been stirred by an article of his in *Y Faner*, I went with youthful braggadocio to "offer my services to Wales!"

But as my work became better known I was invited to speak to societies in Wales, too, and I found myself stressing the necessary qualifications of a truly Anglo-Welsh writer, namely that he should steep himself in all things Welsh to justify the hyphen, although under the influence of conversations with other so-called Celts I began to hope that Anglo-Welsh literature was only a halfway house on the road back to Welsh. Isolated though I was in Manafon I began to toy with the idea of becoming a Welsh writer myself, but was very much in a vacuum. I think that Keidrych like some others of us had a divided allegiance despite his good editorial leadership.

NT.   I wonder if you could say something about the early publishing history of your poetry. The first volume was published, I think, by Keidrych Rhys, and the next two in Newtown. Had you been trying London publishers unsuccessfully before that? Could you say something about your relations with publishers over the years? Though some critics in England seem to want to keep you as a "Welsh upland poet" for evermore, your publishers seem to have allowed you to go your own way, developing and changing your emphasis. Or am I wrong?

My first book of poems was *The Stones of the Field* and was published by Keidrych Rhys from The Druid Press in Caerfyrddin in 1946 with a jacket designed by my wife consisting mainly of a map of Cymru which showed my allegiance. We contributed £60—I never heard whether this was too little or too much. The second, *An Acre of Land,* was a booklet and was published, I can't remember at whose expense, by the Montgomeryshire Printing Company at Y Drenewydd. This was introduced on the BBC program *The Critics* and sold out as a result, necessitating a second impression.

Following the broadcasting of *The Minister* as part of Aneirin Talfan's BBC series *Radio Poems,* a booklet of it was published by the same Montgomeryshire Company. This was about 1951. I seem to remember submitting a collection to one or two London publishers without success. Faber must have been one because I remember a note from T. S. Eliot saying that they couldn't publish them, but he hoped somebody would, which seemed a bit cryptic, but I did realize they were not a part of what he was trying to do in poetry publishing. Nothing else happened until in 1954. Before we left Manafon, I met James Hanley, who on finding I was without a publisher volunteered to find one. I don't know how many he tried, but Rupert Hart-Davis took them and they appeared as *Song at the Year's Turning* during 1955, the year following our move to Eglwysfach. Rupert had considered that an unknown poet should be introduced by a known one so invited me to London to meet John Betjeman. Rupert published my next three or four books and I had a pleasant personal relationship. I think it must have been his influence rather than the poems' merits that won the Heinemann Award and an Arts Council Prize for the best book of poems during the previous three years. He eventually retired, selling to Heinemann. They soon sold to Granada and for a few years I had no personal contact. Feeling that Granada had no great interest in poetry, or at least in my poetry, I asked Rupert's advice, and he suggested Macmillan to whom some of his former staff had removed. My book *H'm* was warmly welcomed by Macmillan's poetry editor Kevin Crossley-Holland and their chief editor Alan Maclean. But I never had the same personal relationship as I had with Rupert Hart-Davis who was, of course, a smaller publisher. However, the change was a convenient posting-house as it followed on a somewhat new departure in my poetry consequent upon my move to Aberdaron. Thus the earlier work about the Welsh hill country, etc., came from the Hart-Davis and Granada houses, the later from Macmillan. The only complication was that in the meanwhile Granada had a fit of remorse or something and offered to re-issue books that had gone out of print. I did not want that, so we arrived at the compromise of *Selected Poems 1946–68*, chosen by me.

As you suggest I have had a free hand from Macmillan, which was generous considering that the earlier style *Selected Poems* proved more popular with a certain type of reader. This was accentuated by their reprinting by Bloodaxe Books, who obtained the right to distribute from Collins, who had taken over from Granada.

NT.   You have never espoused that version of Anglo-Welsh which holds that there can be a literature of Wales in English separate from English literature but also separate from Welsh tradition in Welsh.

But it seems that in the early postwar period you took a more hopeful view of another kind of Anglo-Welsh possibility: that there could be a Welsh literature in English, strongly grounded in a knowledge of Welsh history, language, and literary tradition. What MacDiarmid had done for Scotland and Yeats for Ireland could be done for Wales by writers who properly equipped themselves.

I don't think you maintained this position for long, and am interested to know why. Is it a delusion that repeats itself? After all, Saunders Lewis when young thought he might be the Welsh J. M. Synge. I think you would still advise a young writer in English in Wales to familiarize himself with the national language and traditions, but would you any longer hold out the possibility of building an English-language literature on that basis?

I have already referred to my attitude to Anglo-Welsh writing under Keidrych Rhys's attempt at a renaissance. Vernon Watkins rejoiced in the gift of such a fine medium as English and was unable to understand my dissatisfaction. But Bro Gŵyr was not the sort of area to feel the tensions I experienced. In any case Vernon had no Welsh, whereas I, as I improved, was drawn more into "Welsh Wales" and into the company of people like Euros and Islwyn Ffowc Elis and, of course, Gwenallt after my move to Eglwysfach. I complained once to Saunders about the tension of writing in one language and wanting to speak another and his reply was that out of such tensions art was born. I don't consider myself fit to give advice to any young writer, but I think that after all this time they should know where their allegiance should lie. And in all fairness some of them have learned Welsh. But now that I have thoroughly immersed myself in Llŷn Gymraeg, it seems more impracticable than ever that there should be a hyphenated literature, especially in verse. What is written in Welsh is Welsh literature of varying quality. What is written in English has to strain very hard indeed to merit the description of Welsh writing in English, which is nonsense anyway.

John Barnie.   Welsh Airs (1987) gathers together poems on the theme of Wales written over a number of years and mostly published in earlier collections. In some ways, therefore, it's a Selected Poems. Could you comment on the motivation behind this particular book?

I am old now and there are many younger English speakers in Wales. I was conscious that, since many of the poems were out of print and had not been included in later collections, they were unknown to these younger readers. On the whole I have had my say on the matter of Wales in verse, and do not want to repeat myself. But I believed that some of the poems were still relevant and, therefore, worth reissuing.

JB.   In your autobiography Neb, in prose memoirs such as Y Llwybrau Gynt and in your latest collection of poems The Echoes Return Slow you have created a biography of "R. S. Thomas." Neb is unusual in being written in the third person. Could you say what led you to write it in this way, and whether you are aware of presenting the reader with an edited version of your life which future biographers may consider incomplete?

Some people think I was being falsely modest or that I was joking when I entitled the incomplete autobiography *Neb.* The question of personality arises, which is a complex one. I once suggested that they discuss it on the BBC's *Word in Edgeways* which they did, but not very satisfactorily. Some people aim to become personalities. There is quite a bit about it in Yeats's *A Vision.* I don't think that a really creative being should try to wear a persona. Keats's negative capability is relevant. Borges suggested that Shakespeare himself did not know who he was. I was asked to write *Neb.* It would never have occurred to me to write an unsolicited autobiography, because I am of no importance as a person and have never been at or near the center of so-called important events.

If anything I have written is to have any lasting value, time will decide. It is Keats's feeling that possesses me, too, when I visit a municipal art gallery and look at the rows of "personalities" who became mayors and chairmen and prime ministers and heaven knows what. I feel entirely insignificant. The energy that must have been expended on the becoming of such oppresses me. There must be a point at which a rising personality ceases to be self-conscious, otherwise how explain that peculiar shuffle of ageing "personalities" as they enter a roomful of people who are expecting them? But a creative person must be so open to experience and impressions, so alert and critical of the ideas coming to him, that he is not conscious of his own existence as a person. If there be such an unwise person in the future as to undertake to write a biography of me, he is welcome to enter the morass of trivia which may or may not be open to him. I don't consider it of any importance. Hence the title I gave the short account which I wrote myself. I was approached some while ago for permission to write such by a professional biographer. He did not consider his lack of Welsh an impediment, but how else could he have found out my size in shoes?

JB.   It is tempting for a poet writing in English to view the whole of the English-speaking world as a potential market. How important is it for you to have a readership outside Wales? Has the possibility of such a readership influenced your decision to publish most of your collections of poetry in London?

When I began writing poetry seriously I had what, I suppose, is the young writer's craving for publication, as though the seeing of himself in book form really proves that he is a poet. Since I wrote in English it was to English magazines I submitted my verse, although actually it was an Irishman, Seamus O'Sullivan, editor of *The Dublin Magazine,* who first responded to my work. He advised me to send something to *The New English Weekly,* so it was there that my first poem appeared. But it was *The Dublin Magazine* which published subsequent poems. My submissions of collections to various publishers in London were turned down, and it was not until the events already mentioned that a collection appeared under a London imprint. Certain editors of magazines or newspapers were now asking me for work, so it was no longer necessary to submit. That situation has continued. I have never submitted poems since. As fashions changed, or editors moved, I was rarely asked for a poem, but the habit has persisted. It is evidently a weakness of writers to submit books. Having once had one's first book accepted, there is the need to convince oneself one can "still touch one's toes" and as one writes most of the time, there is generally another collection within a couple of years waiting to be published if the publisher is willing. None of my publishers has harassed me, especially latterly since the decline of interest in poetry in general and my own in particular. I must say that I am increasingly blasé about a so-called readership. I have never frequented London literary circles and some years ago gave up public readings, more especially in England. And now with immigration increasing the pressures on a diminishing Welsh minority, I really care little about trends and fashions in English literary circles. However, I continue to send collections to publishers as they become ready and have a vague interest in how they sell for the sake of the royalties. Since publication is an agreement between publisher and author, I don't see why the publishers should not distribute the work to the best of their ability. I am afraid this is not always the case, especially with poetry, for many different reasons. But I don't think any of these considerations induced me to try to find a London publisher. After all, as far as I remember, there were no reputable publishers of English poetry in Wales, when my first collection became negotiable.

JB.   In 1964 you accepted the Queen's Gold Medal for Poetry. Could you say something about the circumstances which made you decide to accept?

As you know the Welsh situation has deteriorated drastically over the last ten years mainly because of immigration from England. My own attitude has hardened accordingly. I would not now accept the medal. Indeed, this interview is a concession as a result of my relationship with *Planet*. I no longer give interviews in English or accept invitations to go and read my poems in England. Eglwysfach was a very Anglicized village which I, in part, accepted, although I did start a Welsh Society there in an effort to redress the balance. In his letter to me on the occasion, John Masefield spoke of the medal as "a thing of great beauty" so I was also hoodwinked to some extent. I would not describe what came through the post in such terms. I was in Aberdaron by the time of the other hoodwink, known as the Investiture. I remember how on that day twenty-four RAF aircraft flew up the peninsula, reminding me in Auden's words of how "They were there not because, but only just in case." The medal had not been awarded for some years, but such was the indignation at my being given it, that it became almost an annual event to mollify the geniuses that had been slighted.

JB.   You have spoken out in public on a number of issues affecting Wales, most notably on the threat to the Welsh language and its culture, and on nuclear disarmament. Do you see it as a duty of a poet to take a public stand on political and ethical issues?

I think the opposition would be most appropriately voiced in the poet's work, but these days serious poetry has a minority audience. Propaganda poetry is always in danger of rant or jingoism. The ranks of anti-nuclear or pro-Welsh demonstrators are mostly so thin that they tend to attach exaggerated importance to people who have a slight reputation such as poets or vicars, more especially when combined. I have spoken out on both the above issues out of sincere conviction, but I don't go so far as to claim that it is a poet's duty, although he is obviously open to the accusation of living in a dream world, if he does not. I have been invited to give my views and to speak over the media mainly because people thought I had a slight reputation. What a poet like me has to beware is of pontificating about matters on which many lay people are better informed. I like to think that because of his clear-sightedness a poet is less easy to dupe, so in a way does have an obligation to warn his neighbors against the conditioned or stock response.

NT.   What about the worthy causes of people elsewhere? On the whole I think you are not, outside the Welsh context, a signer of letters of appeal and protest in the world's press. Yet you have had things to say about the native American peoples, and I came across the fact that you had broadcast on the plight of the Palestinians, long before that cause was fashionable or supported by oil money. Why did these causes in particular command your support?

"Homo sum. Nihil humanum," etc. I take the view that there are plenty of protesters against world injustice, too few against Welsh. So I tend to confine my protests to Welsh affairs. In the early days of television, I was invited to London by Redifusion, or some such company, to provide a commentary for a documentary on the deprived in Palestine and Hong Kong.

I read *Bury My Heart at Wounded Knee* by Dee Brown, and because of similarities between the history of the Red Indian tribes and Welsh-speaking Wales, I wrote a review of the book in Welsh.

JB.   In the past you have described yourself as a Christian pacifist, yet recently you have also shown an understanding of Meibion Glyndŵr. What, in your view, are the limits to individual direct action? Can a minority's rights be maintained within a mass society governed by majority democracy?

As you know I have always been careful to preface any remarks I make in the context of Welsh opposition with the reminder that I have been a priest of the Church, that my interpretation of the Gospel is pacifist and although a case can be made for the use of force in the condition which Cymru now finds herself in, I am not prepared to incite others to do what I am not prepared to do myself. The ability of most of the general public to think clearly has been eroded by various means. Many people lost their heads completely over my remarks about Meibion Glyndŵr. What I said in answer to a loaded question was that I admired their courage and was glad that the Welsh spirit was not totally subdued. We know that if they are caught, they will be given massive sentences. They know it, too. Therefore it requires courage on their part to risk it. As regards force, I have tried to provoke a debate, because England is very vulnerable here, so is the Church. Many of England's heroes, who were set subjects in school, were butchers. When her existence is threatened, England will always fight. Why is it right for her, but wrong for Wales? Regarding the Church, I have been through it all: the prayers for victory, the prayers for "our boys," the righteous war, condoned and actually supported from popes and bishops down to the rank and file of the clergy. I am pessimistic about the effect of individual action in the world of the mass media and the cash nexus. I think the English tradition tends to favor the gloved fist, but she can be equally ruthless in eliminating what she conceives as a real threat. In an over-populated world hysteria is never far away and many an individual becomes a casualty.

JB.   Do you think there are any circumstances in which it would be possible to regain the Anglicized areas of Wales for Welsh? If not, what, in your opinion, are the likely consequences for the language and for Wales?

To ask if there are any circumstances which I think would lead to regaining Anglicized areas for Welsh is casting a pretty wide net. Even the collapse of the English economy would hardly do it in face of the hordes of English and Anglicized Welsh we have in our midst. But there are a lot of qualifications even for a re-Cymricized Wales. I made my position clear in *Abercuawg*. Under modern conditions there are strong pressures toward uniformity in the Western world. I am not thrilled by the tenants of 210 High Street in some large town's ability to discuss *Citizens* in Welsh or speak Welsh to their dogs on a Sunday morning constitutional in one of the parks. As we know, over-industrialism and over-population are terminal illnesses in Western society, but I cannot foresee a Welsh-speaking green movement taking their place. It is English immigrants or Anglicized Welsh people who are doing most of the experimenting. Cymru Gymraeg has lost most of its pioneers and enterprise people through death or emigration. A Welsh-language daily paper under inspired editorship and Welsh-medium radio and television, independent of London, would help to "de-condition" us. But then that is a dream, is it not? And so the likely consequences are a realization of the Abercuawg nightmare. With the draining of rural Wales of its Welsh-speaking population and the consequent loss of the natural racy idiom, there is only the self-conscious correct Welsh of the new middle-class growing up in the towns. But all this is so much fiddle. As technology is going now, language is at a premium. The forces that are shaping the future of Western society are dehumanizing. But the chief distinction of a human has always been language. I don't like washing Welsh dirty linen in English, so will say no more.

JB.   In a culture such as that of the Welsh which is under threat of annihilation, and in a period of the Earth's history when life itself may be under threat from the human species, what do you think is the function or meaning of art?

I think the use of the word "art" is too wide. I would prefer to confine myself to literature, or even poetry. There are already some very peculiar products appearing under the name of "art" as of music, and they need technical knowledge for their assessment. Regarding literature, I have already partly answered the question in the previous section. Literature has to do with speech. It is the communication of thought and emotion at the highest and most articulate level. It is the supreme human statement. You remember Wallace Stevens's stanza in "Chocorua to Its Neighbour":

> To say more than human things with human voice,
> that cannot be; to say human things with more
> than human voice, that, also, cannot be;
> to speak humanly from the height or from the depth
> of human things, that is acutest speech.

We must remain articulate to the end, with all the overtones that articulation may imply from the drama of Sophocles to that of Beckett. We are certainly contemplating the annihilation of the species for the first time in its history, whether as a punishment for hubris or whether as a result of its own *cupido* and obstinacy. But even at the last hour there are those splendid words of Sénancour: *"L'homme est périssable; il se pent. Mais si le néant nous est reservé, ne faisons pas que ce soit une justice."* I like to think of man, even on his last day on this planet, gazing out into the universe and speaking words of love and of beauty in his native tongue.

JB.   "In the face of this [the relentless destruction of nature in Wales] R. S. knew well why he turned more and more to interest himself in birds" (Neb). Could you say something about your interest in ornithology? And could you elaborate on your statement in Neb?

I have already confessed that I am a romantic, rather like the early Yeats:

> The wrong of unshapely things
> is a wrong too great to be told.
> I hunger to build them anew
> and sit on a green knoll apart.

That dates, doesn't it? We must move with the times; even our art. Speaking as an old man, I, too, caught a whiff of other days when I was young. I have walked westward from Galway into the dark, into the peat smoke and been passed by the kelp carts, with the drivers calling a greeting in Irish. I have been at the birth of the year in Connemara and seen the candlelight in the windows of the cabins along the shores, welcoming it.

I have seen them cutting peats in the Welsh hills, too, and have experienced a traditional welcome in a hill farm and eaten real Welsh lamb, not the stuff that passes for it today. I have known the silence of the countryside before many machines destroyed it and have enjoyed a darkness in which one could see the wealth of the stars and perhaps one light like a flower pinned to some black hill. All changing or changed. I realized it was no good looking for these things anymore. The aircraft, the motors were rending the silence; the lights and glow from the cities and village street lamps were hiding the stars. The wild places are becoming domesticated. Time and distance are being annihilated by speed.

So I turned to the birds. Instead of being asked in to a modernized cottage with the television's St. Vitus's dance in the corner, I went out seeking birds, especially migrant ones. They belong to the open spaces. Over millions of years they have kept to the flyways, many of them migrating thousands of miles with mysterious accuracy. Their sounds are delightful to human ears, yet they are independent of humans. With just a beak they contrive nests of supreme artistry and beauty. The eggs from which they reproduce themselves seem so much more aesthetic than mammalian reproduction. Their conquest of the air through flight has been achieved without any of the uproar and drain on Earth's resources with which man hurtles through space. Ornithology has become a science and there are many experts, of whom I am not one. But there is pleasure, too, in just observing them, and the added pleasure of discovering a new species and of never knowing when you are going to be blessed with the sight of one.

NT.   Would it be true to say that you are more interested in the natural world than the social world? If so, does it set you rather apart from what are sometimes seen as Welsh virtues—a sense of community, cymdeithas, bro, etc. Or perhaps they smack of Welsh vices, the rhetoric with which we console ourselves?

This is partly a matter of upbringing. I was delicate as a child. I was six when we came to live in Caergybi. I seem not to have attended school for a year or two, but was allowed to roam the fields and coast. Even after beginning school I acquired the habit of often going out at first light in the longer days and wandering for a couple of hours before returning for breakfast and so to school. I was happy just to be in the open air and to watch the sea. With my present interest in birds I regret the lack of someone to have started me taking an intelligent interest in them, for I remain an amateur. I was moderately good at games and athletics in school, which helped to commend me to my schoolmates, but later traits manifested themselves which made me awkward in society, arousing reciprocal reactions, so that the old "loner" tendency reasserted itself. Had I come from a different background, which had put me in touch with educated and interesting people, it might have been otherwise. But things being what they were, it would be honest to say that my preference is for the natural world. But mastering Welsh and throwing in my lot with Welsh speakers, in order to become at ease in the language, has meant a kind of cleavage of personality. Although the standard of conversation, with honorable exceptions, had been less high in my socializing with Welsh speakers, I have appreciated their friendliness, and have received much kindness from them. The rift between us arises from what I regard as an exaggerated social orientation among them with a corresponding disinterest in and ignorance of the natural world. *"Does gen i ddim byd i ddweud wrth adar"* is a remark far too common in Welsh circles.

JB. *Could you say something about your reading in the sciences? Astronomy and physics, particularly, appear to be a source of imagery for you, yet at times in your work there seems to be a suspicion of, and perhaps even a hostility toward the scientific mind. Would you say that science and religion are irreconcilable ways of knowing? If they are, is there any reason for preferring one as opposed to the other as a means of exploring reality?*

For obvious reasons my reading in the sciences has had to be by the popularizers of them. I have tried to maintain a slight understanding of scientific doctrines, as they evolve and change, remembering that who marries the spirit of the age will be a widower tomorrow. I have been interested in the tendency of recent physics to harmonize to some extent with Eastern theology and have read some of the works of Fritjof Capra and Paul Davies. To an austere scientist much of my imagery may be reprehensible, but as far as I have understood astronomy, relativity theory, and nuclear physics, I have found images in poetry, which I hope are not too muddle-headed. My joustings with scientists are probably with the lesser fry, because I imagine those of the first rank exercise a wonder at creation which is akin to religion.

It is of applied science as manifest in technology that I am suspicious with its reductionist tendencies, and positively dislike its prostitution to the money power. So it is not pure science and religion that are irreconcilable, but a profit-making attitude to all technology. If pure science is an approach to ultimate reality, it can differ from religion only in some of its methods. It would appear that, following the genetic coding, some are born with a make-up that will lead them along scientific paths to ultimate reality, while others will tend to the religious. But owing to the highly technical nature of science it will be easier for a scientist to be religious, than for a religious specialist to be also a scientist.

NT.   You are sometimes described as anti-technology and there are certainly lines about "the machine" that seem to support this view.

But you have always seemed to me fascinated by the language of science and technology and to be something of an evolutionist. Sometimes I wonder whether you don't see technology as a stage to be worked through on our way to something higher.

Yes, I am, generally speaking, anti-technology. The easy gibe is: why do you run a car, have a telephone etc.? But this is the world that is forced upon us, and it is difficult to be active in such a world without them. But using the machine, as I have, as a symbol for a robotic takeover, it is hard not to be antagonistic. It serves us, but at a price, and the Frankenstein specter is never far off, as science fiction's success shows. The main criticism is that the machine is de-humanizing. It also insulates man from natural processes. The reason I have tried to write poems containing scientific images and which show some knowledge of the nature of science, is because, owing to the enormous part science and technology play in our lives, a divorce of poetry from them would be injurious to the development of poetry and would alienate people from it, as has already occurred to some degree. Science and technology are concerned with vital areas of man's concern, they are therefore taken seriously. So still is religion. The danger to poetry is that it should become a fringe activity, as has already happened to a large extent in England. It has been said that Donne was the last English poet to be still abreast of contemporary knowledge. Granted that modern specialization has made this impossible, what are we to make of a poetry that cannot embrace some scientific knowledge and that is incapable of using words which are daily on the lips of a growing section of the population?

Unfortunately, much critical or trendy opinion is in collusion with this. Poetry which is minor, but slick and lively, cynical and self-conscious, is praised. But poetry which gives hostages to fortune by experimenting and trying to come to terms with the major issues which I have mentioned is pilloried or demolished by having the odd scientific error exposed. The one great weakness of so much of our technology is that it is prodigal of Earth's resources. Green thinking would reverse this to some extent at least. And there is no need to be iconoclastic or to throw out the baby with the bath water. As Gandhi kept the sowing machine, we could be selective. It is the money power that is the enemy rather than the machine, although I find the mind that invents the machine a profound problem. But could a society which had become largely de-mechanized produce a new vocabulary, new ways of thought, and consequently a new poetry?

JB. In a universe where, for example, matter and energy appear to be inter-changeable at the sub-atomic level, what meaning, if any, can be attached to words like "soul" and "spirit"?

I have already referred to the danger of runaway marriage with the spirit of the age. In science, especially at the speed with which it changes, today's orthodoxy can be tomorrow's limbo. The sub-atomic world, like the extra-galactic world, depends to some extent on the imagination. One realizes that the greater the magnification the more territory comes into view at either end of the optic. Because of the concept of infinity, all these spaces are as infinite as they are meaningless to the human observer. So why should not another invisible dimension, infinitely close, be equally valid? "Closer is he than breathing, nearer than hands or feet." Or as Blake cried: "How do you know but every bird that cuts the airy path is an immense world of delight closed by your senses five?"

I am not willing to be browbeaten by the latest scientific "break-through." And maybe we view words like "soul" and "spirit" too much in a Graeco-Judaean context. Taoism, Hinduism, and Zen Buddhism see them rather differently, and, as I have already indicated, sometimes in a way that con-sorts more comfortably with present scientific views than does Christianity.

JB. You have written poems about the probing of science into the nature of the universe and about the retreat of God before that probing. Is it possible, any longer, to contemplate God as other than "that which is beyond the current frontier of our knowledge?"

I may be eclectic, of course, and I do not accept that Christianity is the only way to the kingdom of God or to the beatific vision. But I am orthodox enough to accept Paul's description of God as He "in whom we live and move and have our being." [And to talk about frontiers of knowledge does not imply an ultimate one which the genius of man will one day enable him to cross. Granted that a certain kind of religion has made capital out of a God of the gaps, this does not mean that each closure of a gap is a kind of erosion of the reality of God. There is the God of Ann Griffiths and Mother Theresa as well as of Augustine and Pascal. I sense a limitation of the scope of knowledge in your question. We are becoming so conditioned by the scientific view of things that we are in danger of accepting as truth only an experiment that can be repeated; that is, of accepting as true only that which can be proved. Whereas the use of imagination should remind us that we are surrounded by mystery. We still do not know how or when soul or mind or spirit come into conjunction with the human embryo. And if we cannot prove that the identity survives the death of the body, neither can we prove that it does not. So, yes, I do contemplate or visualize or experience God as other than the last frontier waiting to be crossed.

JB.   Would you consider yourself more a deist now than a Christian? By deist I mean one who believes in the existence of God without necessarily accepting divine revelation. In this context, how do you view Christ?

As you can imagine, I dislike labels. I suppose theist is the term you are after. The bogey of Unitarianism is always round the corner. I find difficulty with Christology, although we no longer go to the stake for heresy. But one can't be too dogmatic either way. "What think you of Christ?" has been a key question for nearly two thousand years. At times his divinity, in its unique sense, seems to me a product of the mythopoeic imagination. At others, the Trinitarian doctrine seems best to do justice to the mystery of personality or the divine economy. But what I reject is deism, understood as the belief in a God who once made the world, and then left it to run by itself, like a self-correcting machine, a pioneer of negative feedback. Of course, this accords with certain mechanistic theories of a certain kind of scientist. But it does no justice to the experience of many artists and religious that the Earth is alive, and even to the views of people like J. E. Lovelock, with his concept of Gaia. I don't want to make it sound just like vitalism. Some would dismiss it as nature mysticism, and certainly it is more to be apprehended via nature, as when in contemplating the stars at night we become aware of the music of the spheres, or in lonely places experience the breathing of the divine being. This is why I dismissed the mechanistic overtones of deism. Is it not analysis and dissection and the growth of the modern conurbation that have come between us and the sense of the living God before whom all created life sings "Holy, Holy, Holy"? We have recalled a great deal recently, with the aid of inspired writers, of how close to a living God most so-called primitive peoples like the Bushman and the American Indian felt before the predatory, pragmatic white man blundered upon the scene. How can one be dogmatic about Christ? He was a poet and drew his imagery largely from nature. I use the past tense, while disclaiming deism. Presumably he spoke Hebrew and Aramaic. How do I talk to a living Christ in Welsh or English? But then there are the bread and the wine.

JB.   You have referred at various times to your reading of Eliot, Yeats, and Wallace Stevens. Do you read the work of younger contemporaries writing in English—Ted Hughes or Seamus Heaney, for example? How would you evaluate their poetry?

I don't keep abreast of contemporary writing in English, or any other language for that matter. I am remote in Llŷn, do not take English papers or magazines, and the libraries' English sections are poor. As some of the work of contemporary English poets becomes available in paperback, I sometimes buy a copy, but without much excitement. I think most contemporary English poetry suffers from a kind of *fin de siècle* enervation. Is there a new T. S. Eliot in incubation? I doubt it. When Ted Hughes burst on the scene a generation ago, he was powerful and verbally alive. There was never much food for the spirit there, and perhaps for this reason he has not maintained momentum. Reading the general adulation of Seamus Heaney makes me wonder if I know what poetry is. Here is a normally good poet receiving abnormal acclaim. I think I understand some of the reasons. Faber were looking for a new poet. Charles Monteith was a Northern Irelander and Northern Ireland is on England's conscience in a way that Wales is not. Robert Lowell also enjoyed an inflated reputation, and Heaney came under his influence. It would have been better had he not. I can see that Heaney's texture is good. England so often has to rely on her fringes for linguistic rejuvenation of her poetry. If I were an Englishman, I should be worried. With science and technology so enormously influential, spawning as they do new words every day, and with the decay of traditional beliefs in God, soul, and the afterlife, surely what England should be waiting for is a poet who can deploy the new vocabulary and open up new avenues, or should I say airways for the spirit in the twenty-first century. But instead of that the critics and reviewers are sold on a poet obsessed with an Irish background that is largely rural, and with his own personal problems. As I have mentioned already, I resent a kind of new treason of the clerks, where poetry is concerned. The old established masters of yesteryear are safe ground, and the studies of Pope or Marvell continue to roll from the presses. But contemporary minor poets are read for titillation rather than as writers worthy of standard treatment in a full-length study, thus helping to downgrade contemporary poetry to a fringe activity of the scientific-technological and politico-economic society in England today. What has become of the great mode of expression in which the English language was supreme? One of the reasons why I gave up *The Times Literary Supplement* was that it would print prose in verse form and it is this prose element in contemporary English verse that is so detracting. Rilke said that a poet's chief duty was to praise. This certainly was to the fore in the Welsh bardic tradition. To do so today is to be called "sloppy" by the trendy reviewers in London. My one great exception would be Geoffrey Hill, who still has many of the virtues to be expected from a serious poet.

NT.   I believe you have said that not much Welsh poetry appeals to you outside the strict meters. That must be an exaggeration when one thinks of Gwenallt, Waldo, Parry-Williams, and others. But perhaps you could enlarge on your position. What Welsh poetry gives you the most pleasure?

I don't like denigrating in English the work of contemporary Welsh poets. I must excuse myself for my inability to get the best out of Welsh poetry. I was thirty when I began learning Welsh and by then English speech and English ways of thought were established. I never aim to criticize Welsh writing because I have no right. I have read the poets you mention, of course, but to be honest I don't get the same satisfaction from them as from others you have mentioned such as Yeats, Eliot, Pound, and Wallace Stevens, nor as I do from some poets in the only other language I can read, namely Valéry, Claudel, and St. John Perse. So with one or two honorable exceptions it is still the earlier Welsh poetry that stirs me, especially in its use of *cynghanedd* to bring out the beauty and associations of our dear names.

NT.   I remember seeing only one published poem of yours in Welsh, a version, or something not too far from a version of "A Peasant." Did you try your hand on other occasions? And why did you give it up? Are we talking about levels of linguistic skill, or something deeper and more mysterious? Is the impossibility of writing poetry in Welsh part of the same tension that makes you a poet at all perhaps?

When questioned on this subject my defense is that I know of no poet any-where who has written major poetry in his second language. It has to do with immediacy and self-consciousness. I have obviously tried my hand at Welsh poems. But beginning learning at thirty was hardly the best way to produce poetry of substance. I failed to satisfy my own poetic standards. So I have now reached a position in old age, when the habit of poetic expression in English is so ingrained that I cannot conceive that I could have written so in Welsh. I cannot see how Welsh as it is now would have been available for the requirements I make upon language. It is a confession which gives me no joy, and one which could be held up to ridicule by a skilled Welsh debater.

NT. Why should prose be so different? On whom, if anyone, have you modeled your Welsh prose? How difficult do you find it to write? Do you perceive yourself as the same person when writing in Welsh?

It used to be acknowledged that poetry was language at its highest level of articulation. Many have been the attempts to define poetry; none have been wholly successful, but there is still a feeling that bears out what I said above, despite the fact that the novel has largely ousted poetry in the public view. Modern fiction has encroached on poetry here and there. But remember Eliot's contention that poetry should at least be as well written as prose. So when I write a poem I am deploying language at a higher tension, in a more concise and memorable way than when writing prose. And its success depends on the naturalness and instinctiveness which comes to me from my mother tongue, my first language, which happens to be English. I am drawing on resources of resonance and memorability which are the fiber of the language as it has been formed over the centuries.

Notice Seamus Heaney's emphasis on this, although he is no more of an Englishman than I am. And all the while I am composing a poem, my critical faculty is active, correcting errors of taste, of sound, and guiding me in my effort to raise the level of the statement to "more than mortal tongue." Because I began too late in Welsh to do this in poetry, I have had to content myself with expressing some things in Welsh prose, which suggests that I do not find it as difficult as poetry. Since moving to Llŷn, where I could at last use the language daily, my Welsh has improved. I am more fluent and deploy a wider vocabulary. Unfortunately, the enjoyment of speaking what should have been my first language has led to garrulity. I talk too much in company, and this coupled with old age has led to a glibness when writing in Welsh. I am dealing with more homely things, so to say, and the precision, which more abstract and educated thought demands, is absent too often. I cannot commend this. It is a slight to the Welsh tradition. The aim should be newness of subject, while retaining the native idiom of good Welsh prose. The question is often asked as to whether I think in Welsh or in English. But it should be obvious that when speaking or writing either, I am thinking in that particular medium, so when I write in Welsh, I am to some extent a different person from the one who writes in English. And in my case the learning of Welsh came so late that I am afraid it could only be imposed or intruded into an embedded Englishness in many ways, although life in Wales from the age of six is bound to have had an effect, too.

JB.   Neb is credited as having been edited by Gwenno Hywyn. Could you comment on the circumstances in which it was written and in what ways the text was edited?

Gwasg Gwynedd had a short series called "Cyfres y Cewri," namely small autobiographies. I was asked to contribute. I don't know what editing entailed. I know Gwenno Hywyn and we had one or two conversations, but there was never any question of interference. I don't remember reading the finished product, but presumably they would have corrected any mistake of grammar or phrasing.

JB.   About the time you published H'm (1972), you experimented much more with stepped, indented lines, and broke syntax more radically across the line. You consolidated this in Laboratories of the Spirit (1975) by dropping the conventional capital letter at the beginning of the line. It seems a major development related to distinct changes in subject matter. This new style is very unlike most contemporary English or Anglo-Welsh poetry—but there are analogies, at least, with the work of American poets like William Carlos Williams. Could you comment on what led you toward these changes?

I left Eglwysfach with its hinterland of Welsh hill country in 1967. I had many uncollected poems at the time and these were published as *Not That He Brought Flowers* in 1968. Looking back both geographically and chronologically from the peninsula, where I then was, I felt I had more or less exhausted that theme. The change of style came with a certain change of perspective and the poems in *H'm* were offered to a new publisher on the advice of my former one, many of whose staff had moved to Macmillan on his retirement. You are correct in thinking that William Carlos Williams was influential in my change of form in certain poems, as being apter for new subject matter and new thinking.

JB.   In your latest collection, The Echoes Return Slow *(1988), short passages, set as prose, are juxtaposed with free verse. There is a formal distinction; yet the prose often has a striking metaphoric expression similar to the verse. What was in your mind when you set the book out in this way? And what distinctions would you make between poetry and prose?*

I was partially influenced by Geoffrey Hill's *Mercian Hymns,* but did not want to imitate him with a prose sequence. Partly I had in mind Coleridge's gloss on the verses in "The Ancient Mariner." It was a kind of counter-pointing. I am not an authority on English prose tradition, but imagine that the two media should be kept strictly apart. This century has seen the encroachment of prose upon poetry, and the deterioration of poetry into bad prose, bad prose set out in poetic form. In shorthand I would say that the difference is in cadence.

JB.   You used rhyme quite often in your early poetry, but later abandoned it. Could you say why?

I was more conventionally motivated lyrically in Manafon. Schubert's quartets and the *C major Quintet* were still echoing in my mind, and rhyme, both terminally and internally, conveyed best my view of the hill country at that time. Later the same hill country seemed to be aside from so many contemporary currents and rhyme seemed to be a trifle too sweet in the attempt to come to terms with those currents.

NT.   Few would think of you as a love poet, yet I have always thought that a small number of your poems would find their way into my anthology of love poetry—I think, for example, of "Not That He Brought Flowers." This seems infinitely delicate, at the edges of what words can be found for, and therefore parallel perhaps with those forays to the edges of what can be said about religious feeling. In a different context, I remember your saying in a lecture that you would have liked to create a woman figure comparable with Kathleen ni Houlihan for whom men would be willing to die. Is this all tantamount to saying that you see yourself as a diffident love poet?

Diffident is the word, is it not? We are all afraid of laughter, at being called soft or sentimental; and certainly such states destroy art. Passion seems to have departed from the poetry I am familiar with in English, Welsh, or French. I shy at the word "darling" which was all too current a while ago. It has something to do with linguistic deflation. Surely most of us would like to write a great love poem to God, to Wales, to our betrothed. It would have to be passionate; but we meander and grow shallow, if subtle.

JB.   The Minister *was a commissioned work, yet it shows a reserve in you for longer, formalized dramatic poetry. You have never followed this up, however. Could you say why?*

I think it is mainly a question of subject matter. When the request came from the BBC I had been thinking about a Welsh Nonconformist minister's position, so was able to elaborate around an already existing poem. But I have not had enough experience of different kinds of people to amass material for another dramatic poem. As you know, I have written other longer poems more recently, but they are about individuals such as Ann Griffiths.

NT.   *You have published two volumes of poetry which take paintings as their subject. Your wife of course is an artist and this must have helped bring you in contact with the visual arts. But over and above this, do you feel a particular affinity for visual art, as against music, say? What is its appeal? Its static quality? The escape from time?*

It is a welcome relief from the obsession with speech and writing to realise the number of other forms of expression, and communication, such as painting, dancing, musical composition and so on. Remember Eleanora Duse's retort when asked to explain what her dance meant: "If I could explain it in words, do you think I would go to the enormous trouble of dancing it?" I try to understand that scientists, too, in mathematics, are engaged in modes of expression which differ only to a degree from those of artists in the broadest sense. Owing to where I live much of my pleasure in painting has had to rely on the secondhand medium of reproduction. It was while musing on those that I wrote two series of poems as pastiches on the original, although through publishing the illustrations in monochrome the publishers lessened the impact of some of the poems. The poems are attempts to comment and to draw out extended meanings in a way which most of the painters would have found reprehensible, because painting has its own plastic and compositional values. The appeal, as you suggest, has much to do with the appeal of reproduction, that an object, place or situation seen with one's eye is not the same as when they are presented by another, be it the artist's brush or the camera. But I am too fond of music to say that my affinity for visual art exceeds it.

NT. Could I then ask you what music you are particularly fond of, and whether, in your view, this has entered into your poetry? And since you have twice mentioned dancing, perhaps I should ask you about that too. Is this a Yeatsian kind of interest?

I am musically uneducated, so am in the position of the man in the street who "knows what he likes." I graduated through Italian opera to chamber music, especially Beethoven, Schubert, Mozart. I do not understand contemporary music technically, so tend to prefer earlier. Apart from madrigals and a few carols I have never been able to stand English song. I like now polyphony, Mozart's operas, and Schubert's songs, but not much later vocal stuff, apart from genuine folk singing such as one hears from a few Irish singers in Irish. But all this tends to make me *laudator temporis acti,* hating modern noise and vocal "ugliness."

All forms of formal dancing appeal to me, ballet and genuine folk dancing. It is the attraction of another mode of expression than speech, the patterns in folk dancing, the gestures in ballet with the underlying reference to the dance of life against the void's backdrop.

The Topography
of R. S. Thomas

Brian Morris

Reprinted from The Little Review, *13/14 (1980): 5–11.*

Neither Manafon nor Eglwysfach is listed in the *Blue Guide to Wales.*[1]
They are too small, no one famous was born or died there, and neither
village contains any monument of architectural or historical importance.
Aberdaron, described as "the remotest village in all Wales," is mentioned
only as the birthplace of Richard Roberts Jones (1780–1843), called "Dick
of Aberdaron," who is said to have taught himself thirty-five languages, and
who never found anything useful to do with any of them. Yet these three
villages, and their parishes, were R. S. Thomas's place of work for thirty-
six years, and nearly all his poetry has been written while he lived in one
or another of them. His self-selected surroundings have exercised a profound and creative influence on his thought and his art, and a mild topo-
graphical meditation may be found to aid exegesis.

Mr. Thomas was born in 1913 in Cardiff, which was then a great
coal-exporting port in the southeast corner of Wales. During the Great War
his father served in the Merchant Navy, and the family lived in various
places, including Liverpool, until they settled in Caergybi (Holyhead) on
the extreme northwest tip of the island of Anglesey in 1918. So his boyhood was spent on the verges of the sea, in ports, and at the extreme edges
of Wales. The importance of "boundaries"—whether the natural barrier
of the sea or the invisible one of the border between England and Wales—
persisted through his training as a theological student at St. Michael's
College, Llandâf. His home was at Caergybi, and Llandâf is a suburb of

47

Cardiff, so his train journey at the beginning and end of term took him almost the whole length of the English-Welsh border, through the area known as "The Marches," the scene of interminable warfare and dispute between England and Wales during the Middle Ages. After ordination, he served his two curacies in the Marches: the first (1936–40) at Chirk, in what was then Denbighshire (where he met and married the painter Mildred Eldridge), and the second (1940–42) at Hanmer, in Flintshire. Both Chirk and Hanmer are small villages in rolling, pastoral, predominantly agricultural country, and though they are geographically in Wales, both are within sight of the English border. As a curate, Mr. Thomas did not have an entirely free choice about his place of work, but it is significant that when, as a priest, he chose his first parish, it was at Manafon (Montgomeryshire), only some thirty miles, as the crow flies, southwest of Hanmer, and still very much on the edge of Wales. In one of his novels the Anglo-Welshman Raymond Williams gives a description of two (fictional) villages which catches the unique flavor of this border area:

> A river runs between Llangattock and Peterstone, and that is the border with England. Across the river, in Peterstone, the folk speak with the slow, rich, Herefordshire tongue. . . . On this side of the river is the quick Welsh accent, less sharp, less edged, than in the mining valleys which lie beyond the Black Mountains, to the south and west, but clear and distinct—a frontier crossed in the breath.[2]

Manafon lies deeper in Wales than that, but the distinction is still valid. The people of Manafon habitually speak English, not Welsh, and in their social and political life they look as much toward the English towns of Oswestry and Hereford as to the local Welsh market towns of Y Trallwng (Welshpool) and Y Drenewydd (Newtown). And, contrary to what one might expect in reading Mr. Thomas's first four published volumes of verse, Manafon is not an exposed hill village, surrounded by moors and mountains, and peopled by peasants more isolated than the sheep they tend. It lies very snugly in a small river valley, the fields are hedged, the pasture reasonably rich, and the hills which lie around it are no more than a few hundred feet high. The village itself is strung out on both sides of a minor road (the B 4390) which connects the equally unimportant villages of Berriew and New Mills; it has no village green, no recognizable "center," and the cottages, bungalows, and houses represent every architectural style (or lack of it) from Tudor to twentieth-century council building at its most starkly functional. The little church of St. Michael and All Angels, which Mr.

Thomas served, is an ancient structure, stone built, with a good timber roof. But it was heavily restored in 1898, its rood screen is uncompromisingly modern, and the overall effect is of a well-kept but quite undistinguished piece of Victorian ecclesiastical rural architecture. It has neither the beauty nor the historical associations of the churches he knew at Chirk and Hanmer. Manafon has nothing of the romantic associations of George Herbert's Bemerton, or even Henry Vaughan's Llansantffraed, but neither does it exhibit the powerful rural squalor of George Crabbe's Aldeburgh. Yet it was in Manafon that Mr. Thomas wrote and published the poems in *The Stones of the Field* (1946), *An Acre of Land* (1952), and *The Minister* (1955). And many of the later poems in *Song at the Year's Turning* (1955) were written during his Manafon ministry.

The very titles of some of these early poems give a fair indication of their tone and content. "Out of the Hills," "A Labourer," "A Peasant," "The Welsh Hill Country," "Cynddylan on a Tractor," "Death of a Peasant," and "The Lonely Farmer," for example, suggest that the poet is concerned to observe the hill farmer, the moorland sheepman, and the isolated laborer rather than to chronicle the social life of the village in the valley. The images and characters of the poems would find few counterparts in Manafon, Hanmer, or Chirk.

> Consider this man in the field beneath,
> Gaitered with mud, lost in his own breath,
> Without joy, without sorrow,
> Without children, without wife,
> Stumbling insensitively from furrow to furrow,
> A vague somnambulist; but hold your tears,
> For his name also is written in the Book of Life. . . .
>
> ("Affinity")

This man is close kin to Twm, whose fate is recorded toward the end of "The Airy Tomb":

> No, no, you must face the fact
> Of his long life alone in that crumbling house
> With winds rending the joints, and the grey rain's claws
> Sharp in the thatch; of his work up on the moors
> With the moon for candle, and the shrill rabble of stars
> Crowding his shoulders. . . .

These are uneducated, inarticulate men, and their utterance must be created for them by the poet:

I am the farmer, stripped of love
And thought and grace by the land's hardness;
But what I am saying over the fields'
Desolate acres, rough with dew,
Is, Listen, listen, I am a man like you. . . .

("The Hill Farmer Speaks")

But the peasant's platitudes and silences remain a problem. In "Enigma,"
Mr. Thomas describes "a man of the fields":

Blind? Yes, and deaf, and dumb, and the last irks most,
For could he speak, would not the glib tongue boast
A lore denied our neoteric sense,
Being handed down from the age of innocence?
Or would the cracked lips, parted at last, disclose
The embryonic thought that never grows?

It was partly to solve this problem that he created the character of Iago
Prytherch:

Just an ordinary man of the bald Welsh hills,
Who pens a few sheep in a gap of cloud.
Docking mangels, chipping the green skin
From the yellow bones with a half-witted grin
Of satisfaction . . .

("A Peasant")

Prytherch appears in many poems in several volumes, and he acts various
roles as spokesman, confidant, opponent, and even *alter ego* for the poet.
Though he is Welsh, he speaks (as the poet always writes) in English, and
this is indicative of the subdued paradoxes, problems, and obliquities which
lie beneath the surface of the "Manafon" volumes. Prytherch and his kin
belong not to the village but to the hills, and the poems of this period find
their origin not in Manafon, but in the hills and moorland of Cefn Coch
above Adfa, more than ten miles to the West. There, the hills, Mynydd y
Gribin and Y Glonc, rise to over fifteen hundred feet, and the land is harsh
and unfertile. But it was while walking there, and talking to the farmers
and laborers who went to form the composite figure of Prytherch, that Mr.
Thomas heard the Welsh language spoken as the normal language of discourse. It became clear to him that he was alienated from these people,
whose way of life fascinated him, by a complicated system of chasms and
barriers. As a rector of the Church in Wales he represented a certain kind
of spiritual, cultural, and social authority. Very few of the hill farmers were

committed Churchmen; some were nonconformist chapelgoers—and since the nineteenth century the chapels have exercised greater influence in Wales than the Church—and many were of no religious persuasion at all. Mr. Thomas was also an import, an outsider. He had not been born and brought up in the area, and so he was not part of that thoroughly known and jealously guarded reticulation of family relationships on which Welsh social life was (and still is) based. Not to be second cousin to someone in the area sets a man apart. He was also a university man, having read classics at the University College of Wales, Bangor, and education was so esteemed in rural Wales that its possessor was marooned on an island of respect. But, above all, he was not "Welsh" in the sense that Welsh was not his first language, and this makes a permanent and irreversible difference. The pure, true Welshman is born in Wales of Welsh parents, and has the Welsh language as his native tongue. Into this élite Mr. Thomas can never enter, for although he learned Welsh as an adult, and speaks it fluently, it is not his first language and never can be. He feels this ultimate exclusion very deeply, and has said that an Anglicized upbringing like his "prevents one from ever feeling a hundred per cent at home in Welsh Wales." Poems about Wales, its history, its culture, and its plight form a steady presence in the poems written at Manafon. The range is wide. There is direct evocation of historical events, like "The Rising of Glyndŵr," and "The Tree"; there are withering denunciations, like "Welsh Landscape":

> . . . an impotent people,
> Sick with inbreeding,
> Worrying the carcase of an old song.

There is satire, as in "A Welshman to Any Tourist," and there are a few glimpses of political utterance, though these are hedged by ironies, shielded by indirections and allusions:

> When we have finished quarrelling for crumbs
> Under the table, or gnawing the bones
> Of a dead culture, we will arise,
> Armed, but not in the old way.
>
>   ("Welsh History")

And to see the significance of the last line of the poem "Wales"— "Gwernabwy's eagle with the sharp claws"—one needs to know the context in the mediaeval Welsh tale of "Kulhwch and Olwen."[3] There is a depth and a complexity in some of these poems about Wales which is by no means evident from their deceptively simple surfaces.

A crucial move took place in 1954. Mr. Thomas exchanged the living of Manafon for that of Eglwysfach, an equally small, rural village, some twelve miles northeast of Aberystwyth on the road to Machynlleth. In some ways it resembles Manafon: it is strung out along the road, the countryside is agricultural, and the minor mountain of Pen Carreg-gopa rises to 1467 feet behind it to the southeast. But it is on the opposite (West) side of Wales, and it looks out over the estuary of the Dovey, which flows into Cardigan Bay only a mile or so away. There are sea birds on the mud flats, and long views. As Manafon lies on the border of England and Wales, so Eglwysfach lies on the border of Wales and the Irish Sea. But, above all, the new parish was about as far into Welsh-speaking Wales as one might get. Aberystwyth, with its University College and the National Library of Wales, is in some ways the cultural capital. It was close enough to have a pervasive influence, yet sufficiently distant to discourage trippers, tourists, and all the machinery of urban life he had sedulously disdained. Mr. Thomas has frequently said that he has always tried to live and work in rural areas among Welsh-speaking Welshmen. He wished and needed to be as close as possible to the roots he could never completely call his own. Eglwysfach would seem to be the perfect place. It did not turn out to be so. As a priest, and the Vicar of a parish, Mr. Thomas was necessarily concerned very closely with parochial affairs, and he found that the people most devoted to the parish and most influential in its administration were not Welsh, but English; they were retired tea planters, ex-military men, and the like, who, in many cases, had retired to this edge of Wales after a life spent in England or abroad, and who had no ancestral or family links with the region at all. Many of the church services were in English, and the national consciousness exuded by nearby Aberystwyth was perhaps less evocative and stimulating than he could have wished. Eglwysfach, like Manafon, was not pure, but mixed; once again, his need as a poet for an essentially and naturally Welsh community had been thwarted.

At Eglwysfach there are certain facts and objects with which he had to live. The Nonconformist chapel at the north end of the village represents that element of stern, pure, but often mean and deadening Calvinism which is an ever-present element in Welsh life. He had written about it at what was, for him, great length, in *The Minister* (1953), but it was a hard spirit, resistant to poetic exorcism. There was the artery of the road through the village, thickening and furring with traffic year by year. There were the visitors, the holidaymakers, the strangers who settled there, diluting the shy, local culture. There was the local "beauty spot," known as "Artists' Valley," just to the south, which was normally the high-water mark for the tourist tide from the seaside resorts. And at the bottom of the narrow cul-de-sac past his gaunt vicarage lay the bird sanctuary.[4] Between the sanctuary and the road stands the church. It is an undistinguished gray stone building, slate-roofed, restored and cared for so that it seems neither ancient nor modern. Inside, with its panelling, its pews, and its gallery, it has a distinctly nineteenth-century atmosphere, plain, frugal, decent, and decorous. Here, for nearly thirteen years, Mr. Thomas exercised his ministry as one of the "Country Clergy" he adroitly describes:

> Venerable men, their black cloth
> A little dusty, a little green
> With holy mildew . . .

To his years at Eglwysfach belong the four volumes *Poetry for Supper* (1958), *Tares* (1961), *The Bread of Truth* (1963), and *Pietà* (1966). To make this assignment is no more than a convenient abstraction, since some of the poems in these volumes were written at Manafon, some look back to that place and its people, and some are proleptic of what were to be his concerns in a later period. Iago Prytherch lives on, and the engagement with him continues in *Poetry for Supper* and later:

> Prytherch, man, can you forgive
> From your stone altar on which the light's
> Bread is broken at dusk and dawn
> One who strafed you with thin scorn
> From the cheap gallery of his mind?
>   ("Absolution")

The hills above Manafon are seductive, but the poet is aware of the succulent bogs of nostalgia:

> The temptation is to go back,
> To make tryst with the pale ghost
> Of an earlier self, to summon
> To the mind's hearth, as I would now,
> You, Prytherch . . .
>   ("Temptation of a Poet")

One senses the specter of W. B. Yeats there, as well as Prytherch's. Eglwysfach presented new horizons. There is a sprinkling of new characters, like Walter Llywarch,

> Born in Wales of approved parents,
> Well goitered, round in the bum . . .

Job Davies, "eighty-five / Winters old," the Puw family, and Rhodri Theophilus Owen. There are some controlled, moving poems about his married life, and others about the seashore, and birds. But two particular developments stand out in the poems of these volumes: a deepening concern with the nature of the Deity, and a more explicit, impassioned commitment to the state of Wales. The first could be easily illustrated by poems like "The Journey" (*Poetry for Supper*), "Dialectic" (*Tares*), or "Souillac: Le Sacrifice d'Abraham" (*The Bread of Truth*). But perhaps the key to the new direction is the title poem of *Pietà*, with its startling, distracting image of the empty cross's agony:

> Always the same hills
> Crowd the horizon,
> Remote witnesses
> Of the still scene.
>
> And in the foreground
> The tall Cross,
> Sombre, untenanted,
> Aches for the Body
> That is back in the cradle
> Of a maid's arms.

The second development, toward an increasingly nationalistic utterance, is as powerful but less easy to chart. "Border Blues," the opening poem of *Poetry for Supper*, is only partly comprehensible without detailed knowledge of Welsh history, mythology, folklore, geography, and the Welsh language:

> *Eryr Pengwern, penngarn llwyt heno* . . .
> We still come in by the Welsh gate, but it's a long way
> To Shrewsbury now from the Welsh border.

Mr. Thomas had never written in the style of "Border Blues" before, but new directions require powerful adjustments. He has never written in quite that style since. A few of the other poems in *Poetry for Supper* are openly concerned with national characteristics, though, as usual, the statements are double-edged:

> . . . Welsh
> With all the associations,
> Black hair and black heart
> Under a smooth skin,
> Sallow as vellum; sharp

Of bone and wit that is turned
As a knife against us
                    ("Expatriates")

As a collection, *Tares* shows a stronger concern with the conditions of life in Wales. Poems like "Abersoch" and "Hyddgen" brood upon places; "Walter Llywarch" examines the cramp and sourness of Welsh social life, in the school and the chapel where he hears "Tales of a land fairer than this"; and in "A Welsh Testament" the poet senses the trap into which the accident of birth has cast him:

> . . . the absurd label
> Of birth, of race hanging askew
> About my shoulders.

The contemporary scene surfaces briefly but clearly here, in a moment of aggressive irony:

> . . . You are Welsh, they said:
> Speak to us so; keep your fields free
> Of the smell of petrol, the loud roar
> Of hot tractors; we must have peace
> And quietness. . . .

The quietness, he points out, would be the stillness of a museum, where everything is tidy, but dead.

The most fiercely nationalistic poems are undoubtedly those which appear in *The Bread of Truth*. The mockery is still there, and strong:

> Why must I write so?
> I'm Welsh, see:
> A real Cymro,
> Peat in my veins . . .
>   ("Welsh")

And so is the withering self-reproach, for later in the same poem he says, "I can't speak my own / Language—Iesu, / All those good words: / And I outside them. . . ." There are other attitudes, and different tones, but they all build up to the savage statement in the last lines of "Looking at Sheep," with which the volume ends:

> Seeing how Wales fares
> Now, I will attend rather
> To things as they are: to green grass
> That is not ours; to visitors

Buying us up. Thousands of mouths
Are emptying their waste speech
About us, and an Elsan culture
Threatens us.
                  What would they say
Who bled here, warriors
Of a free people? Savagely
On castles they were the sole cause
Of the sun still goes down red.

The "Elsan" is a chemical lavatory, much used in caravans, and Mr. Thomas's language here is harshly direct. He remembers Synge's dictum that before language can become human again it must become brutal. The sentiments in these lines would have been applauded by Plaid Cymru, the Welsh Nationalist Party (though the poet has never belonged to it), and the end of the poem might easily be taken to advocate a form of resistance to invasion which transcends the simply verbal. This aspect of the volume escaped most of the London-based critics:

> His subject is not a parish but the bare, inner landscape of atonement. In a deceptively simple and unassuming way, this is a profound and original work.
>
> (A. Alvarez)

Mr. Alvarez missed at least part of the point, but it was not lost on critics and readers in Wales, some of whom were beginning to think of Mr. Thomas as a revolutionary bard. Those who did so were disappointed, for his next collection, *Pietà,* contains no call to arms, no rebel songs. The nationalist strain is submerged, present in poems like "Rose Cottage," "The Provincial," "A Welshman at St. James's Park," and "On Tour," but shifting and evanescent. No one could call these political poems. The wind of change had, once again, changed direction. It may be that the disappointment, the mild frustration at finding that Eglwysfach was not the Welsh Eden to which he was striving to return, bred a kind of resentment, or sense of deprivation, which issued in the overtly nationalistic poems in *The Bread of Truth.* He was searching for a society, a way of life and the objective correlatives of that way of life, which were truly and essentially Welsh, and he had not yet found it. Quite recently he said, cryptically, "when I was at Eglwysfach, I thought reality was a handful of wet earth. I don't think that any more."

He became Vicar of Aberdaron in 1967, and stayed there until he retired from the Anglican ministry at Easter 1978. He spent about a dozen years in each of his three incumbencies, and Aberdaron is in some ways strikingly unlike the previous two. It is a small fishing village and holiday resort, standing at the very end of the peninsula of Llŷn, with the sea on three sides, and wide skies overhead. Three miles out to sea lies the island of Ynys Enlli (Bardsey), one of the earliest Christian settlements in Wales, a place of pilgrimage in mediaeval times, and now abandoned except for the ornithological observatory, which Mr. Thomas visits regularly. The headland above Aberdaron is composed of Pre-Cambrian rock, some of the oldest on earth, anything up to a thousand million years of age. The isolation, the freedom from tourists (at least for nine months of the year), the wide perspectives of sea and sky, the evidences of a world before life began, and a community of farmers, fishermen, and sailors were obviously appealing. But, most important of all, Aberdaron is a Welsh-speaking society. Welsh is the first language of most of the inhabitants; it is the language of conversation in the streets and the shops; church services are predominantly in Welsh. As Vicar of this parish, Mr. Thomas could answer his telephone in the vernacular. At Aberdaron, at last, he could live and work and write in one of the last remaining outposts of pure Welsh Wales. He could write about his homeland from the heart of it.

The strange paradox is that from the time he settled at Aberdaron he has written virtually nothing about Wales.[5] He has abandoned the theme, and his poetry has taken a new direction—not entirely new, for there are precursors and anticipations among the Eglwysfach poems—but the emphasis, penetration, and depth of exploration in his latest four volumes marks them off from his previous work. Iago Prytherch has departed, having served his turn, and it is as if, when he had found the society and way of life he craved, Mr. Thomas was released from the necessity to write about it. This fact illustrates a general truth about his poetry: it takes its origin from dissatisfactions, it broods and breeds in discontent, it is essentially a poetry of search.

When he had found Wales, he intensified his search for God. The 1968 volume, *Not That He Brought Flowers,* sums up the past, and offers hints for the future. There are poems about the Welsh condition, like "Sir Gelli Meurig," satires, like "Welcome to Wales":

> Come to Wales
> To be buried; the undertaker
> Will arrange it for you . . .

There are poems about Welsh history, and there are moments of savage reproach and disillusion, as in the lines from "Reservoirs":

Where can I go, then, from the smell
Of decay, from the putrefying of a dead
Nation? I have walked the shore
For an hour and seen the English
Scavenging among the remains
Of our culture . . .

But the intellectual and political position is no different from that in *Pietà*
or *The Bread of Truth*. What is new is the intensity, the inwardness, of the
search for God in the religious poems. In "The Priest" he seems to have
at last made peace with the status and function of his calling. There are
prefigurations of his interest in science and medicine, as when he writes in
"St. Julian and the Leper" of the sufferer

   . . . contaminating
Himself with a kiss,
With the love that
Our science has disinfected.

But in this volume one image, which has appeared before, takes on an
increased significance. It comes in a poem called "Kneeling":

Moments of great calm,
Kneeling before an altar
Of wood in a stone church
In summer, waiting for the God
To speak . . .

It is a brief poem, and it ends with the line "The meaning is in the waiting." This picture, of a man alone, waiting upon God, who may or may
not speak, is central to the poetry Mr. Thomas has written in the last five
years. It recurs in various forms and guises in poems like "No Answer,"
"Cain," and "Via Negativa," which begins:

Why no! I never thought other than
That God is that great absence
In our lives . . .

The poems of the four most recent volumes, *H'm* (1972), *Laboratories of the
Spirit* (1975), *The Way of It* (1977), and *Frequencies* (1978), are dominantly concerned with the quest for the *deus absconditus,* a search which takes the poet
into new realms of science, philosophy, and theological speculation. The
sense of place has changed, mutated like a gene, and the poetry's concern
with the objects of the physical world is less particular, less directly exegetic.
"Pre-Cambrian," from *Frequencies,* illustrates this new style. It begins:

Here I think of the centuries,
six million of them, they say.
Yesterday a fine rain fell;
today the warmth has brought out the crowds.

"Here" is perhaps the headland of Braich-y-pwll, three miles from
Aberdaron, where the Pre-Cambrian rock forms a prominent border to the
sea, and where the misty rain sweeps in across the Irish channel. The
"crowds" may well be the tourists, who, in earlier volumes, would surely
have earned a line or two of reproach. The landscape of cliffs, weather, and
people now gets no more than a placing gesture. The poem continues:

After Christ, what? The molecules
are without redemption. My shadow
sunning itself on this stone
remembers the lava.

The shadow sunning itself on the headland is another version of the priest
kneeling in prayer at the altar, but the image has become less localized, less
specific. The poem starts from Aberdaron, but it goes on to consider the
world of Zeus, Plato, and Aristotle, and the nuclear bomb. It ends with
the recognition of the need for a faith which will enable the poet "to out-
stare the grinning faces of the inmates of its asylum," and the asylum
covers an area far greater than the borders of Wales. This simultaneous
extension of the range of reference and "interiorization" of the meditation is characteristic of Mr. Thomas's recent poems. If his work has become
less "Welsh" this is because there is less need to find for his new ideas "a
local habitation and a name." One of the poems in *Frequencies* is called
"Abercuawg," which is a place name in a mediaeval Welsh poem; its significance for Mr. Thomas is that no one knows where the place is.

Having found Wales, he has abandoned it. It still matters to him
where he lives, and in his retirement he has settled in a small cottage on
an outcrop of dolerite a few miles out of Aberdaron. *The Blue Guide* to
Wales describes the area:

To the w. extends the bay of *Porth Neigwl* (or Nigel), or *Hell's Mouth*
. . . On the w. side of Porth Neigwl are two National Trust proper-
ties, the *Creigiau Gwynedd* rocks, surmounted by an ancient hill fort,
and *Plas-yn-Rhiw-Manor*.

Perhaps mindful of the fact that the poetry he is now writing presses religious
speculation toward the limits of what, as a priest, he would have regarded as
orthodox, he said recently, "I have retired now, and I'm living at the Mouth

of Hell." The landscapes and people of Wales have been a fruitful source of poems for him in the past. But not any more. His is another journey.

Notes

1. *The Blue Guides: Wales,* ed. Rossiter (London: Ernest Benn Ltd.) and (Chicago: Rand McNally & Co.), fifth edition, 1969. This is the standard guide for tourists.

2. Raymond Williams, *Border Country* (London: 1960), pp. 32–33.

3. See *The Mabinogion,* trans. Gwyn Jones and Thomas Jones (London: Everyman Library, 1949), pp. 125–26. The story mentions the ousel of Cilgwri, the owl of Cawlwyd, and the Eagle of Gwernabwy, among others, as guides in Gwrhyr's search for Mabon. One might note also that the title of Mr. Thomas's poem "The Airy Tomb" is an allusion to the grave of the legendary Myrddin (Merlin), who disappeared into a crystal tomb beneath Bardsey Island, bearing with him the "thirteen treasures of Britain." "Kulhwch and Olwen" was composed to tell the story of the thirteen treasures. See Malory, *Le Morte d'Arthur,* iv. i, and Charles Squire, *Celtic Myth and Legend, Poetry and Romance* (London: n.d.), pp. 339–40. Nothing of this is explicit in Mr. Thomas's poem.

4. The Rectory and the Vicarages Mr. Thomas has lived in have all been gaunt, though with varying qualities of starkness. Manafon Rectory is an elegant, severe, simple Georgian-style house, set apart from the village. The Vicarage at Eglwysfach is an uglier edifice, a house that seems all elbows and knees, though it is not without a certain strength of character. Aberdaron Vicarage is stern and restrained. Large, stone-built, slate-roofed, and hung with slate tiles, it stands isolated in fields above the village. Next to it is an abandoned church. At the end of the nineteenth century the villagers, finding that their twelfth-century church at the edge of the sea was in danger at high tides, with uncharacteristic optimism built a new church on the hill. The optimism was unfounded. A sea wall was built, and the old church of St. Hywyn continues in use. The new church was closed after a few years, and it now stands derelict and mouldering, doors locked and windows broken. The Vicarage surveys this ruin on one side, the sea on the other.

5. To defeat both symmetry and successful generalization, he did publish a small collection *What Is a Welshman?* in 1974, which is wholly concerned with Welsh matters. But it is perhaps in a lighter vein than his other work, and he does not seem to regard it as a major collection.

Keeping His Pen Clean

R. S. Thomas and Wales

M. Wynn Thomas

In a lecture he delivered on December 10, 1938, Saunders Lewis enquired whether Wales had indeed recently managed to produce a distinctive national literature in the English language.[1] At that time Lewis was easily the most dominant figure on the Welsh cultural scene. A founder member of *Plaid Cymru* (the Welsh Nationalist Party), he had recently been given a hero's welcome by a crowd of thousands upon his release from prison. He had served a term in Wormwood Scrubs for setting fire to a bombing school established by the English government, in the teeth of Wales-wide opposition, on a cultural site of historic importance. He was also a giant creative talent—poet, dramatist, novelist, political polemicist, cultural ideologue, and literary critic—whose role in Welsh-language culture has frequently been likened, in terms both of its scale and its radically, innovatively conservative character, to that of T. S. Eliot in Anglo-American culture, or (given the very different political orientation) of Hugh MacDiarmid in the Scottish context.[2]

A mere eight years or so earlier, and the question "Is there an Anglo-Welsh Literature?" would scarcely have been worth asking. In the interim, however, a conspicuously talented generation of anglophone writers from Wales had appeared, the best known of whom, virtually from the outset, was of course Dylan Thomas.[3] These writers came mostly from the concentration of population in the English-speaking south/southeast region of the country, an area which included the depressed coalmining valleys with their associated iron, steel, and tinplate industries, and the great industrial ports of Cardiff and of Swansea. In all its aspects—its threateningly "foreign" language, hybrid culture, proletarian character, militantly social-ist politics, etc.—this region, the product of the late-nineteenth-century boom that had turned south Wales into one of the great cosmopolitan industrial centers of the world, was a nightmarish dystopia to Saunders Lewis, as it was to the cultural constituency he represented.[4]

Lewis (1893–1985) was the most brilliant member of what was virtu-ally the first generation of Welsh-speaking writers and scholars, mostly from a humble rural or semi-industrial background in the north and west, to have been made proudly aware at university of the grandeur and antiquity of a unique native literary tradition extending back some fifteen hundred years.[5] This tradition was perceived as being the very backbone of Welsh national identity, but it was clearly under serious threat—from within, in the curi-ously mixed populist and bourgeois form of the religious Nonconformity which was the drab legacy of the nineteenth century, and (much more catas-trophically) from without, in the shape of the alien, anglophone culture which industrialization had brought to the south. It was perhaps this crisis mentality that energized and sponsored the twentieth-century renaissance of Welsh-language writing, a remarkable cultural phenomenon (broadly comparable, say, to the Southern Renaissance in the U.S.A.) which was at its height in 1938 when Saunders Lewis delivered his lecture.

Given his cultural allegiance, it's not surprising that Lewis draws the lecture to a close by saying "I conclude then that there is not a separate lit-erature that is Anglo-Welsh" (13). His carefully chosen point of compari-son has been Anglo-Irish literature, whose autonomy and national authenticity is based, he argues, on four features absent from the Anglo-Welsh case: first, "a separate world from the industrial civilization of England" (7); second, a form of English which is idiomatically and rhyth-mically distinct from that of England; third, writers like Yeats who con-sciously "write for [their] own race"; and fourth, writers who (again in Yeats's phrase) were "doing something for nationalism." By contrast, "the growth of Anglo-Welsh writing in recent years is the inevitable reflection of the undirected drifting of Welsh national life. It will go on, becoming less and less incompletely English, unless there is a revival of the moral qual-ities of the Welsh people" (14). As for the most famous of Anglo-Welsh writers, his case is dismissed with a benignity that is more apparent than real: "Mr. Dylan Thomas is obviously an equipped writer, but there is nothing hyphenated [i.e., Anglo-Welsh] about him. He belongs to the English" (5).[6]

R. S. Thomas (born 1913) is an almost exact contemporary of Dylan Thomas (born 1914), but he began publishing almost a decade later than the younger man. At more or less the same time (i.e., immediately following the Second World War) he went, spurred by a sudden impulse, on a pilgrimage to visit Saunders Lewis, a man whom he did not know and had never even met. Thomas, no callow impressionable youth but a man of thirty-two, had already embarked on a cultural rite of passage. Having been brought up an English speaker in the busy ferry port of Holyhead, on the overwhelmingly Welsh-speaking island of Anglesey just off the North Wales coast, he had, toward the end of the war, begun to learn Welsh shortly before moving to serve as vicar of Manafon, a rural upland parish in mid-Wales, very near the English border. It was from there that he traveled to Saunders Lewis's home near Aberystwyth. From Lewis, Thomas seems to have received a kind of benediction both on his cultural "conversion" and on his work. In his turn, Thomas was, after a fashion, both paying very personal tribute to Saunders Lewis's intellectual preeminence and, in more general terms, acknowledging the seniority and overlordship of Welsh-language culture. These cross-cultural ties mark him off from the prewar generation of Dylan Thomas and show that he belongs to the group of Welsh writers in the English language—prominent among them being the novelist Emyr Humphreys—who first came to prominence in the postwar years. And although both R. S. Thomas and Emyr Humphreys have continued to write primarily in English, they can both be regarded as the literary sons of Saunders Lewis.

To write in English while remaining a disciple of Saunders Lewis is, of course, to be impaled on a painfully obvious contradiction, since Lewis regarded English as the language of self-alienation and the tongue that threatened the Welsh language (and hence the Welsh nation) with extinction. In some of the early essays of R. S. Thomas, however, there are unexpected signs of hope: "There are signs now that the mantle of writers like T. Gwynn Jones and W. J. Gruffydd [two of the major figures of the modern Welsh literary renaissance] is falling not upon the younger Welsh writers, but upon those of us who express ourselves in the English tongue. We must not grow heady with this distinction and forget that we also are Welshmen. Ireland has contrived to remain Irish despite her use of English, and there is no overwhelming reason why we should not succeed also, provided we can get rid of that foolish epithet Anglo-Welsh" (31).[7] Strictly speaking, this is a heretical view which Thomas quickly abjured, but it could be argued that it has continued, throughout his career, to be operative on the level of his actual writing. One of the interesting paradoxes of his case is that while in his pronouncements, over the decades, he has consistently dismissed the possibility of a Welsh literature existing in English, his poetry has not infrequently fulfilled three of the four conditions Saunders Lewis concluded, from the Anglo-Irish example, were necessary for the creation of a national literature in that language. First, it has confined itself to the non-industrial (and therefore supposedly non-English) regions of Wales; second, it has been clearly written for, and sometimes deliberately addressed to, the Welsh people; and third, it is nationalist in the very spirit of Lewis's own brand of cultural and political nationalism.

There is undoubtedly a sense in which the influence on Thomas's poetry if not of Saunders Lewis himself then of the cultural ideology with which he was so eminently associated is very widely pervasive. A simple example is provided by the poetry of the late forties through the fifties. This is the period when Thomas first came to prominence largely through the eye-catching poems he addressed to the endlessly enigmatic Iago Prytherch, the composite figure he created of the Welsh uplands farmer. The flatly contradictory elements that help make the unpredictable portrait so compelling—rustic boor, child of nature, stoical laborer, elemental man, degenerate brute, etc.—are partly the mirror image of the confused expectations Thomas had brought with him to Manafon. And these in turn had to some extent been fashioned by the concept, assiduously promoted by Welsh-language literary culture for almost a century, of a cultivated rural "gwerin" ("volk"). This was believed to form the bedrock of national life, and was regarded as being the antithesis in quality of those deracinés, the degenerate industrial proletariat. When Thomas sees Iago "fixed in his chair / Motionless, except when he leans to gob in the fire," and concludes that "There is something frightening in the vacancy of his mind" (*SP*, 3),[8] he does so against the background of his earlier (1945) belief that "the health and wealth of a country depends upon its possession of a sturdy, flourishing peasantry" (*Prose*, 22). "Here and there among the upland people," he had then been convinced, "are poets, musicians, pennillion singers, and men possessed of a rare personality" (*Prose*, 23).

Once one is alerted to the poetry's internal connections—infinitely subtle, complex, even elusive though they sometimes are—with this whole socio-cultural context, then it seems that they constitute the very warp and woof of Thomas's whole work. Even the politically induced hatred he has developed of English paradoxically nurtures the tortured passion of his creative appreciation, as a poet, of the incomparable range and power English possesses as a literary medium. The contempt he has shared with Saunders Lewis for the moral spinelessness and genial fudging of his complaisant fellow countrymen translates into the terrible clarity of syllabically weighed utterance in his late, great religious poetry:

```
            I had looked forward
to old age as a time
of quietness, a time to draw
my horizons about me,
to watch memories ripening
in the sunlight of a walled garden.
But there is the void
over my head and the distance
within that the tireless signals
come from.
```
                    (*BHN*, 99)[9]

Underlying this spare syntax of unsparing honesty is also, perhaps, a memory of the qualities of the Welsh-language poetry of the great, medieval period, as identified by Saunders Lewis and others. These qualities were not the supposedly "bardic" ones of visionary rapture and torrential eloquence, but were rather those that Saunders Lewis liked to characterize as "classical" and "aristocratic," namely the epigrammatic terseness of crafted expression.

• • •

Although Thomas has been extensively and deeply influenced by his learned experience of a Welsh-language culture whose chief conscience and custodian was, for him, Saunders Lewis, this is clearly not the place to embark on a comprehensive study of this endlessly branching subject. Instead, I propose to confine myself to some of the poems Thomas has openly and directly addressed to his Wales. There are enough of these to constitute a significant subdivision, or genre, of his poetry, randomly scattered though they originally were throughout the several volumes he published over a period of twenty years or so. This kind of writing was first discernible in the fifties, and it reached its controversial conclusion in 1974, when Thomas published a group of twelve blistering pieces. The sardonic title, *What Is a Welshman?*, he gave to the group was clearly meant to imply that a Welshman is a pretty bizarre phenomenon, resembling an inanimate thing more than he does a real person.[10]

This stiletto-slim collection is worth briefly considering, not least because it tends to be studiously ignored by the many readers who find it too bludgeoningly offensive to mention. It opens with an attack on the south Wales industrial society, and coalfield culture, which has for most of this century been at the sacred heart of an English speaker's image of his

Welshness. Like the sleeper in some medieval dream poem, Thomas lies "on the black hills / black with the dust of coal / not yet mined" (*WW,* 1) and enters the realm of visionary nightmare, experiencing, in surrealistic images, the horrors of a bastardized world. His language of repugnance recalls Saunders Lewis's notorious poem "The Deluge, 1939," where the south Wales of the depression years was imaged in terms of a place where "All flesh has festered its way on the face of the earth."[11] "Here once was Wales," remarked Lewis with obvious distaste, surveying a proletariat supine in its "culture of grease." The social plight of this disorientated people was for him, as it is for Thomas, a symptom of the moral decay that accompanies the loss of the Welsh language. Thomas draws his own poem to a close by imagining the barbed welcome extended by valleys people to one like himself, who comes to them "with a language / filched from the dictionary / of the tribes" (*WW,* 1). They protest that they await his sermon:

> and a pulpit grew up under my feet
> and I climbed into it and
> it was the cage
> of the mine-shaft down down down
> to preach to the lost souls
> of the coal-face reminding
> how green is the childhood
> of a glib people taunting
> them with the abandonment
> of the national for the class struggle
> (*WW,* 1)

This passage culminates with R. S. Thomas's hostile response to the anti-nationalist and pro-British socialism that has dominated south Wales political life for most of this century. But it begins with a wry, self-mocking allusion to the legendary occasion when, as St. David (the patron saint of Wales) was attempting to address a huge congregation in the open air, the ground rose up under his feet to provide him with a natural pulpit. By contrast, R. S. Thomas's elevation proves to be a literal let-down, and the self-mockery which infuses both this opening phrase and the whole of the quoted passage makes, in my opinion, for a much more complex political statement than is usually realized. While not for an instant questioning the truth of his message, Thomas has an eye here for the futility and absurdity of his own prim sermonizing, and seems to see the helpless distance at which history has placed him from his listeners.

The controlled pathos of this passage is, then, a measure of the tensile strength of its political vision, but in other poems in this collection the pathos that is unconsciously elicited is simply a sign of weakness. Thomas's dream (in "He is sometimes contrary") of ancient battles and mythological birds is full of the wistfulness of felt impotence (*WW,* 8); the piece "He agrees with Henry Ford" ends with a wildly grotesque image, as if his imagination had suddenly become dyslexic, in which "Cilgwri's ousel / on my ramshackle aerial / keeps the past's goal / against the balls of to-morrow" (*WW,* 11). Elsewhere in the volume his anger, too, breeds only a weak sarcasm or weaker cliché ("clerks undress / the secretaries with / their lean eyes" [*WW,* 2]), although there are occasional moments of reverberative power: "Anything to / sell? cries the tourist / to the native rummaging among / the remnants of his self-respect" (*WW,* 2).

In the last poem in the volume, however, the unevenness, of tone and of quality, in the writing seems functional and expressive—as if the ferocity of feeling that possesses the speaker makes him careless of taste and heedless of decorum. Accompanying this is a contemptuous sense of the banality of the means by which cultural catastrophe has actually been effected. The subject is the Welsh language and the way it has been "sold" for social advancement. "The decree went forth / to destroy the language"—to describe the clauses relating to the Welsh language in the 1536 Act of Union in these terms is also, of course, to bring in Herod and the slaughter of the Innocents, and when this is realized the celebrated concluding lines of the poem are reinforced by another dark surge of meaning:

> The
> industrialists came, burrowing
> in the corpse of a nation
> for its congealed blood. I was
> born into the squalor of
> their feeding and sucked their speech
> in with my mother's
> infected milk, so that whatever
> I throw up now is still theirs.
>   (*WW,* 12)

That use of the vulgar colloquialism for vomiting is all the more powerful since the linguistically fastidious Thomas so rarely uses slang, and all his resentment at his early helpless and humiliating dependence upon his domineering mother (feelings evident elsewhere in his writing) are here channeled into, and focused in, his attitude toward his "foreign" mother tongue.[12] It should also be remembered that Thomas's actual place of birth was Cardiff, the city that was very largely the creation, in the late nineteenth century, of the mine owners who opened up the south Wales coalfield. As for the title of the poem, "It hurts him to think" means exactly what, with almost brutal plainness, it says. Referring to himself in the third person as he frequently does—in this case conveying in the process a stark sense of self-alienation—Thomas makes it clear that it isn't only the thought of how "the decree went forth," etc., that hurts, but the very process of thinking itself, inseparable as it is in his tormented case from the English language.

The poem is all the more noteworthy because in it R. S. Thomas succeeds in making poetic capital out of the very coarseness of feeling that vitiates several of the other pieces in the collection, and it could be that this coarseness has its origins in the cultural and political disappointments that had ushered in the seventies. After all, the sixties had for the most part been, for Thomas, a relatively hopeful period of political turbulence, during which the bulk of his poetry about the "matter of Wales" was written. Indeed in order to understand that poetry properly one needs to know something about the important events that created the political climate of the period.[13]

In October 1965 many years of nationwide protest in Wales came to a climax when Liverpool Corporation insisted on flooding a mid-Wales valley, that had been home to a Welsh-speaking community, in order to create the reservoir of Tryweryn to service the city's industrial expansion. Embittered reaction to this development included the blowing up of pipelines in the vicinity of the dam, but the large-scale protests were mostly confined to non-violent demonstrations led by the Welsh-speaking intelligentsia. These events helped politicize a whole generation of young Welsh men and women, regardless of language, and contributed to the formation, in the late sixties, of a new nationalist consciousness that manifested itself in both the political and the cultural sectors. In particular, a new group of English-language writers came to the fore who, like the R. S. Thomas of the late forties, began to look to Welsh-language culture both for inspiration and for political orientation.

Welsh-language poets have traditionally played a politically active part in protecting their culture, and so they did at the time of Tryweryn, being prominently involved in the campaigning while also using their poetry either to advertise or to explore the issues that were at stake.[14] R. S. Thomas's poem "Reservoirs" is itself an English contribution to that significant body of literature, but it takes the form not so much of protest as of a bitter elegy for the suicide of a culture. The line breaks form precipices where Thomas's mind pauses to look down with horror into new depths of moral despair: "Reservoirs that are the subconscious / Of a people, troubled far down / With gravestones, chapels, villages even; / The serenity of their expression / Revolts me" (*SP,* 117). Tryweryn becomes his synecdoche for the whole Welsh geopolitical landscape, as Thomas sees mirrored in it the widespread signs of the self-mutilation of a people: "the smashed faces / Of the farms with the stone trickle / Of their tears down the hills' side." And central to Thomas's dark meditations is his sense of being an internal exile—of being a man, in the words of J. R. Jones, the most important Welsh cultural philosopher of the period, whose country has left *him,* rather than he it: "Where can I go, then, from the smell / Of decay, from the putrefying of a dead / Nation?"

The darkness of tone of the poem matches the undertone of pessimism in a historic radio lecture the elderly Saunders Lewis had given in February 1962.[15] He argued that the possibly terminal decline of the Welsh language was not a historical accident, but the rapidly accelerating result of deliberate English government policy. This policy had first been adopted in the Act of Union of 1536 and had thereafter been consistently implemented by means that included the mental colonization by England of the Welsh people. Central still to this ongoing process was the refusal to grant official recognition to Welsh as a language of public administration. Lewis warned that by the beginning of the twenty-first century Welsh would end as a living language if this situation was not immediately challenged and changed. The combination in his apocalyptic lecture of cool argument, searing prophecy, and astute political analysis had a galvanizing effect on his younger Welsh listeners. He had simultaneously provided them with an urgent cause, a powerful motive, and a pragmatically precise yet revolutionary program for action. By the end of the year a group of young *Plaid Cymru* activists had formed *Cymdeithas yr Iaith Gymraeg* (*The Welsh Language Society*). By the end of the decade the society, by then led by prison-tested heroes, could look back on a remarkable program of nonviolent activities which had involved extensive, well-supported campaigns of law breaking designed to gain official state recognition (and status) for the Welsh language.

"The political tradition of the centuries and all present-day economic tendencies militate against the continued existence of Welsh," said Lewis. "Nothing can change that except determination, will power [sic], struggle, sacrifice and endeavour" (*Presenting,* 139). Warmly though R. S. Thomas admired and supported the *Cymdeithas* campaigners, his poetry tended to concentrate broodingly, almost obsessively, on the unpromising facts of the contemporary Welsh situation. He saw the hopes for Wales he shared with Lewis as being everyday doubly confounded—by the ever-deepening inroads made by the English, and by the ever-weakening moral resolve of the Welsh people in general to withstand the process of Anglicization. His nationalist poetry of the sixties—and earlier—is haunted by images of invasion and of internal collapse. "We've nothing to offer you," he says, speaking as "A Welshman to Any Tourist," "no deserts / Except the waste of thought / Forming from mind's erosion" (*SP*, 41). The tone of the observation is typical. Harshly sarcastic, it speaks of a deep hidden hurt, of loathing laced with self-loathing, of a mood of settled political depression, of a feeling of humiliating impotence. It is this particular kind of raw sarcasm—not a controlled explosion of savagery, but rather the by-product of an implosion of dark feelings—that recurs in Thomas's poetry on the subject of Wales. Much rarer are the instances of irony—those occasions when he's able to maintain an inner detachment that comes across at the linguistic level as a poise which enables him to indulge in a kind of cultural *double-entendre*. "You can come in" he airily concedes in "Welcome," "You can come a long way; / We can't stop you. / . . . But you won't be inside; / You must stop at the bar, / The old bar of speech" (*WA*, 21).[16] This is plain enough, but prepares the way for the nice equivocation that follows: "We have learnt your own / Language, but don't / Let it take you in." The sentence turns on its polite axis to warn the outsider that to insist on admittance is also to invite deception.

A year before Saunders Lewis's lecture, Thomas published a poem which included his most fiercely Yeatsian dismissal of his fellow countrymen: "I find / This hate's for my own kind, / For men of the Welsh race / Who brood with dark face / Over their thin navel / To learn what to sell" (*SP*, 71). The prevalence of these and related sentiments in his subsequent poetry came to irritate not only the English-speaking Welsh but also those Welsh speakers who were heartened by the achievements of *Cymdeithas yr Iaith* and the briefly spectacular successes of *Plaid Cymru*. In 1972 Dafydd Elis Thomas, himself soon to become a *Plaid Cymru* M.P., severely criticized "The Image of Wales in R. S. Thomas's poetry."[17] Thomas was accused of "contrasting mythical past with realistic present" (62); of a "middle-class contempt for the ordinary working-class people of the industrial south-east" (63); of an "élitism" involving "the elevation of a small group who have a historical sense" (64); and finally of reducing Wales to an "image of death" (64). Dafydd Elis Thomas illustrated his argument with pointed quotations from the poetry, and ended by tartly observing that "for my generation's poets, being Welsh is not a cause for depression" (66).

There are grounds for supposing that the publication of *What Is a Welshman?* in 1974 was not unconnected with Dafydd Elis Thomas's attack two years previously. The sour venom with which the poet repeated some of his bleak images of Wales in this collection may, therefore, have been in part an answer to what he probably saw as his cocky young critic's callow optimism. However, as the poem "To pay for his keep" shows, R. S. Thomas also had the Investiture of 1969 at the back of his troubled mind. This was the grandiloquent ceremony, held at Caernarfon Castle, at which Charles, as eldest son of the English monarch, was declared Prince of Wales. People of Thomas's persuasion believed, not without very good reason, that the whole event had been cynically arranged and brilliantly stage-managed by the Labour government of the day (in which virulently anti-nationalist Welshmen held key positions) to strengthen and mobilize the British sentiments of the majority of the Welsh people. And whether this had been intended or not it certainly did happen. Moreover the Welsh-speaking community was itself deeply divided in its reactions to the event, split between fierce opposition (leading in extreme cases to acts of physical violence) and qualified support. Tension grew as the Investiture approached and the authorities were then in their turn able to take advantage of the threat and the reality of violence to instigate anti-terrorist measures that included some legally highly dubious but politically very effective police action.

Thomas found confirmation in all this, both of his pessimistic assessment of the popular Welsh character and of his suspicion that the British state would use means foul and fair, crude and subtle, to retain control of the country. From the obvious pun in its title onward, "To pay for his keep" (*WW*, 5) sets out to delineate the scene at Caernarfon in crudely distinct terms that make the poem the verbal equivalent of one of the political cartoons of the day. Thomas enters the mind of the young prince in order to show the Machiavellianism of the ruling mentality. Through Charles's eyes he sees the absurd collection of "respectables" ("rigid with imagined / loyalty"), the mean Caernarfon streets "filthy with / dog shit," and the huge castle, that ostentatious symbol of occupying power, which the politically subtle Charles deplores as unnecessary: "A few medals / would do now." The prince fills the foreground of the poem, but in the distance and beyond his notice is "that far hill / in the sun with the long line / of its trees climbing / it like a procession / of young people, young as himself." This is a shift of moral and political perspective effected by a shift of physical perspective—a device deftly suited to the occasion, since the Investiture had been deliberately conceived of as an inspiring ocular spectacle and actually became a great seductive television spectacular, the modern equivalent of a triumphal royal procession. And in that mention of trees on the far hill beyond the "city" walls of Caernarfon there may also, of course, be just a hint of Calvary to suggest the sacrifices made for the language by the young people of *Cymdeithas yr Iaith* and others.

What Is a Welshman? was, then, a postscript to Thomas's nationalist writing of the previous decade, and it placed a question mark over the optimism generated by the political culture of the period. Thereafter, Thomas has written very few poems directly on the national question. When asked about this he has, on occasions, been mischievously flippant, remarking dismissively that he has wrung that particular dishcloth dry. Left to his own devices, on the other hand, he has volunteered a much more complex and likely answer. In 1966 Thomas became vicar of Aberdaron, a tiny seaside village on the very tip of the "remote" Llŷn peninsula which is part of the rapidly eroding heartland of traditional Welsh-language culture. For him it was the culmination of a lifelong quest for the "true" Wales he had first glimpsed as an English-speaking boy in Holyhead, when he gazed across Anglesey at the magnificent profile of the mountains of Eryri (Snowdonia) in distant Gwynedd. And although Thomas soon found that in Llŷn he was in the very front line of the battle against the Anglicization of Welsh culture and the commercial despoliation of the Welsh landscape, he also found that his daily involvement in the life of the Welsh language made him less anxious to make its fate the subject of his poetry, although he was no less determined to fight for its survival. Since his retirement, in 1978, to live a few miles from Aberdaron, he has continued to be very actively involved in campaigning for various causes—C.N.D., *Cymdeithas yr Iaith,* environmental protection—but his poetry has been almost exclusively one of spiritual search, inspired in part by the great age of the geological formations of the Llŷn peninsula.[18]

• • •

That, then, would seem to be the end of the story, except that in 1987 R. S. Thomas published a collection called *Welsh Airs,* in which he for the first time gathered most of the poems he'd written about Wales into a single volume. Time doesn't stand still in politics any more than in any other sector of life, and to read these poems is in one way to realize how much things have changed over the twenty years and more since most of them were written. For many a contemporary nationalist, Thomas's map of the cultural geography of Wales seems almost to have been reversed by recent historical developments. Rural Wales is well on its way to being lost to the Welsh language, thanks to a massive in-migration of English speakers whose degree of identification with Wales remains a troublingly unknown quantity. Industrial south Wales is no more, but in the remnants of its culture can be found English speakers who have fashioned an authentically Welsh identity out of the industrial history of the valleys. In and around Cardiff— where "a girl relieved herself / of me" and where there is "a stone / doorstep I played / on a while in a brief / ignorance of where I belonged" (*WA*, 36)—there has been an extraordinary increase in the number of Welsh-medium schools. Throughout Wales there are signs that Margaret Thatcher managed to accomplish what the nationalists had failed to achieve: she has managed to produce, in reaction to her unpopular policies, a feeling among Welsh people in favor of a separate Assembly with limited powers. At the same time, the Thatcher revolution may have produced, particularly in the urban belts along the north and south Wales coasts, a generation of individualists uninterested in any kind of collective culture.

This quick social portrait of Wales in the nineties is not prelude to an attack, à la Dafydd Elis Thomas, on R. S. Thomas's supposedly grotesque misrepresentation of the contemporary scene. Rather it is intended to highlight what R. S. Thomas himself wants us to see—the challenging conservatism of the poems defiantly reprinted in *Welsh Airs,* poems that advertise the poet's loyalty to the cultural philosophy he learned in the forties under the tutelage of Saunders Lewis. Here, for the first time between two covers, can be found all those controversial elements in his nationalist poetry that have been listed by Tony Bianchi: "a cherishing [of] all those positions definitive . . . of the ethnic resurgence of the Welsh-speaking middle class: an hostility towards science and urban life as un-Welsh; an equivalent elevation of rural values; an essentialist or ahistorical concept of nationhood, based on a selective view of the past and notions of an organic tradition; a belief in the importance of an élite in defending this ideal, of which the Welsh language is an embodiment; a view of the English-speaking Welsh as alienated and needing to align themselves with these values to overcome this alienation; and above all, the elevation of culture, literature and even 'taste' as the surrogate religion which informs these convictions."[19]

When brought together in a single collection, however, the poems on these themes trace out new and interesting patterns of interconnection. Here, certainly, are those passages and poems in which Thomas jeeringly parodies the crudely pally vernacular of the Anglo-Welsh, but along with them is included "Welsh," the piece in which he adopts that very same vernacular in order to pillory himself: "Why must I write so? / I'm Welsh, see: / A real Cymro, / . . . Only the one loss, / I can't speak my own / Language—Iesu, / All those good words; / And I outside them" (*WA*, 19). Behind this, and at the very bottom, perhaps, of his conversion to cultural nationalism, is a hatred of his snobbishly anti-Welsh mother, and an obsessive desire to "accuse the womb / That bore me" (*WA*, 19). His nationalist poems are that accusation, and to see that intimately personal animus in them is also to notice anew when, as in "Border Blues," Thomas singles a woman out to represent the degeneracy of Wales: "Olwen teasing a smile / Of bright flowers out of the grass, / Olwen in nylons" (*WA*, 10); "the ladies from the council houses: / Blue eyes and Birmingham yellow / Hair, and the ritual murder of vowels" (*WA*, 10).

To personalize Thomas's nationalist poems in this and in other ways is to recover important dimensions of their meaning. "I must," he tells those council house ladies in "Border Blues," "go the way of my fathers / Despite the loneli—you might say rudeness" (*WA*, 11). The sudden, self-protective adjustment of meaning, mid-word, is significant. His nationalist poems are palimpsests in which the underlying loneliness intermittently shows through the overwritten rudeness. That is not, however, to say that he yearns to be reconciled with his people. His nationalist poems are full of a sense that isolation is, in the contemporary socio-political climate, the necessary precondition for integrity. This is very evident in "A Welshman at St. James' Park" where he refuses the invitation, inscribed in the public notices, to become "one of the public," and refuses "to admire birds / That have been seduced from wildness by / Bread they are pelted with" (*WA*, 28). But it is equally a feature of the portrait he paints, under the title "A Lecturer," of the great Welsh-language poet Gwenallt, who is described as an insignificant-looking "little man, / Sallow, / Keeping close to the wall / Of life." This exterior conceals and defends, however, an inner sanctum of genius reinforced by moral courage: "Watch him, / As with short steps he goes. / Not dangerous? / He has been in gaol" (*WA*, 23). There the syntax itself involves the reader in a double-take, as the imperative changes its meaning from an invitation simply to look at this slightly ludicrous figure to a mocking warning to keep a wary eye on him.

The syntax of several of these poems is, in fact, a reliable guide to the deep structure of Thomas's relationship to Wales. The eight uses of the connective "but" in the first two pages of the sequence "Border Blues" shows up the binary pattern of his thinking, his dependence on the dynamics of contrast—particularly between the Welsh present and the Welsh past. There is, indeed, a great deal of the Romantic ironist in Thomas, but he is at his best when he avoids the temptation—which is obviously strong in him— to play a sentimentally simple ideal off against a debased reality. "A Line from St. David's," for instance, is interesting because it dramatizes, very effectively, the way Thomas has been surprised into uncharacteristically garrulous affirmations by the fresh, untainted beauty of the ancient Pembrokeshire landscape, so that he can believe, for once, "That the old currents are in the grass, / Though rust has becalmed the plough" (WA, 18). As for those many poems in which he fiercely attacks contemporary Wales, the problem with them as *poetry* is not, as some of his critics have claimed, that they are somehow politically unfair, but rather that their rhetoric of anger does tend to grow monotonous. There is also the uneven-ness of quality that in Thomas's case seems endemic to this emotionally heightened form of writing. Within the space of a very few lines, such as the following four from "Afforestation," a poem can disconcert the reader by changing from crude invective to an image in which anger and anguish are strikingly fused: "Thin houses for dupes, / Pages of pale trash, / A world that has gone sour / With spruce" (WA, 20). The whole of "Toast" divides cleanly along this fault line, with the overblown and overworked conceit of national decay in the first ten and a half lines eventually giving way to a wearily flat question that sets up, and sets off, the epigrammatic conclusion: "What shall I say / to a people to whom provincialism / is a reasonable asking-price / for survival? I salute your / astuteness and drink to your future / from a wine-glass brimming with acid rain" (WA, 37).

In *Welsh Airs*, R. S. Thomas repeatedly returns to the version of pas-toral he particularly favors, namely the harsh political pastoral. Implicit in this is a bitter satire of the pastoral of rural idyll, as is clear in "Looking at Sheep":

> Yes, I know. They are like primroses;
> Their ears are the colour of the stems
> Of primroses; and their eyes—
> Two halves of a nut.
> But images
> Like this are for sheer fancy
> To play with. Seeing how Wales fares
> Now, I will attend rather
> To things as they are: to green grass
> That is not ours; to visitors
> Buying us up.
> (WA, 25)

Since English Romantic literature (think of Wordsworth climbing Snowdon or visiting Tintern) played its part in developing the Welsh tourist trade by conveniently overlooking the country's society and culture in order to reduce "Wales" to a gloriously inviting landscape, it is appropriate that Thomas should use his own poetry to reclaim, repopulate, and repoliticize the countryside—in short, to *see* "how Wales fares now." He also renames it, using the indigenous names that recall the country's history—Traeth Maelgwn, Hafod Lom, Hyddgen, and Llanrhaeadr-ym-Mochnant, this last being the name of the little hamlet where in 1588 Bishop William Morgan produced the magnificent Welsh Bible which for centuries has been the bible (in the secular sense) of Welsh writers: "The smooth words / Over which his mind flowed / Have become an heirloom" (*WA*, 32).

"Welsh Airs" can also, clearly, be read as "Welsh heirs," and the whole volume then becomes a study in sharply contrasting applications of that term, with "The Patriot" placed near "The Provincial," and versions of the past ironically shadowing a present that sees a people "quarrelling for crumbs / Under the table, or gnawing the bones / Of a dead culture" (*WA*, 9). But even as it actually stands, the title of the volume is politically pointed. "Welsh Airs" is a phrase that brings to mind genteel Victorian collections of melodies from "the land of song"—the sentimental epithet by which an anxiously ingratiating Wales made (and perhaps still makes) itself respectable in the eyes of the English world. During the course of *his* collection Thomas plays several variations on this politico-musical theme. At one point, for instance, he recalls a familiar Welsh hymn's affirmation that in heaven the golden harp's song will continue forever, only to sharply change key by observing that "the strings are broken, and time sets / The barbed wire in their place" (*WA*, 13). Elsewhere Welsh people sing hymns that are "not music / so much as the sound of a nation / rending itself, fierce with all the promise / of a beauty that might have been theirs" (*WA*, 43).

Another musical term appears in "Fugue for Ann Griffiths," the title of his splendid, long, concluding poem about one of the greatest of Welsh hymn writers. Ann has traditionally been regarded as the heroine of Welsh Nonconformity, and indeed Thomas himself appreciates the way her hymns blow the dust off the Welsh language "week by week in chapel after chapel" (*WA*, 51). Yet the terms in which he celebrates her tend to remove her from the tender care of those decaying chapels he elsewhere so mistrusts, those grim killjoy institutions whose "varnish / Wears well and will go / With most coffins" (*WA*, 34). He depicts her as a spirit in rapture and a pilgrim soul, "her face, figure-head of a ship / outward bound" (*WA*, 51). It is an unorthodox view of Ann, slightly reminiscent of the one offered by Saunders Lewis in a famous public lecture when he, too, intrigued Nonconformists by removing her from their charge and placing her in the more exalted spiritual company of the great European mystics.[20] His lecture was an inspirational event, and it could well be of such occasions that R. S. Thomas was thinking when he wrote in "The Patriot": "Those who saw / For the first time that small figure / With the Welsh words leaving his lips / As quietly as doves on an errand / Of peace-making, could not imagine / The fierceness of their huge entry / At the ear's porch" (24).

Unidentified though he is in "A Patriot," Saunders Lewis is the openly avowed subject of another poem in *Welsh Airs,* a piece that is important enough to need quotation in full:

And he dared them;
Dared them to grow old and bitter
As he. He kept his pen clean
By burying it in their fat
Flesh. He was ascetic and Wales
His diet. He lived off the harsh fare
Of her troubles, worn yet heady
At moments with the poets' wine.

A recluse, then; himself
His hermitage? Unhabited
He moved among us; would have led
To rebellion. Small as he was
He towered, the trigger of his mind
Cocked, ready to let fly with his scorn.

(*WA,* 44)

This penetrating portrait can also be read as a revealing self-portrait of R. S. Thomas himself in his old age. The details fit both characters in almost every respect, except that Thomas is considerably taller than his subject! Of course the likeness here to Thomas is entirely unintentional, yet it is by no means fortuitous. He has, after all, for almost half a century, instinctively developed his relationship to Wales along the demanding, unyielding lines laid down in both the life and the work of the extraordinary man he first met at the end of the last war. This particular poem therefore simply confirms the impression left by *Welsh Airs* as a whole when it shows us that R. S. Thomas is indeed, in many important respects, Saunders Lewis's [Anglo-] Welsh heir.

Notes

1. Saunders Lewis, "Is there an Anglo-Welsh Literature?" (Cardiff: Cardiff section of the Guild of Graduates of the University of Wales, 1939).

2. See Alun R. Jones and Gwyn Thomas, eds., *Presenting Saunders Lewis* (Cardiff: University of Wales Press, 1973); Bruce Griffiths, *Saunders Lewis* (Cardiff: University of Wales Press, Writers of Wales Series, 1979). The plays of Saunders Lewis have been translated, in four volumes, by Joseph P. Clancy (Llandybie: Christopher Davies, Vols. 1–3, 1985, Vol. 4, 1986).

3. For the history of modern Welsh writing in English, see Roland Mathias, *Anglo-Welsh Literature: An Illustrated History* (Bridgend: Poetry Wales Press, 1986); Glyn Jones, *The Dragon Has Two Tongues* (London: Dent, 1968).

4. The history of Wales during this period is covered in Kenneth O. Morgan, *Rebirth of a Nation: Wales, 1880–1980* (Oxford: Clarendon Press, and Cardiff: University of Wales Press, 1981).

5. See Emyr Humphreys, *The Triple Net: A Portrait of the Writer Kate Roberts* (London: Channel 4 Television, 1988), and the relevant entries in Meic Stephens, ed., *The Oxford Companion to the Literature of Wales* (Oxford: Oxford University Press, 1986).

6. Dylan Thomas's relationship to Wales is revealingly discussed in "Lord Cut Glass, Twenty Years After," in Roland Mathias, *A Ride Through the Wood* (Bridgend: Poetry Wales Press, 1985), 57–78; and in James A. Davies, "A Picnic in the Orchard, Dylan Thomas and Wales," in Tony Curtis, ed., *Wales: The Imagined Nation* (Bridgend: Poetry Wales Press, 1986), 43–65.

7. R. S. Thomas, "Some Contemporary Scottish Writing" (1946), in Sandra Anstey, ed., *R. S. Thomas: Selected Prose* (Bridgend: Poetry Wales Press, 1986), 29–40.

8. R. S. Thomas, *Selected Poems, 1946–1968* (London: Hart-Davis, MacGibbon, 1973, Granada reprint, 1980).

9. R. S. Thomas, *Between Here and Now* (London: Macmillan, 1981).

10. R. S. Thomas, *What Is a Welshman?* (Swansea: Christopher Davies, 1974).

11. "The Deluge, 1939," in Joseph P. Clancy, trans., *Twentieth Century Welsh Poems* (Llandysul: Gomer Press, 1982), 75–77.

12. Thomas's relationship to his mother was, of course, more complex than this. For its influence on his poetry see "Songs of Ignorance and Praise: R. S. Thomas's poems about the four people in his life," in M. Wynn Thomas, *Internal Difference: Studies in Welsh Writing in English* (Cardiff: University of Wales Press, 1992).

13. An excellent introduction to this whole background can be found in Ned Thomas, *The Welsh Extremist* (Talybont: Gwasg y Lolfa, 1973, reprinted 1978).

14. See Alan Llwyd, *Barddoniaeth y Chwedegau* (Felindre: Cyhoeddiadau Barddas, 1986).

15. Saunders Lewis, *Tynged yr Iaith* (Caerdydd: BBC, 1962). For a translation, see G. Aled Williams, "The Fate of the Language," in *Presenting Saunders Lewis,* 127–41.

16. R. S. Thomas, *Welsh Airs* (Bridgend: Poetry Wales Press, 1987).

17. Dafydd Elis Thomas, "The Image of Wales in R. S. Thomas's Poetry," in *Poetry Wales,* 7:2 (Spring 1972), 59–66.

18. R. S. Thomas's own account of his life can be found in his autobiography *Neb* (Caernarfon: Gwasg Gwynedd, 1985). For an English version see Adele Sarkissian, ed., *Contemporary Authors, Autobiography Series,* 14 (Detroit: Gale Research, 1986), 301–13. I am grateful to my friend, Dr. Tony Brown, UCNW Bangor, for this reference.

19. Tony Bianchi, "R. S. Thomas and His Readers," in *Wales: The Imagined Nation,* 69–95.

20. An excellent introduction to her work is provided by A. M. Allchin, *Ann Griffiths* (Cardiff: University of Wales Press, Writers of Wales series, 1976; reprinted in new format, 1987).

Humanus Sum

A Second Look at R. S. Thomas

R. George Thomas

*Reprinted from The Anglo-Welsh Review, XVIII:42 (1970): 55–62.

R. S. Thomas is the finest living Welsh poet writing in English: this fact in itself is an ironic comment on the nature of the cultural life of Wales in the twentieth century and the poet would be the first to appreciate and savor the irony of the situation. For he, more clearly than any of his contemporaries, is specifically concerned with one small area of recognizably Welsh life and, more sharply than they are, is motivated by a desire to capture the essential quality of the national voice. Like them, he is compelled to use the English language for this purpose—a hard fact of linguistic experience that he seems continually to regret and that is expressed in numerous disguises in his poems—and, like them, his reputation has flourished among English readers outside Wales. In this hard soil his poetry continues to grow and, like his own characters who scratch a bare living from the agricultural Welsh wilderness, he returns again and again to his task, patching the gate and turning the stiff clod. The harvest, in terms of quantity, is a bare but adequate one; its quality improves with each year's tillage, for

> the heart's roots
> Are here under this black soil

at which he labors.

Since the publication of his early selected verse in 1955, R. S. Thomas has published five slim volumes of poetry: *Poetry for Supper* (1958), *Tares* (1961), *The Bread of Truth* (1963), *Pietà* (1966) and *Not That He Brought*

Flowers, which was published as the 1968 Christmas Choice of The Poetry Book Society. His first collected volume, *Song at the Year's Turning* (1955), gained the Heinemann Award for Literature, and last year he received a major award from the Welsh Arts Council. He is now fifty-six years of age, a priest of The Church in Wales, who has deliberately kept to the backwaters of rural life because he feels more at home with the old humanities than with the impetus and direction of an urban technological society. In the Book Society Christmas Bulletin he claims that "the poet of the new age may already have been hatched in some incubator or other. For myself I cannot boast even a guitar. I play on a small pipe, a little aside from the main road. But thank you for listening." Here in prose, with a warning touch of irony, is the essential quality of the poet: deliberate withdrawal, severe concentration, clearsighted purpose, ironic detachment, a half-concealed pride in his chosen role, absolute truth of bare statement, and a grateful awareness of his growing audience. But the verse texture contains an additional quality—the poet's humility before his self-imposed and self-impelling task:

> I have failed after many seasons
> To bring truth to birth,
> And nature's simple equations
> In the mind's precincts do not apply.

and yet

> the old lie
> Of green places beckons me still
> From the new world, ugly and evil,
> That men pry for in truth's name.

His reputation as a poet rests securely on the force and power with which he follows this uncompromising quest.

Not That He Brought Flowers, with its ambiguous and wavering title, has forced me to review his poetry of the last decade and to clarify my own attitude to it. I find this a most difficult undertaking, chiefly because the poet has refused to stand still while critics, reviewers, and publicists (myself among them) have neatly pigeonholed his achievement, saving themselves the effort of close reading while they patted him on the back for being so ruthlessly and successfully his old uncompromising self. Nothing could be further from the mark: this poet, who pries for truth as much into his own heart as into the real or imagined lives of his parishioners, rejects falsity, posturing, and clichés—even those he has himself inspired. The open-eyed stance he offers to the late twentieth century may be as inflexible and old-fashioned as W. G. Grace at the wicket, but his "eye" is not self-deceiving. Unlike those who have talked of the earth because they

> have been reared on its reflections
> In art or had its behaviour
> Seen to

his belief, like ours, must be dipped

> Not in dew nor in the cool fountain
> Of beech buds, but in seas
> Of manure through which they squelch
> To the bleakness of their assignations.

The actors in this poem ("Look") are two cronies who stand aside from modern science, modern medicine, and a welfare society, but the poem is not a simple knocking exercise. The poet offers no easy dogmatic textbook answer; repeatedly he hammers on the door of his faith

> for anything
> Rather than this blank indifference.
> Than the neutrality of its answers, if they can be called answers,
> These grey skies, these wet fields,
> With the wind's winding-sheet upon them.

Some years ago it seemed to me that the voice of compassion and belief was less apparent in R. S. Thomas's poetry than the exclamations of satire, hungry insufficiency, and despair. Latterly, successive volumes have laid bare the uncompromising wrestle with faith that gives these hard-seeing poems their skeletal rectitude and spare force:

> Beauty
> Is how you say, and the truth,
> Like this mountain-born torrent
> Is content to hurry
> Not too furiously by.

In this latest volume there is a widening of interest, both in imagery and in themes, and a greater flexibility of rhythm and tone without any slackening of grip on "the truth" that is central to all his verse.

Not That He Brought Flowers is especially remarkable because it contains no poems about Iago Prytherch. This is a significant omission. Iago made his first appearance in Thomas's poetry a quarter of a century ago and he has stayed on. In all previous volumes the Iago poems recur almost like the "sure touch" of a professional beggar: the poet returns constantly to this well-worn patch—the fixed life of the hill farmer—in search of some assured certitude about his own attitudes to mid-twentieth-century urban civilization. The plight of Iago is the plight of the decaying depopulated Welsh hillside farms; he is an uncertain repository of a way of life that, stated explicitly in political terms, could become the cradle of an enduring Welsh way of life which, the poet believes, should be maintained and extended against the false values of an invading English culture. In some subtle way Iago has become part of the poet's mind, an *alter ego:* the peasant is tied to his soil and animals; the priest is tied to his faith and his parishioners; the poet is anchored to his craft and cannot let go. Not surprisingly, then, Iago is valued for his capacity to endure and to accept:

> There is no forward and no back
> In the fields, only the year's two
> Solstices, and patience between.
>
> • • •
>
> He will go on; that much is certain.
> Beneath him tenancies of the fields
> Will change; machinery turn
> All to noise. But on the walls
> Of the mind's gallery that face
> With the hills framing it will hang
> Unglorified, but stern like the soil.

This is not the whole of Prytherch; he is many-faceted and, in Coleridge's sense, he is a true poetic symbol. ("A symbol is characterized by a translucence of the special in the individual, or of the general in the special, or of the universal in the general. Above all by the translucence of the eternal in and through the temporal. It always partakes of the reality which it renders intelligible: and while it enunciates the whole, abides itself as a living part in that unity, of which it is the representative.") Curiously, but not irrelevantly, Coleridge too had been attracted by the example of an ordered existence that is "one method employed in the formation of the understanding" offered to us by the laborer and the artisan. "He organizes the hours and gives them a soul; and that, the very essence of which is to fleet away, and evermore *to have been,* he takes up into his own permanence, and communicates to it the imperishableness of a spiritual nature. Of the good and faithful servant, whose energies thus directed, are thus methodized, it is less truly affirmed that he lives in time, than that time lives in him. His days, months, and years, as the stops and punctual marks in the records of duties performed, will survive the wreck of worlds, and remain extant when time itself shall be no more." Such Coleridgean rhetoric is far removed from the stark visual sketches of Prytherch that are present in all of Thomas's verse, but the underlying concern of both poets is the same, although Thomas never allows rhetoric to falsify his observation. Iago, conceived in wartime and developed against the background of Hiroshima, always partakes of present reality:

> And Prytherch—was he a real man,
> Rolling his pain day after day
> Up life's hill? . . .
>
> Could I have said he was the scholar
> Of the fields' pages he turned more slowly
> Season by season, or nature's fool,
> Born to blur with his moist eye
> The clear passages of a book
> You came to finger with deft touch?

Iago as symbol consciously becomes another side of the poet's own mind. Even though he is someone "I don't know / Really":

> He has become part of me,
> Aching in me like a bone
> Often bruised. Through him I learn
> Emptiness of the bare mind
> Without knowledge, and the frost
> Of knowledge, where there is no love.

The theme of Prytherch is an inexhaustible one in the poetry of R. S. Thomas and it accumulated in *The Bread of Truth* almost like a boil that must be lanced. In "Servant" the poet defines the consolatory nature of his frequent recourse to this treasured memory of the archetypal peasant and, with a typical ruthless clarity, indicates the deficiency of this symbol:

> You served me well, Prytherch.
> From all my questionings and doubts;
> From brief acceptance of the times'
> Deities; from ache of the mind
> Or body's tyranny, I turned . . .
> To where you read in the slow book
> Of the farm . . .
> > Not that you gave
> The whole answer. Is truth so bare,
> So dark, so dumb, as on your hearth
> And in your company I found it? . . .

> Is not truth choice,
> With a clear eye and a free hand,
> From life's bounty?

It would be over-dramatic and quite untrue to suggest that this poem is a turning point in the verse of R. S. Thomas; yet, as Prytherch disappeared from the poetry[1] like an unsmiling Cheshire Cat, a new note of hope, a tougher exploration of joy, love, and reverence certainly color the verse that follows. The numerical count of poems is against such a conclusion but tentatively in *Pietà*, and certainly in *Not That He Brought Flowers*, there are new themes and different characters that help to variegate the canvas and soften, without blurring, the overwhelming sense of solitude and isolation that dominates the verse.

Pietà is calmer in mood and more varied in theme than most of the earlier volumes: the poems often show a greater concern to record observation, often without comment from the poet. The wryness that too often has turned inward and bitten like despair into the earlier poems is now frequently used for satiric purposes. Rhodri Theophilus Owen (like many similar euphonious characters in Dylan and Gwyn Thomas) is a pleasant caricature and a reminder of the Welsh gift for self-mockery:

> Don't mention roots
> To Rhodri: his address
> Is greater than the population
> Of Dolfor . . .

Rhodri "is cool," with no taste

> For the homeland with its pints
> Of rain water.

Similarly "A Welshman At St. James' Park," with its easy echo of the officialese of public notices

> (I am invited to enter these gardens
> As one of the public, and to conduct myself
> In accordance with the regulations;
> To keep off the grass and sample flowers
> Without touching them)

combines a sustained irony with a sharp satiric comment:

> I am not one
> Of the public; I have come a long way
> To realise it,

and ends with a neat implied comment on a theme that the poet has often thundered out like a tub-thumper—the separateness of two nations:

> I fumble
> In the pocket's emptiness; my ticket
> Was in two pieces. I kept half.

For me this is a subtler and more effective tone than the loud anger of some of his earlier tirades; controlled anger bites deep. There are many stops to R. S. Thomas's ear for conversational undertones: the sharp eye is reinforced by a sensitive ear despite the ever-present tendency to denounce with a too forceful use of shock words that makes the chance encounter of "The Dance" as savage as some of the last poems of Yeats. Yet as he brings his mind to observe, in and for observation's sake, "learning to bring only my wonder to the contemplation" of things, the later poems offer moments of rest and peace that act as a counterpoise to "the underlying despair / Of what should be most certain in my life":

> There is loveliness growing, where might have been truth's
> Bitterer berries. The reason tempers
> Most of the heart's stormier moods.

Even the ugliness of some Welsh towns can now be turned aside with a jest:

> The people cannot translate
> Beauty. I must forgive them.
> They sin in Welsh.

Some years ago I wrote a short study of R. S. Thomas's poetry based on his first three collected volumes. At that time I was puzzled by the absence, so I thought, of the spirit of compassion that one could expect to find in the poems of a Christian priest. I glimpsed its presence most securely in the developing figure of Prytherch, especially in two fine poems in *Poetry for Supper:* in the one the poet denies that he had made fun of Iago's gaunt figure and unlovely habits—

> My poems were made in its long shadow
> Falling coldly across the page;

in the other poem ("Absolution") the poet makes magnificent amends for the errors of his own tone and the blindness of his readers:

> Prytherch man, can you forgive
> From your stone altar on which the light's
> Bread is broken at dusk and dawn,

One who strafed you with scorn
From the cheap gallery of his mind?

Surely it is in the clear yet humble tone of such poems that Welshmen must learn to detect the sincerity with which R. S. Thomas castigates our national faults. He is under the lash himself, both as poet and priest, as poems like "Service" and "They" make quite clear when read in their entirety. In like fashion, one could elaborate the newly emergent themes of the family unit in the last three volumes: the family as an agency of disruption as well as a key to self-knowledge. The pattern of development of this slowly maturing poet becomes clearer with hindsight: the priest and his parishioners, the father and his family, the peasant and his earth, the birds' conflict with nature, the poet's wrestle with himself and words, the believer's renewed struggle with his faith; these are the concentric circles that surround the far-from-still center of R. S. Thomas's poems.

Slowly the voices through which he speaks are multiplying and the *personae* of his verse are showing a protean quality. I detect, too, a loosening of the texture of the verse. Until recently, R. S. Thomas seemed to favor two kinds of structure. One was a short sharp burst of a poem, frequently of sonnet form with an octosyllabic line and the merest hint of an assonantal rhyme, and with a clear-cut antithesis between octave and sestet: this was a favorite form for the Iago poems and the sharp protests of his peasants. The other frequently used structure was a longer wavering poem of short lines, throughout which fairly long sentences were broken up by taut, jerky phrases, frequent questions, and vitriolic phrases that were offered to the reader in the tone of a calm un-Welsh litotes. These two structures are still the norm of his latest volume, but one detects a new form that replaces some earlier experiments with dialogue. Poems like "After the Lecture," "The Priest," "That," "Tenancies," "Concession" (that gives the volume its title), and "A Grave Unvisited" are based on a longer line unit and although they still present a thesis and an antithesis, their tone is more relaxed, the meditative ideas dominate over the visual images, and there are fewer last lines that clap a resounding finish (a merely verbal synthesis?) on the inner movement of the progressing argument that usually forms the core of each poem. Illustration would be tedious, however necessary, especially quotation in print, because R. S. Thomas is essentially a poet to be read aloud; all I can suggest is that interested readers should take down these poems and judge for themselves. Their effect on me over the last nine months is the nearest approach I can find to the change in Yeats's *Tower* volume, which itself was a later fulfilment of his 1900 essay on "The

Symbolism of Poetry" with its prophecy of the change in the manner of English poetry once we had accepted that poetry moves us because of its symbolism: "We would cast out of poetry those energetic rhythms, as of a man running, which are the invention of the will with its eyes always on something to be done and undone; and we would seek out those wavering, meditative, organic rhythms, which are the embodiment of the imagination, that neither desires nor hates, because it has done with time, and only wishes to gaze upon some reality, some beauty." There is much in R. S. Thomas's poetry that cuts across the easy, *fin de siècle* optimism of Yeats in 1900, but the wavering, meditative, organic rhythms are a pronounced feature of this latest volume in which the poet seems to open, unambiguously for the first time, a small window into the inner sanctum of his hardly won faith. Such poems add a new dimension to his poetry and one that sympathetic young listeners will readily understand. Such poems, born of a "willed gentleness," are like parables that are as candid as any of Edward Thomas's poems and as cautiously insistent on the need for faith as the verse of George Herbert. Their most welcome explicitness of the poet's frequent cry in all his poetry, that he is a man like us, comes through his poem on the migrant martins:

> . . . it is I they build
> In and bring up their young
> To return to after the bitter
> Migrations, knowing the site
> Inviolate through its outward changes.

Note

1. In his poem, "The Grave," published in *The Anglo-Welsh Review*, No. 41, R. S. Thomas asserts

> I know that under
> The bright grass there is nothing
> But your dry bones. Prytherch,
> They won't believe that this
> Is the truth.

But these dry bones seem to have some life in them and, judging by this single poem, the ghost of Prytherch may take a detached interest in contemporary Welsh politics.

Via Negativa

Absence and Presence in the Recent Poetry of R. S. Thomas

J. D. Vicary

Reprinted from Critical Quarterly, 27:3 (Autumn 1985): 41–51.

The publication of *H'm* in 1972 marked a change of direction in R. S. Thomas's work. Despite continuities between the earlier and later poetry, the sense of a radical break has been noted by those who welcome and by those who regret his recent development—and indeed by Thomas himself. The change has been partly a change of subject matter. The country (in both senses) in which he has lived, and its population, are no longer the major stimuli. In an interview on Radio Cymru, broadcast in 1983, he said that, while feeling "more of a Welshman, a straightforward Welshman" than before, he no longer felt the need "to write like a Welshman."[1]

Instead, his religious concerns, always evident, have come to dominate his poetry. Problems of Christian belief, the complexity of religious experience, and their particular contemporary forms, preoccupy poems which range from explorations of states bordering on a blank despair to speculations, in a language that can be traditional but also restlessly modern, on the nature of God. Not all his poetry can be characterized in this way, the main exceptions being the short (twelve poems) *What Is a Welshman?* (1974) and the sequence of poems relating to impressionist paintings that make up the first part of *Between Here and Now* (1981). But it is the religious poetry that forms the central and distinctive body of work. It is interesting to note that Thomas's most recent selection, *Later Poems*

(1983), includes only one poem from *What Is a Welshman?*, and two from the first section of *Between Here and Now.*

R. S. Thomas has always been a religious poet. He has written about the role of the priest in relation to his parishioners, and he has tested his beliefs against his perceptions of those who feel no need to share them. His sense of the "spiritual" has been made to confront the insistent pressures of the "natural" and "material." The countrymen and women among whom he has found himself have spoken to him as "voices of the earth," demanding that he

> dip belief
> Not in dew nor in the cool fountain
> Of beech buds, but in seas
> Of manure through which they squelch
> To the bleakness of their assignations.
>
> ("Look")

The challenge to belief is notably physical. In the earlier poetry particular observations of people and places provided the occasions for Thomas's religious reflections. Even his most introspective poems tended to be given a local habitation. One thinks of poems which feature the priest in his church, and of the importance of the church as building, where "the dry whisper of unseen wings" comes from "Bats not angels, in the high roof" ("In a country church").

In the later poems these mediating contexts and occasions frequently drop away, and the subjects of Thomas's meditations are abstracted from any tangible surroundings. The extent of the change can be gauged from the terms that have been used to describe Thomas's earlier work. Calvin Bedient, for example, writing about the poetry that precedes *H'm,* praises Thomas for his "passionate naturalness," for "the grateful dependence of his senses on the world." For Bedient, Thomas is a "natural poet" who "never tires of speaking of what is around him."[2] It would not be possible to use these terms of Thomas's work since *H'm.* Instead we find Thomas, in the opening poem of *Laboratories of the Spirit* (1975), writing of:

> the emerging
> from the adolescence of nature
> into the adult geometry
> of the mind.
>
> ("Emerging")

By giving "mind" its head and by relegating "nature" (in one sense at least) Thomas has divided his readers. He has placed himself in a tradition of meditative and speculative religious poetry, claiming, in "Groping," a poem from *Frequencies* (1978), that "The best journey to make / is inward. It is the interior / that calls."

Verdicts on this development have varied. A. E. Dyson, who sees Thomas as "among the five or six greatest poets to have written in English in this century,"[3] has based his claim precisely on the volumes of the 1970s. On the other hand there have been dissenting voices. Andrew Motion, for example, accuses Thomas of moving toward "a didactic abstraction."[4] Colin Falck, reviewing *Frequencies,* writes that Thomas "seems finally to have abandoned the saving rituals of Prytherch country for abstruser meditations about God himself. The poetic loss is great . . ."[5] Andrew Waterman has said that Thomas's later poems "fall towards the mere higher prattle of a metaphysically worried man."[6]

These negative judgments, whatever their merits, do at least encourage us to look closely at the type of religious poetry that Thomas has come to write. This poetry is largely concerned with states of doubt, loss, abandonment, absence. We are led to ask whether it is possible to make good poems out of such negative terms. Is there an aesthetics of absence, as well as a theology of absence, that would justify Thomas's poetic strategies? To put the question another way, are Thomas's poems in fact as abstract and discursive as some have seen them?

Thomas has certainly come to question the dependence of his senses on the world. He has also questioned the relationship between language and the world. As he writes in "Abercuawg":

> I have no faith
> that to put a name to
> a thing is to bring it
> before one.

Thomas's skepticism about language has become one of the central subjects of his poetry, and is closely connected to his religious concerns. If the poet cannot be confident about the naming of things, how much less confident must he be about the naming of God? The naming of God is a difficult matter. Thomas occupies a position where the name precedes him, "ubiquitous / in its explanations," as he puts it in "Waiting," a poem from *Frequencies.* It is these explanations that have to be unpicked so that the poet can get behind the name, not to the "thing" itself, but to the gap that separates name and thing.

The word "God" is an empty space waiting to be filled with whatever meanings the poet projects into it. At the same time it necessarily comes laden with the weight of past associations. The poet is both free and constrained, and it is the acceptance of this dilemma that gives Thomas's later poetry its particular character. The closing lines of "Waiting" provide an appropriate introduction:

> Young
> I pronounced you. Older
> I still do, but seldomer
> now, leaning far out
> over an immense depth, letting
> your name go and waiting,
> somewhere between faith and doubt,
> for the echoes of its arrival.

In 1963 Thomas edited *The Penguin Book of Religious Verse*. One of the features of the anthology was its generosity to poems that others might not have considered as religious at all. As he put it in his introduction, Thomas wanted to produce a contemporary anthology which would appeal to a "modern sensibility that might wish to include more under the title 'Religious' than traditionalists could accept" (p. 10). One part of the book was called "Nothing," and Thomas defended its inclusion in the following terms: "Poems such as the 'terrible' sonnets of Gerard Manley Hopkins are but a human repetition of the cry from the Cross: *'Eloi, Eloi, lama sabachthani!'* The ability to be in hell is a spiritual prerogative, and proclaims the true nature of such a being" (p. 11). The experience of "Nothing" was part of the "experience of ultimate reality" which was how Thomas defined religion, and he ended his introduction by saying: "Without the section entitled 'Nothing' I feel that the contents of this anthology would have been incomplete and its poetry the poorer" (p. 11).

None of this surprises a reader of Thomas's recent poetry. A negative title seems appropriate for much of his work since *H'm*. His poems frequently announce their "true nature" by their "ability to be in hell," the place where God is absent. They remain "religious" because this absence implies, elsewhere, a presence. It is a theological absence they explore, one that only has meaning because of the tantalizing proximity of its opposite term.

What is more surprising in Thomas's introduction is the confidence of his positive claims for poetry, for religion, and for the relationship between the two. His position is derived unashamedly from Coleridge: "The nearest we approach to God, he [Coleridge] appears to say, is as creative beings. The poet, by echoing the primary imagination, recreates. Through his work he forces those who read him to do the same, thus bringing them nearer the primary imagination themselves, and so, in a way, nearer to the actual being of God as displayed in actions" (p. 8). This formulation is not a recipe for religious poetry as such, but it does bring poetry and religion into close alignment. Thomas's commitment to a Romantic theory of imagination is explicit: "The world needs the unifying power of the imagination. The two things which give it best are poetry and religion. Science destroys as it gives" (p. 9).

This theoretical admission of a debt to Romanticism is interesting because it runs counter to much in Thomas's poetic practice. His own poetry, early as well as later, has been marked by a distrust of imagination as much as by a faith in its power. It would perhaps be more accurate to say that he distrusts imagination exactly because of its power. The imaginative capacity to idealize and transform, to create an autonomous world, is one that Thomas views with misgiving, on moral as well as aesthetic or philosophical grounds. He has always been fascinated by what resists transformation, what punctures the self-sufficiency of the aesthetic. It is for this reason that Iago Prytherch emerges in the early poetry as Thomas's antagonist. In "A Peasant" Thomas says of Prytherch:

There is something frightening in the vacancy of his mind.
His clothes, sour with years of sweat
And animal contact, shock the refined,
But affected, sense with their stark naturalness.
Yet this is your prototype . . .

Here, Prytherch's contact with the non-human, with the earth and with animal life, is a guarantee of reality. Refinement is equated with affectation, an attempt to gloss over a basic and inescapable material condition. If there is an element of presumption in Thomas's attribution of mental vacuity to Prytherch, nevertheless its function is clear. Thomas needs to believe in the emptiness of Prytherch's mind because he also wants to hint at the emptiness of the mind itself, when it distances itself from the material. Prytherch is the "prototype" not despite but because of "the vacancy of his mind." The presumption involved in Thomas's judgment of Prytherch acts as a corrective to the opposite presumption of the mind.

A later poem, from H'm, "The Epitaph," opens:

You ask me what it was like?
I lived, thought, felt the temptation
Of spirit to take matter
As my invention, but bruised my mind
On the facts . . .

The temptation is as important as the resistance to it. The later poems bring to the foreground the tension between the claims of the imagination to create, or discover, significance, and the refusal of the world to submit to its demands.

Thomas's confrontation with Romanticism in his own poetry is, then, marked by conflict. Coleridge himself gives his name to a poem in the 1955 collection, *Song at the Year's Turning*. In it the Romantic thinker serves as a warning rather than an inspiration. Coleridge's is a "vain philosophy" and its vanity is exposed by its inability to grasp the bruising fact. It is vain in two senses, both wrong-headed and arrogant in its assumption of the superiority of mental operations that ignore contingency. Confronted by a material world, the reality of which eludes his philosophical categories,

> He felt his theories break and go
> In small clouds about the sky,
> Whose nihilistic blue repelled
> The vain probing of his eye.

Thomas's later poetry has made this distrust of the imagination into a central theme, while at the same time allowing itself considerable speculative scope. The pull of imaginative freedom and the restraints of skepticism become the actual material of the poetry. His poems only rarely exhibit the confidence in "the unifying power of the imagination" expressed in his Penguin introduction, but the Romantic appeal is still felt. Yeats, who saw himself, famously, as one of "the last romantics,"[7] features, by name or allusion, in several of the later poems. If Thomas's most recent assessment of Yeats is that "He leads us to expect / too much" ("The Cones"), it is nevertheless the extravagance of the earlier poet that accounts for the force of the fascination.

Between Here and Now has another poem called "Waiting," retitled "Waiting for It" in *Later Poems*, either way a characteristic title. The poem begins, "Yeats said that," and goes on to record a loss of faith in Yeatsian rhetoric. The hubristic claims of such eloquence are countered by the values of patience and reticence. To the question, "What counsel / has the pen's rhetoric / to impart?" Thomas answers, in the final lines of the poem:

> Now
> in the small hours
> of belief the one eloquence
>
> to master is that
> of the bowed head, the bent
> knee, waiting, as at the end

of a hard winter
for one flower to open
on the mind's tree of thorns.

The poem compares an early, "delighted," encounter with Yeats to a later, less trustful reading. The recording of a change of response is important, but so too is the continuing engagement with Yeats. The poem's success is paradoxical. Its values are those of continence and self-denial. It preaches an austere sobriety partly motivated by self-disgust:

Fingers burned, heart
seared, a bad taste
in the mouth, I read him

again, but without trust
any more.

But despite, or because of, its warnings against rhetoric, the poem becomes, triumphantly, its own contradiction, for it is undoubtedly "eloquent," and eloquent in a Yeatsian way, in its resolution of conflict through symbol (a traditional symbol with immediate religious associations), and in its sense of an affirmation that is asserted in the face of all that would deny it. The ending of the poem is ambivalent in a way that is typical of Thomas. The poem is about waiting, the postponement of spiritual gratification, but the last two lines bring the apparently deferred hope into the present of the poem. The form of the poem does not simply match its subject. The poem closes on an image, rather than opening on to an uncertain prospect. The movement of the poem, again typically, is from an open beginning to an achieved conclusion. "Yeats said that"—the poem begins *in medias res,* as an apparently arbitrary interruption in a preceding conversation. It then moves, by way of its unanswered questions, to a concluding statement which rhetorically, by rhythm as much as by image, resolves in paradoxical form the tensions of the poem. The effect is to balance the negative and positive elements, the resistance to rhetoric and the achieved eloquence.

I want to stress the importance of the symbolic conclusion and its relation to the meanings of "belief." Belief on the one hand implies a discursive procedure, the testing of propositions under intellectual pressure. The poem alludes to this meaning. "In the small hours of belief" it is the mind's difficulty in holding on to positions that is in question. But belief can also mean commitment to truths not rationally arrived at, as when "belief" is contrasted with "knowledge." In "Waiting" the intellectual aspect is there—it is the *mind's* tree of thorns from which the hoped-for flower may bloom—but the poem itself does not deal directly with rational challenges to belief, nor is the wished [for] resolution expressed in rational terms. There are two logics operating in the image of tree and flower, one based on continuity, the other on contrast. On the one hand, if the tree is a tree of the mind, then the flower should also be of the mind. On the other hand, and as strongly, there is a disjunction between tree and flower. The waiting, "the bowed head, the bent / knee," imply a suspension of mental activity, a lenten abstinence aptly symbolized by a tree of thorns. The flower that will bloom on, not from, this tree, appears as a symbol of grace operating on a level that supersedes that of rational enquiry. The symbolic mode of the poem suits a theology that is skeptical of the mind's ability to create certainties out of its own sufficiency. At the same time the use of symbol suggests a confidence, in religious terms, faith, in a truth that can be evoked but not defined.

The word "waiting" itself conveys this ambivalence. Is it a waiting in hope or unhope? In one sense hope is deliberately denied as being premature, a false rhetorical optimism inappropriate to the poem's penitential posture. On the other hand one could argue that the logic of the images works against such neutrality. The small hours promise a dawn as winter promises spring. If the poem has a "message" it is a contradictory one, summed up in the final image of the flower which does not exist, whose tense is the future, and which is nevertheless present in the poem. The closing symbol carries what force it does because of the reticence which surrounds it. It emerges as the "one flower" from the ascetic "tree of thorns" which constitutes the poem. The affirmation it embodies exists only in the context of an insistent denial.

This sense of a denial which is occasionally redeemed in ways that are not explicable by reference to a rational understanding of belief dominates much of Thomas's later work. The theology of his poetry from *H'm* onwards could appropriately be given the title of one of the poems from that volume, "Via Negativa." The title refers to the Christian mystical tradition which is based on a sense of the inadequacy of human attempts to give expression to the experience of encounter with the divine. In the introduction to his translation of the medieval *Cloud of Unknowing*, Clifton Wolter describes the *via negativa* in the following way: "*Via negativa* starts from the unknowability of God. . . . He cannot be understood by man's intellect. The truths of religion about him can, but not himself. When the mind faces him who is absolutely different it 'seizes up'; it becomes blank before a knowledge it can never assimilate because it can never understand the first thing about it; it enters a cloud of unknowing."[8]

In his introduction to *The Penguin Book of Religious Verse* Thomas alludes to this tradition when he draws a distinction between mystic and poet. To the mystic "the *Deus absconditus* is immediate; to the poet He is mediated. The mystic fails to mediate God adequately insofar as he is not a poet. The poet, with possibly less immediacy of apprehension, shows his spiritual concern and his spiritual nature through the medium of language, the supreme symbol" (p. 9). Here the comparison is to a considerable degree in the poet's favor—that "possibly" is a discreet qualification—and Thomas is of course a poet. But in his later poetry, the poet's lack of immediacy of apprehension is more strongly felt, and is not necessarily compensated [for] by the ability to "mediate God." What is mediated, rather, is the lack of apprehension itself, the sense of a limitation which is both spiritual and linguistic.

For one following the *via negativa,* the imagination is a dubious gift. The creation of symbols, far from mediating religious truth, may become an obstacle between the individual and God. *The Cloud of Unknowing,* for example, warns against the use of images in contemplation, however devoutly conceived these images may be. Thoughts about God, or images of God, are, for the contemplative, to be covered "with a thick cloud of forgetting, even when they are holy and promise well to achieve your object," and "the vigorous working of your imagination, which is always so active when you set yourself to this blind contemplation, must as often be suppressed."[9] In more recent times, Simone Weil has written in much the same vein: "The imagination is continually at work filling up all the fissures through which grace might pass. . . . We must continually suspend the work of the imagination filling the void within ourselves."[10]

Here is Thomas's "Via Negativa":

Why no! I never thought other than
That God is that great absence
In our lives, the empty silence
Within, the place where we go
Seeking, not in hope to
Arrive or find. He keeps the interstices
In our knowledge, the darkness
Between stars. His are the echoes
We follow, the footprints he has just
Left. We put our hands in

His side hoping to find
It warm. We look at people
And places as though he had looked
At them, too; but miss the reflection.

I find Weil's terms useful for a reading of the poem. Thomas keeps his imagination tightly reined so as not to fill the fissures through which grace might
pass. On the contrary, it is exactly a sense of the void that he wants to
evoke—"absence . . . silence . . . interstices . . . darkness . . . echoes . . .
footprints." The question is, whether poetry can be made from such neg-
atives. If God is silent, is not silence also the proper human response?
"Presume not God to scan" says Pope, and Thomas is aware of the dangers
of such presumption. But Thomas is a poet, and must speak, as the mystics
have traditionally done, or we would have no record of them. The result is
a language about God, more accurately about the human approach to God,
which is based on negative terms. God cannot be encapsulated in a poem
because he eludes all human categories. What can be expressed is the sense
of an absence which only has meaning as, specifically, the absence of God.
In evoking the distance between the human and the divine, the poem simultaneously denies and affirms. The poem exists in "The Gap," the title of
the first poem of *Frequencies,* which:

> is
> the narrowness that we stare
> over into the eternal
> silence that is the repose of God.

In this sense, the frustration of the *via negativa* is also its reason for being.
The spiritual quest is valid *because [of],* rather than in spite of, the fact that
there is no earthly hope of its fulfilment.

It is this first sense of the poem that justifies its title, but it is a far from
adequate summary of its effects. The poem is more than the statement of
an impossible position. If it were that alone, it would be vulnerable to the
charge of abstraction that has been leveled at Thomas. It is important to
note the ways in which the impression of abstraction is countered in the
poem. First of all, there is Thomas's sense of the dramatic. As with
"Waiting," only more obviously, the poem plunges straight into an argument with its opening words—"Why no!" Thomas alludes to, without
specifying, a position or positions that exist outside [of] and prior to his
lines, and it is this engagement with imaginary adversaries that provides the
context of the poem. The polarized adversaries implied by the poem are
perhaps those, on the one hand, who would insist on too presumptuous a

theology of presence, and those, on the other hand, who fail to see Thomas's sense of absence as being meaningfully theological at all. Thomas's *via negativa* turns out also to be a *via media,* a refusal of the black-and-white view that between faith and unbelief there is no neutral ground.

Secondly, the tendency toward abstraction is checked within the poem itself. Thomas plays off the general and the particular, the abstract and the personal. He does this through his deployment of line breaks. Questions of belief are sharply subjectivized by this device. God is not just "that great absence" but—after the necessary pause—"that great absence / In our lives," and his generalized "silence" is similarly localized as "the empty silence / Within." The question of God's existence outside the self is nicely poised against an inner experience.

There is also a movement away from abstraction in the progress of the poem. The poem changes direction in the eighth line. After the impersonal terms, "absence . . . silence . . . knowledge," we move to the more intimate suggestions of "echoes" and "footprints." These shift the tone of the poem from philosophical speculation to a more personal register. Although the images still convey absence, it is an absence felt, metaphorically, through the senses. Thomas, treading here a more conventionally acceptable poetic domain, suggests thereby a growing personal engagement with his material. The initial "public" contact with an imagined interlocutor is displaced by the language of private discovery. The movement to the personal is also accompanied by a greater confidence in the object of the poem's search. Absence *need* not imply a presence elsewhere, but footprints certainly do. Similarly, silence may be just a negative but echoes are audible. What we find, in fact, is that the poem is dramatic in a further sense than in its assumption of an audience. It traces a development, and one which qualifies its initial premises. The negative way turns out not to be such an absolute road as might at first appear. The metaphorical presence of echoes and footprints suggests that the poem can, tentatively, make positive claims.

The next lines intensify the sense of personal discovery while at the same time rooting the poem in a more public domain, one that is specified as Christian by the biblical allusion. This is deftly done, for the image of the wound in Christ's side follows easily from the image of God's footprints. The contact is here at its most intimate, but is also generalized by the reference to a collective body of tradition. The paradox of presence in absence is expressed most intensely in this image. God is here, given body, but contact with him is still through an absence, a hole, and the unanswered hope prevents any collapsing of the sense of distance and separation.

The last three lines are flat, anti-climactic. After the probing into depth, into the opening in God's body, we are brought back to a general and sweeping survey of surfaces, surfaces which are opaque and unhelpful. The project of the poem, the pursuit of God, is arrested before any conclusion is reached, and we are left with the space, the hole in God's side, kept open.

This account should suggest something of the complexity and compression, achieved by deceptively lucid means, which is characteristic of Thomas's most successful writing. Before leaving the poem I want to look more closely at its biblical reference. The passage from which the image is derived concerns the nature of faith:

> Then saith he to Thomas, Reach hither thy finger, and behold my hands; and reach hither thy hand, and thrust it into my side: and be not faithless, but believing. And Thomas answered and said unto him, My Lord and my God.
>
> *(John* 20: 27–28)

The use of the allusion allows for at least two interpretations. It may be seen to give weight to a positive reading since, in the gospel, the doubter is finally convinced. But another reading is possible. The comparison between the doubting Thomas of the gospel and the doubting Thomas of the poem may be ironical, since the biblical character is granted the consolation of immediate and tangible evidence for belief, which is denied to his twentieth century namesake.

However, this point needs to be taken a stage further, for the contrast between belief based on irrefutable evidence and a faith in what is intangible and invisible is precisely the point of the biblical narrative itself: "Jesus saith unto him, Thomas, because thou hast seen me, thou hast believed: blessed are they that have not seen, and yet have believed" (v. 29). With the biblical passage in mind, the images of echo and footprint may serve as models of what faith might be, while at the same time suggesting its tantalizing, and in one sense hopeless nature.

A reading of "Waiting" and "Via Negativa" brings us close to the central subject of much of Thomas's poetry of the last decade. This subject is the complex relationship between faith and doubt, between a theology of presence and a theology of absence. His exploration of this area is, in his best poems, neither didactic nor abstract, but depends heavily on paradox and ambiguity. "Waiting" and "Via Negativa" are situated, typically, in the gap between affirmation and negation. In the vacated footprint, absence and presence are intimately connected.

Notes

1. R. S. Thomas, *Selected Prose,* ed. Sandra Anstey (Bridgend: Poetry Wales Press, 1983), p. 16.

2. Calvin Bedient, *Eight Contemporary Poets* (London: Oxford University Press, 1974), pp. 53, 56–57. Bedient's book, though published in 1974, deals with the earlier work. A poem from *Pietà* (1966) is referred to as "recent" (p. 53).

3. A. E. Dyson, *Yeats, Eliot and R. S. Thomas: Riding the Echo* (London: Macmillan, 1981), p. 303.

4. Andrew Motion, *The Review of English Studies,* XXXIV: 133 (February 1983): 111, in a review of W. Moelwyn Merchant, *R. S. Thomas* (Cardiff: University of Wales Press, 1979).

5. Colin Falck, *The New Review,* 5: 1 (1978): 121.

6. Andrew Waterman, "The Poetry of Geoffrey Hill," in *British Poetry since 1970: A Critical Survey,* ed. P. Jones and M. Schmidt (Manchester: Carcanet, 1980), p. 88.

7. In "Coole Park and Ballylee, 1931."

8. *The Cloud of Unknowing,* trans. Clifton Wolters (Harmondsworth: Penguin, 1961), pp. 15–16.

9. *Ibid.,* p. 65.

10. Simone Weil, *Gravity and Grace,* trans. Emma Craufurd (London: Routledge & Kegan Paul, 1963), pp. 16–17.

R. S. Thomas

The Landscape of Near-Despair

Robert Nisbet

Reprinted from Planet: The Welsh Internationalist, *35 (1976): 26–30.*

Every poet is, ultimately, a product partly of his social and political situation, and rarely more so than when, like R. S. Thomas, he flatly rejects many of the values of the society or societies surrounding him. It is important, in Thomas's case, to examine the social rôle and stance which he, the poet-priest in the isolation of depopulated areas, has adopted.

The society of England and Wales since the Butler Education Act of 1944 has been the society of the new meritocracy. It was the age of the I.Q. test, the 11-plus examination, "O" level, "A" level, degrees. With these have come, increasingly, social mobility, town-dwelling, metropolitanism, often a pseudo-cosmopolitanism. For rural Wales, this has meant depopulation, a drift away of the most active and able young. "Getting on" has meant in practice an inexorable movement from Machynlleth to Cyncoed or Croydon.

The poet who opts out of all this is contending with the values of the new meritocracy, and this conflict is relatively straightforward. A more insidious enemy is found in the set of alternative values which any society will produce as a safety valve—never real values, in fact, but fictional clichés, a set of dewy-eyed aspirations which simply placate the "hiraeth" and the disillusion from time to time.

For a society in which city-dwelling has become semi-obligatory, a vague belief in the country is inevitable, a pastoral idyll flickering through the margarine adverts. A society which believes, obsessively, in the Ph.D., will want and need also to believe in the rustic sage, the sheep-farming philosopher; "The Archers" will provide him. A society in which "home" has become somewhere you visit will often have a very cosy, very glib picture of home. And Wales, for the exile, is always that little bit better in nostalgic memory. With the real values, there will be alternative values, and they will so easily become glib clichés, misty falsehoods. It is this untruth, as much as the obvious target of his society's real values, which must be a main target of the poet who has opted out.

What will one look for, then, in the poet who commits himself to rural Wales, attempts to celebrate an impoverished and declining rural society in an age of urban affluence? The commitment itself, in the obvious sense of actually living there, must be inevitable. One would then ask, I think, that the poet offer, in some way, a real set of alternative values to those of the meritocracy on which he has turned his back. And, with the cliché alternatives firmly in mind, one will ask, inevitably, that the poet render his values, celebrate his people and place, with a rigorous absence of sentimentality.

There are moments when Thomas *is* sentimental, when the picture of Iago Prytherch's rural Welsh life becomes a little too rustic, a little too heroically Welsh. The poem "Too Late" (a poem admittedly, which laments Prytherch's selling out to "the cold brain of the machine"), celebrates a little too easily the life of the hill farmer

"Contented with your accustomed ration
Of bread and bacon, and drawing your strength
From membership of an old nation."

But what is most notable is that such moments *are* rare. Thomas's most striking characteristic by far is his scrupulous, even harsh, avoidance of sentimentality. The poem "Where to Go" could define both his social role and his poetic stance very crisply, right at the outset. He will have no truck with any pastoral dream, with any contentment or satisfaction with the rural Welsh, on his own part or on the part of the Welsh themselves or of outsiders who would project their compensatory cliché picture on to the Welsh landscape, to reassure themselves that all is well:

The serenity of their expression
Revolts me, it is a pose
For strangers, a water-colour's appeal
To the mass, instead of the poem's
Harsher conditions.

His role as a poet is bound up with this, a deliberate depiction of the harsher contours, a flat refusal to pander to any of the social clichés which threaten always to drown a poetry of rural Wales in a tide of self-indulgence.

One can pick out, one by one, the cliché beliefs, the sentimental untruths, about rural Wales, and detect, in Thomas's dealing with them, always the same approach: the harsh and unsparing handling of the scene and the attitudes. What one often has to dig a little bit harder to find is the nugget of hope which will often do no more than glimmer briefly in the heavy bulk of his daily experience.

For the city-dweller, it is an axiom that the country is always there to be visited. It's fundamentally dishonest, of course, involving a draining away of the life of the countryside and a glib expectation that the new urban society can turn back to it at will for a fortnight's annual respite. But Thomas's attitude to the tourist is savagely unsparing. "Where to Go" is scathing in its description of the English on the beach:

> Scavenging among the remains
> Of our culture.

"Welsh Seaside" is equally unwelcoming:

> . . . On the conveyor belt
> Of their interests they circle the town
> To emerge jaded at the pier,
> To look at the water with dull eyes
> Resentfully, not understanding
> A syllable. Did they expect
> The sea, too, to be bilingual?

The accommodation of the tourist, and the emotional distortion necessary to provide it, are pictured here as a form of prostitution.

But there is no glib national pride behind this spurning of the stranger. National pride, possibly, but the picture of Welsh nationhood which appears in "Welsh Landscape" is bleak, to say the very least: one of

> . . . an impotent people,
> Sick with inbreeding,
> Worrying the carcase of an old song.

There is a dark resentment in this poem, of "the spilled blood," the memory of "strife in the strung woods," and Wales as a country in which one can only live in the past. It's an unwelcoming landscape, sardonic almost in its savage self-effacement. But then, in the midst of the pessimism, hope flickers. At the end of the poem (the lines quoted above), is the "old song."

There is perhaps a stirring of pride here, as there is, I think, in the depiction of the language.

> The soft consonants
> Strange to the ear.

The language is strange perhaps, and unwelcoming, but to Thomas himself, I would feel, a source of grim pride.

Thomas's landscape, equally, is never a national park amenity. There is no "watercolour's appeal" here, but very much "the poem's Harsher conditions." The landscape in the poem "Evans" reaches almost total bleakness:

> . . . the drip
> Of rain like blood from the one tree
> Weather-tortured.

But, again, there is a tough pride asserting itself occasionally in the very harshness of the setting. The poem "The Country Clergy" celebrates quietly, drily, and sadly the lonely lot of the rural priest, does so with an edge of defiance and pride in

> . . . their lonely thought
> In grey parishes.

It is in the very loneliness, the very absence of color, that Thomas seems to find his source of real pride. Likewise in "Welsh Landscape." It is the spilling of blood, the injustice that "went to the making of the wild sky." One does not feel, given the bitterness, that Thomas would want the sky to be any other way. In the grayness of the one poem, the hostility of the other, in the unwelcoming quality overall, there is perhaps something real for him, an integrity.

Yet another stock belief would lament the way in which our society will draw the life away from rural Wales by depopulating it; it is a belief, indeed, to which even this essay would largely subscribe. Yet Thomas is still prepared to face the other harsh side of the picture, in "Family Farm":

> Grandfather or grandmother, gnarled hands
> On the cheque-book,

the children waiting "with angry patience," "waiting for someone to die." Even here, the flicker of consolation is flecked with fear. The final bird song is

> . . . the terrible accompaniment of the song
> Of the blackbird, promising love.

Similarly, in his handling of the people of his parishes and of their lives, Thomas's tone can deepen into real pessimism. Certainly there is never any blithe acceptance of any role as "prophet of the common man" or the like; on occasions, indeed, he suggests a real resentment of the fact that his lot is linked to those of the Iago Prytherchs of this world. "The Country Clergy" pictures the parish priest sympathetically enough; then comes the real bitterness:

> . . . And yet their skulls,
> Ripening over so many prayers,
> Toppled into the same grave
> With oafs and yokels.

The same "oafs and yokels" picture emerges in "On the Farm," in the descriptions of Dai, Huw, and Llew Puw, three seemingly subnormal, hulking peasants. Then, in this desperate setting, the hope stirs briefly:

> And lastly there was the girl:
> Beauty under some spell of the beast.
> Her pale face was the lantern
> By which they read in life's dark book
> The shrill sentence: God is love.

The need posed to dig the nugget of hope out of a pit of near-despair is typical of Thomas. The final axiom, "God is love," is emphatic enough in isolation, triumphant even. But this is no easy triumph. The hope is a "shrill sentence"; this particular crying-out of the human spirit emerges, in context, as a scream almost of desperation.

We might well look at the poem "Evans" for a good example of Thomas's handling of people and place, to note this same abiding tendency of his, to root his hopes in a deep bedrock of near-despair. The setting of "Evans" is quite startlingly spare, as a count of the adjectives alone ("bare," "gaunt," "black," "cold," "stark," and so forth) will easily show. And yet, in the midst of this utterly stark picture, there *is* perhaps a glimmer of some sort of warmth, to me at least, in the reference to

> . . . the gaunt kitchen
> With its wood fire, where crickets sang
> Accompaniment to the black kettle's
> Whine . . .

A bleak sort of comfort perhaps, but one which is never at odds with the overall dreariness, and one which convinces more for that reason. One can say the same for the poem's more fundamental point: Thomas's compassion for

> . . . that sick man
> I left stranded upon the vast
> And lonely shore of his bleak bed.

What is important here is what is left unsaid; there are no ministerial words of comfort, only an uncomfortable mingling of pity and despair. Again, perhaps because of the juxtaposition, the pity convinces more.

But, if one is to treat of Thomas's handling of people, and to deal with his ability to go beyond the stock response, one must come back finally to Iago Prytherch. In the grim landscape of Thomas's small-scale personal mythology, Prytherch is a key figure, and his quality establishes most clearly Thomas's role in relation to the characters both of the new meritocrat and of the cliché-sage who is the opposite of, the counterpart to and, ultimately, the creation of, the meritocrat himself.

The point hardly needs laboring that Prytherch himself is the fundamental opposite of the educated, sophisticated, city-dwelling, and traveled meritocrat in the direction of those values our sons and daughters and we ourselves, are usually headed. What might be questioned, of course, is the degree to which Prytherch can be regarded, in any sociological sense, as typical or representative. It's doubtful; his fearsome isolation and vacancy *are* at odds with most of the chapel and Eisteddfod-based traditions of many parts of rural Wales. But I doubt if Thomas is really aiming, in the creation of Prytherch, at social realism. Prytherch suggests more, to me, a myth and, in a curious way, an ideal: a bleak assertion of all those elements of rural life which are most at odds with meritocratic values.

As a myth, Prytherch is an intense and savage creation. If his depiction was to be achieved satisfactorily, it had to be done without sentimentality. It had to be clearly seen that he was crude and ignorant, and that his horizons, within the meritocracy's terms of reference, were desperately limited. Anything else would have led to the spawning of another television cliché. And still, given that, the dignity had to come through, if any sort of alternative value was to be achieved.

"A Peasant," the first creation of this character, doesn't perhaps succeed too well in blending the elements of ignorance and dignity which impel Thomas in Prytherch's direction. The crudity is there clearly enough: the "spittled mirth," the "clothes, sour with years of sweat," Prytherch gobbing in the fire. But the movement at the end toward the establishing of the peasant as

> . . . a winner of wars,
> Enduring like a tree under the curious stars

is perhaps a little too violent; the transition is too forced and the crudity and dignity never really fuse into an integrated whole.

In another sense, the poem was certainly unsuccessful, as is shown by the simple fact that its sequel, "Iago Prytherch," had to be written. This would seem to be, though, for different reasons—because the crudity had come through with too much force, and Prytherch's coarseness was more than the meritocracy could take. Yet, paradoxically, it is the very lack of success in getting through to the reading public which is perhaps a measure of Thomas's complete success in another direction: in getting so far away from the rural-stage stereotype that the poem met with blank incomprehension.

The reason lies probably not, though, in the simple crudity of the details. It is more, I think, in a single line:

> There is something frightening in the vacancy of his mind.

This is a society which lives by qualifications, and in which "wisdom" is a neglected word, is the ultimate heresy. Thomas *had* to be making fun, or feeling pity. In fact, as the line says, he was frightened, an emotion which simply indicates the fact that some sort of quality in Prytherch was beyond him. For this reason, perhaps, the final celebration of the peasant is too glib; Thomas does not, in this poem, fully come to terms with this frightening vacancy.

He had to continue. Such a coming to terms was essential if he were to offer a real alternative value. It is the poem "Iago Prytherch" (for me, one of Thomas's finest) which seems to me to do this. It is more subdued and the spare but delicate respect for the peasant:

> . . . crouched at your slow
> And patient surgery under the faint
> November rays of the sun's lamp

comes beautifully through. Most importantly, Thomas returns, successfully it seems to me, to this vacancy of Prytherch's mind,

> . . . science and art
> The mind's furniture, having no chance
> To install themselves, because of the great
> Draught of nature sweeping the skull.

It is this "draught of nature" which is the ultimate solution, the final value, and they [sic] are the solution and the value of the priest—perhaps also, of the poet—for at the heart of the idea is mystery. We know in part and we prophesy in part; it is the meritocrat, not Prytherch, who would pretend otherwise.

The figure of Prytherch is left, I think, as Thomas's major achievement,

> . . . your dark figure
> Marring the simple geometry
> Of the square fields with its gaunt question.

This is the "dark figure" which finally disturbs and challenges the values of an I.Q. society. The "geometry" image has about it all the qualities of the school subject and a neat, all-round slotting into place, an ultimate glibness. The "gaunt question" is that most inconvenient and embarrassing of attributes in a society which is moving too rapidly ever to stop and concern itself with mystery. But this is the essence of Thomas's most fundamental of alternatives. It's the alternative of the priest and the poet, one which carries sufficient integrity and body to illuminate briefly, as in similar glimpses of aspiration, his own personal landscape of near-despair.

R. S. Thomas

Poet-Priest of the Apocalyptic Mode

William V. Davis

Reprinted from South Central Review, 4:4 (Winter 1987): 92–106.

R. S. Thomas, an Anglican priest who has lived in several small Welsh villages most of his life, has been a visible figure in the landscape of contemporary poetry for some time, but, until recently, only a background figure. That he has moved to the foreground is the result of a major shift in his work which began with the publication of *Pietà* (1966), when Thomas turned abruptly toward the apocalyptic.

If, as Thomas J. J. Altizer has said, ". . . ours is an apocalyptic or eschatological time, a time of the end of what we have known as history, consciousness, and society, then the Christian theologian is called to a new task, a task of mediating what he has been given as apocalyptic faith and vision to a new eschatological time and destiny."[1] And A. M. Allchin considers the relationship "of the poet who is also a priest" as raising "the question of the relationship between poetry and the Christian faith in its most acute form," since "on the one side there is the free creative activity of the imagination ranging over the whole creation, on the other the bound service of a crucified God."[2] R. S. Thomas, as poet and priest, is ideally suited for confronting the apocalyptic moment of recent history, and he has stressed the equal importance of both his professions in defining his position.

Although he acknowledges that "the two professions of priest and poet are so divorced in the public eye as to be quite beyond the possibility of symbiosis,"[3] Thomas joins them:

A lot of people seem to be worried about how I combine my work as a poet and my work as a priest. This is something that never worries me at all. . . . any form of orthodoxy is just not part of a poet's province. . . . A poet must be able to claim . . . freedom to follow the vision of poetry, the imaginative vision of poetry. . . . And, in any case, poetry is religion, religion is poetry. The message of the New Testament is poetry. Christ was a poet, the New Testament is a metaphor, the Resurrection is a metaphor; and I feel perfectly within my rights in approaching my whole vocation as priest and as preacher as one who is to present poetry; and when I preach poetry I am preaching Christianity, and when one discusses Christianity one is discussing poetry in its imaginative aspects. The core of both are imagination as far as I'm concerned. . . . My work as poet has to deal with the presentation of imaginative truth.[4]

At least since the publication of *H'm* (1972), Thomas has been working definitively within an apocalyptic mode, and in *Frequencies* (1978), his most important and most powerful book to date, his use of that mode comes to climax. I wish to consider here this book and its tradition in some detail.

In *Frequencies* Thomas confronts the apocalyptic theme head-on in a way fully in keeping with his poetic as well as his theological traditions. Indeed, in *Frequencies,* the dark night of the soul first announced in *H'm* and developed in *Laboratories of the Spirit* (1975), is brought to fruition in a way which, for Thomas, must seem inevitable. Whereas many contemporary apocalyptic poets follow a path which seems to end in a kind of philosophical black hole, Thomas follows the more traditional mystic way which, although it is every bit as dark, holds out a ray of hope at the end. In this sense Thomas is best considered in terms of his literary contemporaries and in terms of their more "classic" tradition, rather than in comparison with the younger apocalyptic poets at work around him. He is best compared to poets of his own age, or older, poets like William Butler Yeats, Wallace Stevens, Dylan Thomas, and John Berryman, or, perhaps to his closest temperamental contemporary, Theodore Roethke.

Both Thomas and Roethke live and write "near the abyss."[5] And for both poets the business of poetry and the business of life are almost identical, and are ultimately defined in theological ways. Roethke's well-known statement, "I believe that to go forward as a spiritual man it is necessary first to go back,"[6] is clearly exemplified in his work,[7] and a similar path might well be charted through Thomas's recent work. It is enough to note here that both Thomas and Roethke, each no doubt influenced by Yeats, rather visibly follow the traditional mystic tradition toward what Roethke described in his essay "On 'Identity'" as his central poetic concern, an "heightened consciousness" which forces a "break . . . from I to Otherwise, or maybe even to Thee."[8]

Thomas has said:

> The need for revelation at all suggests an ultimate reality beyond human attainment, the *mysterium tremendum et fascinans*. And here, surely, is the common ground between religion and poetry. But there is the question of the mystic. To him the *Deus absconditus* is immediate; to the poet he is mediated. The mystic fails to mediate God adequately in so far as he is not a poet. The poet . . . shows his spiritual concern and his spiritual nature through the medium of language, the supreme symbol. The presentation of religious experience in the most inspired language is poetry.[9]

Roethke might be made to speak for both poets when he says, "God for me still remains someone to be confronted, to be dueled with."[10] Such a confrontation requires the poet to deal with the presence of the absence of self in the context of an ontological and epistemological crisis which only the poetry of apocalypse can confront. Thus, for Thomas (as for Roethke), the dark night of the soul hints inevitably at the final union with the divine.[11] Indeed, it seems only in such a context (and here Thomas and Roethke differ) that one can account for the otherwise incredible poetry which Thomas has been producing in the last several decades—poetry which, I think, has been conspicuously misread or misunderstood because it has not been considered in terms of the apocalyptic mode.[12] In contemporary apocalyptic poetry there comes the time, at the end of a dark night, when light begins to flicker if not fully flame. This usually occurs only at the end of a considerable period of doubt and questioning, often over a fairly long period of time. Because Thomas is prolific and because he lives and works within a fully defined and active apocalyptic period, and because of his theological training and his pastoral responsibilities, the time frame for his initiation into and his movement through the traditional stages of this process has been significantly reduced. Thus, as soon after *H'm* (1972) and *Laboratories of the Spirit* (1975) as *Frequencies* (1978), we find Thomas already into the final stage of the process.

Frequencies opens with "The Gap," a poem which immediately announces the rupture which has occurred between his earlier poems and those in this book. Clearly, there has been a "gap," a shift. This "gap," this "narrowness that we stare / over into the eternal / silence that is the repose of God," is described, interestingly enough, in terms of the word "word." Here Thomas neatly combines his literary and theological theme through reference to the "word," which is at once the words of his poetry and the Word (*logos*) of his theological tradition. Words are the only way the Word may be able to cross over "the gap" between God and man.

"The Gap" begins:

God woke, but the nightmare
did not recede. Word by word
the tower of speech grew.
He looked at it from the air
he reclined on. One word more and
it would be on a level
with him; vocabulary
would have triumphed. He
measured the thin gap
with his mind. No, no, no,
wider than that! But the nearness
persisted. How to live with
the fact, that was the feat
now. How to take his rest
on the edge of a chasm a
word could bridge.[13]

What then? The poet, having established the necessity of the process and initiated the apocalyptic possibility, becomes the vehicle for its completion. Thus, in "Present," the second poem in *Frequencies,* we find Thomas saying:

I am at the switchboard
of the exchanges of the people
of all time, receiving their messages
whether I will or no.

(9)

The poet, at the point of "exchange" between powers, between man and God, is like the prophet of an earlier age. Much of the difficulty, for poet and prophet, for priest as intermediary, has to do with the fact that:

He was like
anyone else, a man with ears
and eyes,

that:

> he was driven
> to his knees and for no reason
> he knew,

that:

> He had no power to pray.
> His back turned on the interior
> he looked out on a universe
> that was without knowledge
> of him and kept his place
> there for an hour on that lean
> threshold, neither outside nor in.
>
> (10)

Therefore, if "you want to know his name? / It is forgotten" (10). And because of all this "we wait for the // withheld answer to an insoluble / problem . . . in the torn / light that is about us" while "the air / echoes to . . . inaudible screaming" (11). In such a world, "God breathes within the confines / of our definition of him" (45). This then is the place for poetry in the world, a place which only poetry, prophecy having been banished, can fill.

As we have seen, Thomas speaks of "the common ground between religion and poetry" and goes on to deal specifically with the problem of the *Deus absconditus* in terms of the contrast between the mystic and the poet. Where "the mystic fails to mediate God adequately insofar as he is not a poet," the "poet . . . shows his spiritual concern and his spiritual nature through the medium of language, the supreme symbol."[14] Again, Thomas here defines religion "as embracing an experience of ultimate reality, and poetry as the imaginative presentation of such" and asserts that "the presentation of religious experience in the most inspired language is poetry."[15]

It is this "significance / of an absence, the deprecation / of what was there, the failure / to prove anything that proved this point," (20) which becomes crucial to an understanding of Thomas's recent poetry. This "periphery I comprehend" (18) is complicated, even at times confusing, but is important to an understanding of Thomas's poetry.

"Shadows" is a significant poem.

> I close my eyes.
> The darkness implies your presence,
> the shadow of your steep mind
> on my world. I shiver in it.

It is not your light that
can blind us; it is the splendour
of darkness.
                    And so I listen
instead and hear the language
of silence, the sentence
without an end. Is it I, then,
who am being addressed? A God's words
are for their own sake; we hear
at our peril. Many of us have gone
mad in the mastering
of your medium.
                    I will open
my eyes on a world where the problems
remain but our doctrines
protect us. The shadow of the bent cross
is warmer than yours. I see how the sinners
of history run in and out
at its dark doors and are not confounded.

                    (25)

Here, in the inevitable chiaroscuro of the apocalyptic mode, Thomas uses the play of light and dark in a traditional manner, but combines the shadow imagery at the end of the poem with the image of the "bent cross." The cross, the crucial Christian symbol, has been used in varying ways by Thomas over the years. This "tree / with its roots in the mind's dark / . . . the original fork / in existence"[16] has become his obsessive symbol for the complexities and doubts which modern man faces. "Cross," is, as well, a crucial word in his vocabulary, suggesting, simultaneously, the cross of Christ and a point of intersection or exchange from one state to another. Such rhetorical crisscrossing is typical of Thomas's work, both thematically and structurally, and it functions effectively both ways.

In *Frequencies,* the image occurs, significantly and finally, in the poem "Epiphany" where

                    Far

off from his cross in the wrong
season he sits at table
with us with on his head
the fool's cap of our paper money.

                    (50)

A. E. Dyson raises the question which such imagery suggests when he asks: "Is there something *in* the Cross . . . which by its actual nature bypasses theology and, at the level of language and image, testifies to itself?" Dyson suggests what may well be Thomas's answer to such a question: ". . . the image of evolved man, alone in a creation where God is dead, is held in exact silhouette against the other image of Christ on the Cross, when God is absent. If the Christian religion has this paradox at its heart, perhaps it is not irrelevant of modern doubt after all, but simply an anticipation of it by 2000 years."[17]

Thomas has been exploring such theses throughout his career, but in recent years he has become obsessed with them. "In Church," from *Pietà* (1966), and "The Empty Church," from *Frequencies,* read as companion poems and make for an interesting comparison in terms of their assumptions and of Thomas's apocalyptic obsessions.

IN CHURCH

Often I try
To analyse the quality
Of its silences. Is this where God hides
From my searching? I have stopped to listen,
After the few people have gone,
To the air recomposing itself
For vigil. It has waited like this
Since the stones grouped themselves about it.
These are the hard ribs
Of a body that our prayers have failed
To animate. Shadows advance
From their corners to take possession
Of places the light held
For an hour. The bats resume
Their business. The uneasiness of the pews
Ceases. There is no other sound
In the darkness but the sound of a man
Breathing, testing his faith
On emptiness, nailing his questions
One by one to an untenanted cross.[18]

THE EMPTY CHURCH

They laid this stone trap
for him, enticing him with candles,

as though he would come like some huge moth
out of the darkness to beat there.
Ah, he had burned himself
before in the human flame
and escaped, leaving the reason
torn. He will not come any more

to our lure. Why, then, do I kneel still
striking my prayers on a stone
heart? Is it in hope one
of them will ignite yet and throw
on its illumined walls the shadow
of someone greater than I can understand?

(35)

"In Church" attempts to "analyse" the quality of the silence after a
service. The speaker, in the emptied church, has "stopped to listen" as the
caught air "recomposes itself" for the vigil it has kept since the church was
built around it. The prayers of the congregation have failed to animate it.
Only the darkness (the shadows) is alive, with the blind bats and the man's
breath, as he tests "his faith on emptiness," using his own air (his breath)
to compose and recompose the prayers of his poem, "nailing his questions
one by one to an untenanted cross."

In "The Empty Church" the church itself is "this stone trap" to
which men have hoped to attract God "like some huge moth." But, having been burned once before, "He will not come any more to our lure."
The church, a "stone trap," is to the world what the heart (also stone) is
to man: both are traps to catch God. Man's prayers are like flint struck on
his stone heart in the hope of creating a spark which will ignite—if only
to create an illusion—"the shadow of someone greater than I can understand" on the empty wall of the church.

In both of these poems, as in so many of Thomas's poems, the emptiness becomes a sign or symbol for an original presence which it has displaced or replaced: the "untenanted cross"; the "empty church."

"The Possession" (33) is an important transitional poem. The speaker,
"a religious man," "looking around . . . with . . . worried eyes / at the
emptiness," wants to believe. "There must be something," he says—even
as he thinks there is "nobody there!" His "fused prayers" only allow him
to reflect on the "infinite darkness between points of light" which he
knows are only stars.

Thomas has always been drawn to images of reflection and he uses these
images in several ways simultaneously. Reflection suggests contemplation,

distortion, and mediation as well as the throwing back, shadowlike, as pictures or echoes, of images or sounds from mirrors or mirror-like surfaces. Perhaps something very much like Heidegger's notion of man's "throwness" is implied by Thomas's use of such images. Various meanings come to bear on lines like "All I have is a piece / of the universal mind that reflects / infinite darkness between points of light" (33). Indeed, as Calvin Bedient discovered, even in Thomas's early work, there is an "ambiguity of reflection" which is the "central and stubborn meaning" of his poetry.[19]

The poems which immediately follow "The Possession,"—"Gone?" (34) and "The Empty Church" (35)—focus the transition which "The Possession" details just as "Waiting" (32), the poem which immediately precedes "The Possession," implies it. In "Waiting" the speaker "leaning far out / over an immense depth," speaks God's name and then waits "somewhere between faith and doubt, / for the *echoes* of its arrival" (32; [my italics]).[20]

The next important poem, intriguingly enough, is called "Perhaps." It begins:

> His intellect was the clear mirror
> he looked in and saw the machinery of God
> assemble itself? It was one that reflected
> the emptiness that was where God
> should have been. The mind's tools had
> no power convincingly to put him
> together. Looking in that mirror was a journey
> through hill mist where, the higher
> one ascends, the poorer the visibility
> becomes.
>
> (39)

This:

> . . . could have led to despair
> but for the consciousness of a presence
> behind him, whose breath clouding
> that looking-glass proved that it was alive.
> To learn to distrust the distrust
> of feeling—this then was the next step
> for the seeker?
>
> (39)

Here, the "clear mirror" of the intellect reflects on the "emptiness . . . where / God should have been" but discovers that man's mind is unable to make of these imaginary figments anything substantial, and that his "reflections"[21] become increasingly misty "the higher / one ascends." Curiously, the breath clouding the mirror "proved" the "consciousness" of "a presence" which is absent. This paradox is followed by a series of paradoxes, each detailing an absence which seems to imply a presence, or the presence of an absence: the "crossing / of a receding boundary which did not exist"; the yielding "to an unfelt pressure"; the "looking up / into invisible eyes." All of these paradoxes suggest the possibility, even the plausibility (note that the title is *not* a question even though much of the poem is) of "the ubiquity of a vast concern" with which the poem ends, an important inching forward toward the realization of the apocalyptic moment in which *Frequencies* ends.

"Emerging," a poem which draws some direct parallels between this book and *Laboratories of the Spirit* (the opening poem of *Laboratories* is also called "Emerging"), begins a dialogue of the speaker with himself which will run to the end of the book. Indeed, this "pilgrimage," as the last poem in *Frequencies* would have it, is Thomas's parallel with and response to the age-old journey to a holy place. The difference is that his pilgrimage is not a physical journey but a metaphysical quest and it arrives not at a site but at insight.

> Well, I said, better to wait
> for him on some peninsula
> of the spirit. Surely for one
> with patience he will happen by
> once in a while. It was the heart
> spoke. The mind, sceptical as always
> of the anthropomorphisms
> of the fancy, knew he must be put together
> like a poem or a composition
> in music, that what he conforms to
> is art. A promontory is a bare
> place; no God leans down
> out of the air to take the hand
> extended to him. The generations have
> watched there
> in vain. We are beginning to see
> now it is matter is the scaffolding
> of spirit; that the poem emerges
> from morphemes and phonemes; that
> as form in sculpture is the prisoner
> of the hard rock, so in everyday life
> it is the plain facts and natural happenings

that conceal God and reveal him to us
little by little under the mind's tooling.

(41)

"What he conforms to / is art." ". . . he must be put together / like a poem or a composition / in music. . . ."[22] This God, if he is there, if he was ever there, must needs be found by the mind moving and merging upon itself. Through such musings, through poetry and music, things unseen but sensed begin to emerge until, finally, "This great absence / that is like a presence" ("The Absence," 48) presents itself for the mind's consideration. But even such possibilities, illusive and perhaps hallucinatory, are transitory, temporary structures, "scaffoldings," built to support and sustain something more stationary and permanent. This suggestion is in keeping with traditional apocalyptic notions, which always portend something more permanent—and imminent; something, as Thomas would have it, that is still "emerging." Such self-creation, "the mind's tooling," is a mental operation, a metaphorical/metaphysical maneuver for the sake of some kind of sanity in the midst of a world gone (and continuing to go) awry.[23]

As we look at the remaining poems in *Frequencies* it is difficult not to notice how much Thomas, poet and priest, must have wrestled with such notions. He has been able to deal with such matters, perhaps been forced to such answers, because he finds himself living "in a contemporary / dwelling in country that / is being consumed"; because he is "A being with no / view but out upon the uncertainties / of the imperatives of science" ("Semi-Detached," 42). And what he has found and brought forward for view is something as elusive and rare as a white tiger, but "breathing / as you can imagine that / God breathes within the confines / of our definition of him" ("The White Tiger," 45). Here, like the rare bird in "Sea-Watching," "It is when one is not looking, / at times one is not there / that it comes," and thus "its absence / was as its presence" (*Laboratories of the Spirit,* 64). This presence of an absence is typical of poems in the apocalyptic mode, and it is Thomas's answer to the questions he has posed.

The questions have been raised; answers are needed. Appropriately, "The Answer" immediately follows. The poet asks, "Is there no way / other than thought of answering / its challenge?" (46). The answer he makes to his question is the priest's answer, given in theological terms.

> There is an anticipation
> of it to the point of
> dying. There have been times
> when, after long on my knees
> in a cold chancel, a stone has rolled

from my mind, and I have looked
in and seen the old questions lie
folded and in a place
by themselves, like the piled
graveclothes of love's risen body.

(46)

But if this is now, or ever was, an answer, it is not answer enough to
sustain man, as the next poem, "The Film of God," makes plain. Even
though we now have cameras "sensitive to / an absence as to a presence"
(47), they seem to "see" nothing "and we are still waiting" (47). In such
circumstances, what must one do? "The Absence" is Thomas's answer.

It is this great absence
that is like a presence, that compels
me to address it without hope
of a reply. It is a room I enter

from which someone has just
gone, the vestibule for the arrival
of one who has not yet come.
I modernise the anachronism

of my language, but he is no more here
than before. Genes and molecules
have no more power to call
him up than the incense of the Hebrews

at their altars. My equations fail
as my words do. What resource have I
other than the emptiness without him of my whole
being, a vacuum he may not abhor?

(48)

"The Absence" is the climax of Thomas's poetry in the apocalyptic
mode, and it has behind it the whole sequence of his thinking from *H'm*
onward.

The central poem (and the thematic center) of *H'm* is "Via Negativa,"
in which God is defined as:

. . . that great absence
In our lives, the empty silence
Within, the place where we go
Seeking, not in hope to
Arrive or find.

(*H'm*, 16)

Again, the significance of the absence of God's presence, a typical apocalyptic obsession, haunts all of Thomas's poetry since *H'm*. For Thomas, this is "the common ground between religion and poetry."[24] It is this prescient presence of absence which Thomas, as poet, tries to "mediate." If God "keeps the interstices / In our knowledge," is only "the darkness / Between stars," still we can posit his presence *by* his absence. With such faith "We put our hands in / His side hoping to find / It warm" (*H'm*, 16). In such a situation, "new explorers" can "change our lives" because they can "interpret absence / as presence," as Thomas says in a poem called simply "They."[25]

Thus, "The Absence" begins with the conclusion to which Thomas's work to date has come, as "this great absence / that is like a presence . . . compels / me to address it." Into this room "from which someone has just / gone, the vestibule for the arrival / of one who has not yet come" the speaker enters in awe only to discover that "he is no more here / than before." Such a conclusion after so long a quest leaves the poet on the verge of ultimate despair as he acknowledges that even these words have failed to evoke anything but absence. All that is left to hope beyond hope for is that the emptiness that "his" absence makes in the "whole / being" of the poet may, paradoxically, elicit a "vacuum he may not abhor." This is a curious argument. Still, if one is in the habit of finding absences mysteriously filled with presences, it is possible to assume that a "vacuum" would be an open invitation to such a "presence" and that such a filling, were it to occur, would ultimately be as close as man could come to the fulfilling of his need for a presence beyond himself.

The apocalyptic moment having been defined in this inevitably paradoxical way, *Frequencies* draws quickly to a close. The three remaining poems each raise again what has become by now Thomas's constant theme, but they do something interesting and slightly different with it by forcing outward questions inward, into the mind's domain. "Balance," after briefly invoking Kierkegaard[26] at the beginning of the poem, after stating, "I have abandoned / my theories, the easier certainties / of belief" (49), concludes with two questions:

> Is there a place
> here for the spirit? Is there time
> on this brief platform for anything
> other than mind's failure to explain itself?
>
> (49)

"Epiphany," likewise, opens with a question: "Three kings?" (50). The answer to the question of the manifestation of divine presence in the world is provided by the very Christ figure who "Far / / off from his cross in the wrong / season . . . sits at table / with us with on his head / the fool's cap of our paper money" (50). Thomas's pun on "fool's cap" is typical. On the one hand the dunce's cap which the savior wears is meant to remind us of our inability to see and understand anything beyond the immediate reality of our "paper money," symbol of a reality we never see but nonetheless believe in. On the other hand, the "fool's cap" may simply be a reference to a sheet of standard-size writing paper, called fool's cap in Britain. This meaning may imply that Thomas is turning the irony another time, suggesting that the paper which holds the words of the epiphanic moment is used to make mockery of the moment.

"Pilgrimages" is the final poem in *Frequencies*. It begins:

There is an island there is no going
to but in a small boat the way
the saints went, travelling the gallery
of the frightened faces of
the long-drowned, munching the gravel
of its beaches. So I have gone
up the salt land to the building
with the stone altar and the candles
gone out, and kneeled and lifted
my eyes to the furious gargoyle
of the owl that is like a god
gone small and resentful.

(51)

The pilgrim asks, "Am I too late?" Then wonders, "Were they too late also, those / first pilgrims?" (51). It is a question which echoes down the centuries, and it is the question which haunts Thomas's recent work, *his* pilgrimage, as he acknowledges here at the end of it: "It is I / who ask" (52). "He is such a fast / God, always before us and / leaving as we arrive" (51). "There is no time on this island, . . . the tide / has no clock" and "events / are dateless." Thomas acknowledges that his quest is not unique, but typical—however unique it is for him at the moment. He asks:

Was the pilgrimage
I made to come to my own
self, to learn that in times
like these and for one like me
God will never be plain and
out there, but dark rather and
inexplicable, as though he were in here?

(52)

Thus, *Frequencies* ends, with an answer which is a question. It is a question with which the poetry of apocalypse has always had to deal since answers are never finally, fully available. The pilgrimage itself must be answer enough.

Frequencies ends, but the reverberations of this evocative book continue as the various accumulated meanings of the title work back and forth through the poems and through our readings of them. In "One Way," in *Between Here and Now*[27] Thomas speaks of "refining / my technique, signalling / to him on the frequencies / I commanded"—without success. Perhaps his success is more definitive on the human level. As he says in "Threshold," the final poem of *Between Here and Now*, ". . . what balance is needed at / the edges of such an abyss" (110).

Aptly enough, the last poem in Thomas's most recent book is titled "Prayer." In it Thomas imagines his grave, "not too far from Baudelaire" and "not too far" from "the tree of science":

> somewhere within sight
> of the tree of poetry
> that is eternity wearing
> the green leaves of time.[28]

In this Edenic metaphor for present existence, the "tree of poetry" becomes, for Thomas, equivalent to the tree of knowledge. And the fall into the present carries with it the prayer that, in an apocalyptic age, the poet-priest may be able to find salvation in the word, if not in the world. What balance is needed on the edge of such an abyss.

Notes

1. Thomas J. J. Altizer, "Imagination and Apocalypse," *Soundings: An Interdisciplinary Journal,* 53:4 (1970): 398.

2. A. M. Allchin, "The Poetry of R. S. Thomas," *Theology,* 72:605 (November 1970): 490.

3. R. S. Thomas, "A Frame for Poetry," *The Times Literary Supplement,* March 3, 1966, 169.

4. "R. S. Thomas: Priest and Poet," a transcript of John Ormond's BBC film for television, broadcast April 2, 1972, and published in *Poetry Wales,* 7:4 (Spring 1972): 52–53.

5. *The Collected Poems of Theodore Roethke* (New York: Doubleday, 1975), 129.

6. Theodore Roethke, "Open Letter," in Ralph J. Mills, Jr., ed., *On the Poet and His Craft* (Seattle: University of Washington Press, 1965), 39.

7. See my article, "The Escape Into Time: Theodore Roethke's 'The Waking,'" *Notes on Contemporary Literature*, 5:2 (March 1975): 2–10.

8. Mills, 25.

9. R. S. Thomas, Introduction, *The Penguin Book of Religious Verse* (Harmondsworth: Penguin, 1963), 9.

10. Mills, 26. Cf. Thomas's acknowledged debt to a poem like Francis Thompson's "The Hound of Heaven."

11. Both Roethke and Thomas might best be described as "nature mystics." Indeed, Thomas so described himself in the BBC film of 1972. Recently, Thomas has again attempted to define his mystical tendencies—and to deal with the "misunderstanding and misinterpretation on the part of the critics" in terms of this notion. (See "R. S. Thomas Talks to J. B. Lethbridge," *Anglo-Welsh Review*, 74 [1983]: 47–48.)

12. As Martin Buber says, "The apocalyptic writer has no audience turned towards him; he speaks into his notebook. He does not really speak, he only writes; he does not write down the speech, he just writes his thoughts—he writes a book." ("Prophecy, Apocalyptic, and the Historical Hour," in Buber's *Pointing the Way* [New York: Harper & Brothers, 1957], 200.)

13. R. S. Thomas, *Frequencies* (London: Macmillan, 1978), 7. Hereafter, all references to *Frequencies* will be included, in parentheses, in the text.

14. See n. 9 above.

15. See n. 9 above. Cf. "R. S. Thomas Talks to J. B. Lethbridge," 55.

16. R. S. Thomas, *Laboratories of the Spirit* (London: Macmillan, 1975), 5. Hereafter, all references to *Laboratories of the Spirit* will be included, in parentheses, in the text.

17. A. E. Dyson, *Yeats, Eliot and R. S. Thomas: Riding the Echo* (London: Macmillan, 1981), 304. This image of the cross, as I have tried to show, goes back in Thomas's work to the seminal and explicit reference of "Amen" in *Laboratories of the Spirit* (5). Dyson considers "Amen" one of the two poems in *Laboratories of the Spirit* (the other is "Rough") which "I cannot pretend fully to understand," although he sees it as "a poem poised at a cross-roads" (312, 317).

18. R. S. Thomas, *Pietà* (London: Rupert Hart-Davis, 1966), 44.

19. Calvin Bedient, *Eight Contemporary Poets* (London: Oxford University Press, 1974), 67.

20. Cf. W. S. Merwin: "In an age when time and technique encroach hourly, or appear to, on the source itself of poetry, it seems as though what is needed for any particular nebulous unwritten hope that may become a poem is not a manipulable, more or less predictably recurring pattern, but an unduplicatable resonance, something that would be like an echo except that it is repeating no sound". ("On

Open Form," in Stephen Berg and Robert Mezey, eds., *Naked Poetry: Recent American Poetry in Open Forms* [Indianapolis: Bobbs-Merrill, 1969], 270–71). Cf. my article on Merwin as an apocalyptic poet, "'Like the Beam of a Lightless Star': The Poetry of W. S. Merwin," *Poet and Critic,* 14:1 (1982): 45–56.

21. Cf. "The central and stubborn meaning of Thomas's work is . . . the ambiguity of reflection. Existence and action, as Jaspers remarks, display an 'endless ambiguity': 'anything can mean something else for reflection.' Only eternal knowledge is finite—which helps explain why Thomas, one of the most restless of men, refers himself to it." (Bedient, 67)

22. Thomas sounds like Wallace Stevens, a poet he is clearly fond of and has been "influenced" by, as I have tried to show. (See my article on Thomas and Stevens, "'An Abstraction Blooded': Wallace Stevens and R. S. Thomas on Blackbirds and Men," *The Wallace Stevens Journal,* 8:2 [1984]: 79–82.) Thomas has said that, for him, there is no "newer voice" in English poetry than Stevens, who "comes nearest to expressing the situation" of the moment ("R. S. Thomas Talks to J. B. Lethbridge," 56).

23. It is interesting to remember, in terms of this poem, that Thomas lives at the very tip of the Llŷn peninsula in northern Wales, at a place called Aberdaron, not far from Porth Niegwl, "The Mouth of Hell."

24. See notes 9 and 11.

25. R. S. Thomas, *The Way of It* (Tyne and Wear: Ceolfrith Press, 1977), 28.

26. Thomas, at about the same time these poems were written, was thinking of Kierkegaard in another context. In a lecture he delivered in 1977, entitled "The Creative Writer's Suicide," he said, "In his book, *The Present Age,* Kierkegaard posed a profound and important question: Does man have a right to let himself be killed for the sake of truth?" Thomas uses this Kierkegaardian question as the basis for his talk on "the creative writer." It is clear that much of what he says here has a direct bearing on his own work. (See R. S. Thomas, "The Creative Writer's Suicide," *Planet,* 41 [January 1978]: 30.) Cf. also Thomas's poem, "Kierkegaard," in *Pietà* (18), and his reference to Kierkegaard in the BBC television documentary on Thomas mentioned above, as well as "R. S. Thomas Talks to J. B. Lethbridge," 54–55.)

27. R. S. Thomas, *Between Here and Now* (London: Macmillan, 1981), 95.

28. R. S. Thomas, *Later Poems: A Selection* (London: Macmillan, 1983), 214.

R. S. Thomas's
Poetry of the Church of Wales

Donald Davie

Reprinted from Religion & Literature, *19:2 (Summer 1987): 35–47.*

In 1972 R. S. Thomas's ninth collection of poems (there have always been too many of them) had the arch and unpromising title, *H'm*. It marked a turning point in Thomas's writing, and the turn that he made alienated some who had admired him. Their discontent was voiced by John Wain in one of his lectures as Professor of Poetry at Oxford:

> R. S. Thomas . . . is a particularly depressing example of the damage caused to a poet's work by the flight from form; his subject-matter has always been rather lowering (depopulation of the countryside, depopulation of the human heart through the decay of beliefs, etc.). But there was a time when the depressing nature of what Mr. Thomas conveyed was irradiated and made beautiful by his beautiful sense of rhythm and sound. The poems in *H'm* offer no such consolation.

And Wain quoted in support of this contention "Via Negativa":

> Why no! I never thought other than
> That God is that great absence
> In our lives, the empty silence
> Within, the place where we go
> Seeking, not in hope to
> Arrive or find. He keeps the interstices
> In our knowledge, the darkness
> Between stars. His are the echoes
> We follow, the footprints he has just

Left. We put our hands in
His side hoping to find
It warm. We look at people
And places as though he had looked
At them, too; but miss the reflection.

Here, Wain contended, "the lowered, daunted quality of the subject matter is matched by the same characteristics in the expression"; whereas "in
the days when Mr. Thomas made graceful, lyrical poems about being
daunted, he was telling us that the negative experience was being contained
in a mind, and expressed by a sensibility, that was reaching beyond, attaining something positive."

The response is clearly and forthrightly expressed, it is understandable, and certainly it was widely shared. But it is open to certain objections.
In the first place, and most importantly, it must be questioned whether the
subject matter of "Via Negativa" is, as John Wain confidently takes for
granted, "lowered, daunted." Thomas's other poems suggested, and were
to suggest, that a God who "keeps the interstices / In our knowledge, the
darkness / Between stars" was a concept not daunting but consolatory. The
religious mind finds its consolations in regions where the secular mind discerns only forbidding bleakness, and just that paradox or seeming paradox
is what R. S. Thomas's later poems resolutely explore. If one's worst fear is
that technological man may extend his knowledge to the point where no
mysteries are left in the universe, then a God who can be relied on always
to reveal gaps in that knowledge is a God to be thankful for. The way of
negation, the "Via Negativa" of the title, is thus one of the ways to transcendence; this is what traditional Christian thinking affirms, and the poem
endorses that traditional understanding.

Secondly, one may question Wain's implicit assumption that the poetry
he calls "lyrical" characteristically works by expressing "lowering" apprehensions in a sweetly formal way that makes them paradoxically exalting.
That some poetry works on us in that way need not be denied. But to take
that way of working as a norm runs the risk of overvaluing a suave melan-
choly, the poignantly managed dying fall. It is a risk that English readers of
Wain's generation are particularly prone to, enamored as they mostly are of
Philip Larkin, that poet of very lowering apprehensions indeed. The least
one can say is that the poet of *H'm,* though for that matter of earlier collections also, had no interest in being lyrical on that understanding of "lyric."

All the same, John Wain undoubtedly had a point: the R. S. Thomas
of the 1970s certainly went to great lengths to offend and disappoint the
reader's ear. As soon as we consider how to read "Via Negativa" aloud, we

can see where that offensiveness is: in the enjambments, the run-overs. As the reading voice turns from the third line into the fourth, and again from the fourth into the fifth, it encounters after two syllables the jarring stop that had been denied it (where it would not have jarred) at the end of the verse line. There are not much less-jarring enjambments where the fifth line turns into the sixth, and the seventh into the eighth; a particularly abrupt one, on to a single syllable, where the ninth line turns into the tenth; and another, only one syllable more lenient, where the eleventh line turns into the twelfth. Of course such abrupt or violent enjambments are an invaluable resource available to the poet; but when they are resorted to so frequently in a short poem (which is a sonnet only on the understanding that all fourteen-line poems are sonnets), the trick seems to be a mere mannerism, one that denies even minimal integrity to the verse line. Where the verse line is concerned—and "verse" comes from *versus,* the *turn* (from one line into the next)—John Wain's allegation, "flight from form," seems not excessive. Wain called "Via Negativa" "a fine poem," but then, on second thought, "a fine piece of writing"; it would be more accurate to say (teasingly, yet in all seriousness) that it may or may not be a fine poem, but it certainly isn't a fine piece of verse.

This is not always the case. In "The Calling," from the next collection *Laboratories of the Spirit* (1975), the enjambments—not just between lines but between quatrains—are similarly violent; yet in every case there is rhetorical justification. That is to say, they are expressive, and therefore an aid rather than an impediment to the voice that would read the poem aloud:

> And the word came—was it a god
> spoke or a devil?—Go
> to that lean parish; let them tread
> on your dreams; and learn silence
>
> is wisdom. Be alone with yourself
> as they are alone in the cold room
> of the wind. Listen to the earth
> mumbling the monotonous song
>
> of the soil: I am hungry, I
> am hungry, in spite of the red dung
> of this people. See them go
> one by one through that dark door
>
> with the crumpled ticket of your prayers
> in their hands. Share their distraught

joy at the dropping of their inane
children. Test your belief

in spirit on their faces staring
at you, on beauty's surrender
to truth, on the soul's selling
of itself for a corner

by the body's fire. Learn the thinness
of the window that is
between you and life, and how
the mind cuts itself if it goes through.

In this fine poem the line endings overridden so imperiously are in the service of a saturnine, even savage, wit—consider how in the fourth quatrain the line endings link "distraught" with "inane." It is not how we imagine a Christian priest contemplating his flock; but in that case we had better (so the poem implies) revise our notions, and not suppose that either Christian charity or pastoral care precludes the Yeatsian arrogance that is invoked in the third and fourth lines. (Thomas alludes to Yeats continually: something too little noticed by those who, finding him for the most part a rural person, have typed him as a Wordsworthian poet, gray and good and sober—that is not at all his character.)

Even so, Thomas's ruthless enjambments became in the 1970s, and have remained to the present day, such a prominent feature of his style— sometimes to affective purpose, more often not—that it is hard not to see this as a tic, a mannerism. It is as if this sole device constitutes for him a prosody; and we may legitimately protest that a respectable prosody must comprehend a good deal more than this. Before I am through, I shall venture to suggest how and why this came about. If I am right, the matter cannot be explained as simple misjudgment in the niceties of verse writing as a craft; on the contrary it involves us in sympathetically speculating about what it means nowadays to be, as Thomas is, a Welshman, and a Welshman who writes in English.

Moreover, this is a Welshman of a very special kind, in one crucial respect unrepresentative. For Thomas, who was born in 1913, spent his working life (he has now retired) as a priest of the Church in Wales, that is to say of the Anglican Church. I am not aware that Thomas has ever explained—why should he?—what impelled him to that particular priesthood rather than some other. But it sets a gulf between him and many, indeed most, of his fellow Welshmen. I do not have any statistics, but am willing to believe what is commonly assumed: that the religious experience of the Welsh people, in Wales and out of it, is characteristically focused on "chapel," not on "church"; that is to say, that many more of them worship with the nonconformist dissenting sects (for instance, the Baptists) than with those who recognize, as the head of their Church, the monarch of the United Kingdom. I am picking my words with some care, for these are potentially very inflammable considerations. In England the Church of England is described just so, as "of England"; whereas the Church of Scotland is *not* the Anglican Church, and in Wales the Anglican Church is scrupulously described as the Church not *of* Wales but *in* Wales. Neither in Scotland nor Wales, nor for that matter in Ireland, is the Church that R. S. Thomas served the *established* Church, as it is in England. In Wales the Anglican Church is no more privileged, among other Protestant churches, than is the Episcopal Church of America among other Protestant churches in the U.S.A. Indeed, Welsh nationalists (and R. S. Thomas is ardently one of them, as we shall see) sometimes conceive of the Anglican Church in Wales as profoundly alien, an ecclesiastical extension of the English drive, sustained through centuries, to subjugate Welsh culture to English. To be a Welsh patriot while serving as priest of what was originally and is persistingly an *English* church—this is the anomaly, as some see it, of the condition that R. S. Thomas chose and lived with.

The effect of this, poetically, can be seen most clearly by comparing Thomas's poems with those of the *English* Anglican poet who with characteristic generosity took note of Thomas's first collection, parochially published from an obscure Welsh printing house, and enthusiastically launched him before a metropolitan audience. This was John Betjeman, later Poet Laureate, a lesser poet than Thomas and yet not just the quaint and comical rhymester that he was for too long supposed to be. Betjeman followed up laudatory newspaper reviews by introducing in 1955 Thomas's *Song at the Year's Turning: Poems, 1952–1954*. Betjeman's poems of Christian experience, though early and late they often turn on such uncomfortable matters as mortality and original sin, are nevertheless *cosy* as Thomas's are not; Betjeman when he attends church is aware of participating in a socio-political as well as a religious ritual, whereas Thomas the Welshman when he attends or officiates at worship has, and can have, no such confidence. For him the worship has a religious significance, or none at all; and to judge from his poems, "none at all" is the bleak verdict that his demanding consciousness often passes on his priestly endeavors. Of the many poems that the poet-priest has addressed to his parishioners, we may take as typical "To Church":

You sat in the stone church;
To what secret prayers
Did your lips say, Amen?
The preacher spoke from the high
Pulpit, his quick words
Bounced on your mind's crust.
You were not there to learn
Agility of a creed
Grown nimble from keeping
Its balance on smooth tongues.

You sat in the tall pew;
No new vows were wrung
From your hard heart, pardon,
Hovering on the air,
Had no place to go.
You went down on your knees
With the rest; the priest's blessing
Fell on you like the tree's
Shadow in which at last
Your crossed bones were buried.

There are several ways in which the bones in the grave can be said to be
"crossed"; but one sense of the word surely is that the bones have had the
sign of the cross made over them. If so, this line and the poem as a whole
may be thought to express the Anglo-Catholic and Roman Catholic faith
that such consecrations by a priestly hand are efficacious even if they stir no
responsive feeling or understanding on the part of the person consecrated.

When this poem first appeared (in *Poetry* for May 1962) it was accompanied by "This," typical of many poems that derive from the poet-priest's
pastoral care for his parishioners outside of church. One such parishioner,
doubtless a woman, speaks:

I thought, you see, that on some still night,
When stars were shrill over his farm,
And he and I kept ourselves warm
By an old fire, whose bars were bright
With real heat, the truth might ripen
Between us naturally as the fruit
Of his wild hedges, or as the roots,
Swedes and mangolds, he grew then.

No luck; the thoughts hopefully sown
On such evenings never could break

The mind's crust. Keeping my own
Company now, I have forsaken
All but this poor basement of bone,
Where the one dry flame is awake.

We may reasonably take this poem as an example of that suavity which John Wain liked in Thomas's earlier collections, which he deplored the lack of when in the 1970s Thomas's style became harsher, more rebarbative. And it is true that the enjambments here are managed with a liquid ease that Thomas later would not pause for; as it is also true that the formal decorum of the sonnet, for instance in regard to rhyme, is here respected as it would not be later. Yet this decorum is largely illusory or superficial: it is notable for instance that only one line, the sixth, can be scanned as iambic pentameter, though that is the meter which traditional decorum requires for the English sonnet. (The other lines are accentual tetrameters, and indeed Thomas's meters are nearly always accentual, despite the rough and uncertain rhythms which accentual meters lend themselves to, as against the stricter requirements of the accentual-syllabic.) The signs were always there that Thomas's observance of traditional forms was grudging, mutinous, and temporary. But the signs were overlooked by Thomas's English admirers like, of all people, Kingsley Amis (who declared that Thomas's earliest poems moved him to tears).

They were overlooked also by such American readers as took notice of him. Calvin Bedient for instance, writing of Thomas in his *Eight Contemporary Poets* (1974), decided that "Reading Thomas one learns to endure the glare of emotion; one learns again a kind of innocence." Thomas, Bedient said, "is an anachronism, a poet of feeling in an age of intellect"; and further, he claimed, "Thomas never really challenges the mind. His appeal is all to feeling. . . ." Such a misreading was barely understandable even in 1974; for how could Bedient discern an "age of intellect," after the feelingful excesses of Anglo-American poetry and public behavior in the 1960s? Today it is quite inadmissible. Bedient to be sure had bad luck, for he wrote just too soon to take account of the new turn that Thomas's poetry was taking in the 1970s. Yet Thomas, I have suggested, was at that point merely taking off the wraps—he had always been an intellectual poet, and a rebellious one.

However it may have been with English readers like Wain and Amis, it is plain how this American reader went wrong. Calvin Bedient had a hazy and inaccurate idea of the Anglo-Welsh poetic tradition that R. S. Thomas inherited, a tradition represented in Bedient's mind by Gerard

Manley Hopkins, who so far as I know conceived of himself always as a Victorian Englishman, and by Dylan Thomas, an urbanized and Anglicized Welshman who spoke no Welsh. If we are to get our poet into sharper focus, we need to do rather better than that in conceiving what it means to be a Welsh writer in the present century. And first we must recognize the force and the validity of Welsh nationalism.

Because Welsh nationalism is less of a *political* force than Scottish, not to speak of Irish, the outside observer tends to think that Welsh nationhood is something merely picturesque and sentimental, which the English may safely indulge. In fact, however, just because the political assimilation of the Welsh has gone further than with the Irish and the Scots, and because accordingly the English are readier to indulge what they see as endearing Welsh foibles, the Welsh writer's attitude to English culture is peculiarly exacerbated and in many cases peculiarly intransigent. It turns for him, far more than for his Irish and Scottish peers, specifically on matters of language. For on the one hand Welsh is far nearer being, as a practical possibility, an alternative national tongue than Gaelic is for the Irish and the Scots; yet on the other hand the English spoken and written by Welshmen differs from metropolitan English, lexically and grammatically, much less than the English of Ireland or Scotland does. Accordingly, the Welsh writer who writes in English feels especially guilty at doing so, although he cannot contrive a third option such as Hugh MacDiarmid contrived for Scotland with Lallans or "synthetic Scots." Anglo-Welsh, Anglo-Irish, Anglo-Scottish are three hyphenated compounds that ought as it were to lie parallel one with another; but this is not so—the three conditions, though similarly painful in a way that few English or Americans recognize, are in important ways unalike.

The predicament, and the pain of it, are touched on rather more often in R. S. Thomas's earlier poetry than later. But the dilemma has not been solved, and if Thomas set it aside in his poetry he has not set it aside in his politics nor in his sense of himself as an artist responsible to his nation. In 1978, in an address originally delivered in Welsh, he spoke of it heatedly, as some may think with anguish:

> This devilish bilingualism! O, I know about all the arguments in favour of it: how it enriches one's personality, how it sharpens one's mind, how it enables one to enjoy the best of two worlds and so on. Very likely. But to anyone in Wales who desires to write, it is a millstone around his neck. . . .
>
> A foreign language! Yes. Let nobody imagine that because there is so much English everywhere in Wales it is not a foreign language. . . .

An Anglo-Welsh writer is neither one thing nor the other. He keeps going in a no-man's land between two cultures. . . .

Woe that I was born! Who has suffered, if I have not suffered? For I bear in my body the marks of this conflict. . . .

What emerges elsewhere in this extremely personal testimony is the fact that Thomas writes in English because (he spells this out, and it does him honor) his Welsh was too lately and too laboriously acquired, for him to be critical enough of his own performances in that language. What seems to follow, however, is that accordingly he regards English as the medium that an unkind fate has condemned him to. And indeed Thomas says nothing to suggest that he regards English other than grudgingly, even resentfully. This is surely a very uncommon way for an artist to feel toward the medium that he is working in. And the oddity is highlighted by the way in which, when Thomas speaks of the poetic tradition in Welsh, he dwells admiringly on its formal intricacies. For, as we have seen, his way with such elegances inherited from the *English* tradition—for instance, those of the English sonnet—is quite brutally rough-and-ready.

There is a striking contrast, in certain poets from the Irish northeast who attracted in the 1970s much admiring attention outside Ireland. Not only Seamus Heaney explicitly, but Derek Mahon and Michael Longley almost as plainly, were in love with the English language, and with English poetry of the past as manifesting that language raised to its highest power. Indeed in 1968–1970, the years of their first collections, these Irishmen made deft and accomplished use of the traditional English resources which too many English poets were then rejecting, often with contumely. The Irish, it seemed, could embrace the English tongue without any suspicion that by doing so they betrayed their Irishness. But the Anglo-Welsh poet could have no such confidence. His namesake Ned Thomas sees R. S. Thomas as subscribing to the desperate view held by other Anglo-Welsh nationalist writers of the 1970s: "one was writing poetry in English so as to render that poetry unnecessary in the Wales of the future." Surely no Irish nor Scottish poet was ever driven to this logical but lunatic extreme of prolonging a tradition in the devout hope that it would soon be extinguished.

These questions do not arise with a poet whom R. S. Thomas was from time to time prepared to consider one [of] his Anglo-Welsh peers: the author of *The Anathemata,* David Jones, who died in 1974. One of the humiliating embarrassments for the hyphenated cultures in the United Kingdom is the over-abundance of borderline cases; the English reader is understandably though too easily bemused when John Buchan is presented to him as a Scottish writer, Louis Macneice as Irish, Edward Thomas as

Welsh. David Jones is not one of these; it is plain that his ancestral Welshness was crucial to his sense of his own identity, and also that that inherited allegiance was a principle of, and a motive behind, the one interminable poem which, as now appears, he spent most of his life putting together. Jones, however, though an Anglo-Welshman, was in a very different situation from R. S. Thomas. London-born, having never achieved more than an inaccurate smattering of Welsh, and having spent little time inside the Principality, Jones was moreover deeply attached to the British army with which he had served on the Western Front in 1916, in a regiment where London Cockneys fought beside Welsh-speaking Welshmen—an experience which he commemorated movingly in his long-meditated *In Parenthesis* (1937). From then on he seems to have devoted himself to re-creating, with a wealth of archaeological learning, that era in the history of the British Isles when Englishman and Welshman were not yet at odds since both were citizens of Roman Britain. It was entirely consistent that Jones as a young man should have joined the Roman Catholic Church; for the worship of that Church, so long as it was conducted in Latin, preserved for the linguistically sensitive the memory of that Romano-British unity. Jones thus avoided the Anglo-Welsh predicament by tracking back through recorded and legendary history to the point where the predicament had not yet arisen. For that reason one finds in Jones no resentment of the English donation to Wales, beyond a certain tetchiness with those periods of English culture when it seems to have attended more to other connections (e.g., French) than to the Celtic.

Some who sought to excuse Philip Larkin's exclusion of David Jones from *The Oxford Book of Twentieth-Century English Verse* pleaded that, whereas at times Jones had indeed written finely in English, none of that writing was in any strict sense poetry. It would have made more sense, and a better apology, if they had contended that whereas Jones's writing was undoubtedly poetry, very little of it—and that not the best part—was in verse. For the verse line, and the niceties of turning from one verse line into the next, Jones very seldom showed any susceptibility at all; and in his letters, whenever he is required to comment on rhythm and meter and the relation between them, his remarks are puerile. In this if in little else he is at one with his fellow Anglo-Welshman R. S. Thomas: it is English verse that they do violence to, not English poetry.

Jones's stance, however, is Olympian. It is R. S. Thomas who has articulated and suffered through the predicament of the modern Welshman. The analogy with the Irish, partial though it is and potentially misleading, is illuminating. If we compare Seamus Heaney with his formidably accomplished and cosmopolitan fellow Northern Irishman, Derek Mahon, the comparison cannot resolve itself into asking which is the better poet. Rather, Heaney has chosen to enter himself in a league that Mahon, perhaps honorably judging himself unqualified, has chosen not to compete in: that is to say, the aspiration by the poet to be the voice of his people. Heaney and Thomas have chosen to act out, in their lives as reflected in their writings, the role and the predicament imposed in our times on the generic Irishman in the one case, the generic Welshman in the other. This is presumptuous, and in both cases the presumption has been fastened on, and derided, by the poet's compatriots: Heaney in Ireland, and R. S. Thomas in Wales, have been prophets without much honor in their native countries. But the presumption is allowable, and indeed necessary, in the case of those who aspire to be *national* poets. Contrary to what is often supposed, a national poet addresses his own nation far more than he addresses foreigners on behalf of that nation. Such a poet holds up a glass in which his nation shall see itself as it is, not as it is thought to be in some beguiling image available alike for internal and external consumption. So one has heard Welsh people complain that while Thomas's unflattering portrait of the Welsh is faithful, he should have registered it only in Welsh, not in a language that foreigners can read. So too Heaney is extolled much less wholeheartedly in Ireland than in the United Kingdom and the U.S.A. Affronted by the presumption of a Heaney or a Thomas, who impudently offer in their words and stanzas to enact the dilemmas not of themselves only but of entire nations, many readers may understandably prefer the beguiling modesty of Derek Mahon or (though the case is admittedly very different) of David Jones. But it is the presumptuousness of Thomas and Heaney that keeps the faith with great national poets of the past—or for that matter of the present, as in the case of many subjugated nations of Eastern Europe.

That last reference is not altogether gratuitous, at least not for those who may be asking themselves how Thomas the Welsh patriot can be reconciled with Thomas the Christian believer and Christian priest. For we have news of how in Poland, and less certainly in Czechoslovakia and Hungary and Romania, priests of the Roman Church and also sometimes Lutheran and Calvinist pastors seem to have taken upon themselves, as an extension of their pastoral functions, the safeguarding of their respective nationhoods—if only to the extent of preventing their nations from being torn apart by internal strife. We observe the same exertions by clerics, white and black, in South Africa. Of course, the comparison is out of all proportion. In these countries the stakes are higher, and the risks of pursuing such a course are much greater. R. S. Thomas is not likely to be murdered or thrown into prison. Yet the principle, it may be thought, is the same. "The Church in Wales"—and in that formulation "Wales" gets as much emphasis as "Church."

I have been suggesting that there is in R. S. Thomas a perhaps intermittent but certainly persistent animosity toward English culture; and that this appears not in what his poems say, but in their way of saying it. In other words the clues are to be found, with this poet as with any serious artist, precisely in his *art*, in how he handles his artistic medium. For Thomas that medium is the English language and the English verse-line; and like John Wain I find Thomas handling that medium with a peculiar gracelessness which he has indulged more and more over the years. That is of course, and is meant to be, a damaging comment. Damaging, and yet not quite damning. For grace or gracefulness, though we are right to look for it in poetry and to feel resentment when it is denied us, is not traditionally held to be a *sine qua non* of poetry. It is not even, if we may trust the wisest authorities through the centuries, one of poetry's highest attributes. These thoughts and admonitions come to mind when we look at the best of the undoubtedly bleak and craggy poems that have come from R. S. Thomas in recent years. One of these is a poem overtly on the Old Testament theme of Cain slaying his brother Abel, but in fact and more urgently on the New Testament themes of Incarnation, Crucifixion, and Redemption. Thomas's treatment of these sacred matters seems at first sight deeply shocking:

> Abel looked at the wound
> His brother had dealt him, and loved him
> For it. Cain saw that look
> And struck him again. The blood cried
> On the ground; God listened to it.
> He questioned Cain. But Cain answered:
> Who made the blood? I offered you
> Clean things: the blond hair
> Of the corn; the knuckled vegetables; the
> Flowers; things that did not publish
> Their hurt, that bled
> Silently. You would not accept them.
>
> And God said: It was part of myself
> He gave me. The lamb was torn

From my own side. The limp head,
The slow fall of red tears—they
Were like a mirror to me in which I beheld
My reflection. I anointed myself
In readiness for the journey
To the doomed tree you were at work upon.

This is graceless in the ways we have looked at earlier. But to speak for myself, faced with something so uncompromising in its treatment of matters so troubling, I can accept that the poem has to be graceless if it is to be (as it surely is) sublime and tragic and austere.

Negativity and Language in the Religious Poetry of R. S. Thomas

Vimala Herman

*Reprinted from ELH, 45:4 (Winter 1978): 710–31.

> At the back of all there surely has to be a creed, a fundamental state-
> ment put in language that does not jar with every reality we know
> about the world. We don't want to be put off with serpents and fig-
> leaves and sacrificial lambs. We want a creed in modern English, sir.
> And we can't find it![1]

Thus spoke a young man to a vicar in H. G. Wells's novel *Babes in the Darkling Wood*, and if we substitute Welsh peasants, barren moors, and cold country churches for the sacrificial lambs, serpents, and fig leaves, the statement could probably be hurled with equal truth at R. S. Thomas by the reader. What strikes one most powerfully about Thomas as priest-poet is the seeming absence of a creed, or a "fundamental statement" of apparent unbelief which conflicts radically with traditional Christian assumptions regarding the nature of God and belief. The fact is all the more curious when one recalls that Thomas has been a practicing priest for over thirty years. Yet the nature of religious experience in the verse is peculiarly ambivalent, enigmatic, and negative in tone. In the poem "H'm," the preacher's inarticulation, his inability to speak of God's love, illustrates the readers' perspective on Thomas as a religious poet.

> and one said
> speak to us of love
> and the preacher opened

his mouth and the word God
fell out so they tried
again speak to us
of God then but the preacher
was silent . . .[2]

What does one make of this kind of poetry? Such inarticulation about
God on the part of God's deputy would seem to create disturbing currents
of betrayal. The poem with its rush of words unbroken by traditional stops
and starts of punctuation, paradoxically amounts precisely to a statement—
about nothing, or a something that defies articulation. The run of words
including in its wake the insistent verbal onslaughts of the questioners coa-
lesces both question and answer about God into a fundamental gesture of
inadequacy. The inability to answer and the demand for answers are held
in tension, in a circular movement, the one continuously generating the
other. The final result is a statement about the impossibility of making statements about God and belief, which signals the absence of a mode of
confirmation, an easily available "creed in modern English, sir" that could
be given and accepted and thus break the circle. And it is the significance
of this "negative moment" as it may be termed, that is crucial for an understanding of Thomas as a religious poet. It is a moment that is manifest in
the poetry as a central absence, a loss of anchorage, a mystery, a lack of final
reference, which subverts the assertiveness of language and makes it falter.
God exists in Thomas's poetry, but the features are transformed. The God
of Thomas does not reside in regions of ineffable plenitude, but in a context of alienation. He is not a rationalist God—a God of enlightened justice and beauty—but a Dark God, basically unknowable, distanced, silent.
Consequently, for Thomas, the basic problem in his religious poetry appears
to be the problem of not knowing, and for a religious poet, it is not only a
crisis of belief but also a crisis of language. For what can a priest say about
a God he cannot know? And how would language articulate such negation?
The absence of a center—of an authoritative, referential presence, from
whom meaning may be derived—sets into motion the process of reconstruction of meaning in another way, out of the drifting bits of faith and
doubt, from fleeting and unauthorized moments of intensity, in neutral fragments of language. The stringency of Thomas's accounting of the "negative moment" in his poetry can be seen to explain the characteristic effects
of his work—the troubling ambivalence of statement, the instabilities of
tone, which disturb the reading by its demand for attentiveness on the part
of the reader to *its* predicament, and its subsequent refusal to award the
reader with any position of security.

As priest, the question of a religious reality and of knowledge of that reality for the Christian worshiper is obviously crucial. God as Truth, as "Ultimate Reality," is the object of knowledge and of faith, and the mediation of that reality, Thomas sees, as the task of the religious poet. Thus, Thomas defines religion as "embracing an experience of ultimate reality" and poetry as "the imaginative presentation of such."³ For the poet, the force of "imaginative" is important, for it is here, within the creative act itself, that Thomas posits compatibility between religion and poetry. He invokes Coleridge's conception of Imagination, and stresses the role of the primary imagination as the agency for the perception of truth—the ultimate reality that is seen to govern existence. The creative act is thereby a religious act, a repetition in some analogous way of the original act of creation, which can bring men nearer to God.

> The poet, by echoing the primary imagination, recreates. Through his work he forces those who read him to do the same, thus bringing them nearer the primary imagination themselves, and so, in a way, nearer to the actual being of God as displayed in action.⁴

The creative act, the imaginative perception must, however, be manifest in the order of language for it to be an adequate act of mediation. The significance that Thomas attaches to the role of language in the task of mediation accounts for the preference that he shows for the poet over the mystic. To the mystic,

> Deus absconditus is immediate; to the poet He is mediated. The mystic fails to mediate God adequately insofar as he is not a poet. The poet, with possibly less immediacy of apprehension, shows his spiritual nature, through the medium of language, the supreme symbol.⁵

The process of mediation, however, is highly problematic, and the crisis of faith and language explored in the poetry is the product of the religious framework that is constructed on the basis of the transcendence of Truth. The positing of an Ultimate Reality to underwrite the finite reality of the world has resulted in a *gap* in the schema, which is to a great extent endemic to the religious discourse itself. By definition, the finite, of which language is a part, cannot either capture or contain the Infinite, and is not to be identified with it. The surplus of reality available to the "Ultimate" or Infinite level renders the finite inadequate in its relation to Truth. It is an old problem that generates a new crisis. In Thomas's poetry, the excess of reality renders God not nonexistent but unknowable. The Ultimate, Unknowable Reality that must be mediated creates problems for the poet, for language falls short both of description and of address. For how is

Ultimate Reality to be known or mediated? At what level of encounter can Truth be validated? The existence of the "gap," the central darkness that defies language and meaning, conditions radically the nature of the mediation that Thomas sees as the task of the religious poet. Since neither Reality nor Truth are simply given nor easily assured, language cannot deputize for a prior Reality that its propositions can embody. The poet as amanuensis sensitively transcribing Reality for consumption is also inadmissable. Instead, the mediatory act demands the confrontation of the mystery, the address to darkness, and the construction of both faith and meaning is undertaken according to the limits and possibilities set by the condition of negation— the premise governing the religious framework. Religious poetry is consequently produced, constructed, in the various strategies that realize in language the nature of the space between God and Man in the unequal tension of the Infinite God and the finite self that structures the framework. The precarious, uncertain process of constructing knowledge and the passage toward meaning take priority over the description and ratification of the object of knowledge. The content, the meaning, both of selfhood and the nature of God—and therefore of religious experience itself, which constitutes the poetry—is continually in the making, "under construction" as it were, as the different effects of the "negative moment" are explored. The displacements, substitutions, alterations of perspective, by which the process is articulated, sets into relief the linguistic and religious problems of a schema that has decentered its referent. But the threatened meaninglessness is resolved within the terms set by the schema, by making the negative systematically productive of meaning, but in such a way as to preserve the discontinuities and gaps that it generates and also by absolving the finite in its finitude as a mode of meaning. Within this strategy, the reading of religious poetry is transformed from an act of innocent assimilation of a fixed truth, to a process of work, of attention to the various practices of writing, which, while renouncing identification with an origin or source beyond the text, must yet undertake to establish meaning within the void of such a separation. The anxiety of reading parallels the anxiety of the religious subject whose identity, constructed in void, must know itself as redeemed.

The most consistent feature of God to appear in the poetry is his absence. The earliest manifestation of this is to be found in the poem "In a Country Church."

> To one kneeling down no word came,
> Only the wind's song, saddening the lips
> Of the grave saints, rigid in glass;

> Or the dry whisper of unseen wings,
> Bats not angels appear in the high roof.[6]

The seeker waiting for affirmation of his Christian identity—kneeling in prayer and waiting for the God to speak in the poem—remains unaffirmed. No word comes. God is absent, both in the soul of man and in the world outside. The spiritual meaning of the material is missing. The wind is just wind, not the breath of the spirit. Bats not angels appear in the high roof. The deliberate emphasis on the finiteness of these images questions the expected investment of spiritual significance in them. Similarly, in the poem "In Church,"[7] nothing in the building seems to capture the spirit of God. The church remains just a building unanimated by God's presence in spite of man's prayers. The phrase "the hard ribs of the body" insists rather on its material presence. The silence intensifies the absence, the absence the silence. The only disruption is the breath of man as he waits unanswered in the darkness confronted by an untenanted Cross. In the poem "Service,"[8] the experience of God's absence becomes particularly poignant within its context of a ritual communication, a service to a God who is not there. In this situation, the sense of alienation from God and Man is acute, and prayer becomes an exchange of noncommunication.

The nonpresence of a spiritual truth vested in the material fact raises the problem of the nature of reality and of knowledge of it. The impossibility of grasping an Infinite truth creates the ambivalence regarding the "truth" as presented by experience. Nature, which should normally reveal "evidence" of its Creator, remains mute under interrogation, stubborn in its materiality, silent to the challenge of any other truth.

> And God said: How do you know?
> And I went out into the fields
> At morning and it was true.
>
> Nothing denied it, neither the bowed man
> On his knees, nor the animals,
> Nor the birds notched on the sky's
>
> Surface. His heart was broken
> Far back, and the beasts yawned
> Their boredom. Under the song
>
> Of the larks, I heard the wheels turn
> Rustily. But the scene held;
> The cold landscape returned my stare;
>
> There was no answer . . .
>
> ("Amen")[9]

Likewise, the central statement of the poem "Parry"[10] appears to be, "God exists, I do not know," the speaker attempting to parry the questions about God, as knowledge is not given, or the knowledge found is not that which is sought. The interminable nature of this refusal as constituting the nature of reality itself is captured in the poem "That." The anonymity of the title indicates the anonymity of reality, the obscurity of which remains inviolate regardless of the violence of the interrogation.

> It will always win.
> Other men will come as I have
> To stand here and beat upon it
> As on a door, and ask for love,
> For compassion, for hatred even; for anything
> Rather than this blank indifference,
> Than the neutrality of its answers, if they can be called answers,
> These grey skies, these wet fields,
> With the wind's winding-sheet upon them . . .[11]

The absence of God's presence in the world renders the finite world neutral. The very heterogeneity of the finite world creates problems for the priest, problems of value.

> I praise you because
> I envy your ability to
> See these things: the blind hands
> Of the aged combing sunlight
> For pity; the starved fox and
> The obese pet; the way the world
> Digests itself and the thin flame
> Scours. The youth enters
> The brothel, and the girl enters
> The nunnery, and a bell tolls.
> Viruses invade the blood.
> On the smudged empires the dust
> Lies and in the libraries
> Of the poets. The flowers wither
> On love's grave. This is what
> Life is, and on it your eye
> Sets tearless, and the dark
> Is dear to you as the light.
>   ("Because")[12]

The poem is constructed through the neutral balance of positive and negative. The pendulum of the argument alternates between the two poles.

Praise, envy; the brothel, the nunnery; the starved fox, the obese pet; the blind hands and the sunlight; and maintains the equilibrium between them. The repressed anguish, however, makes a fleeting appearance in the semantic load of "tolls" in "the bell tolls," which is negated by the "tearless eye" of the compassionate observer to whom "dark" and "light" are equally "dear." The tolling bell is structurally significant for it captures the sense of loss for alienated man and a world bereft of significance and hints at the disavowal of this position of compassionate neutrality by the priest. The neutral swing of the pendulum is in fact a toll for this state of affairs.

The quest for God through the movements of the soul or through creation has produced a negative "No Answer." Consequently, the frustrations of the unknowability of God and the impossibility of addressing him permute variously the image of God that can be known and addressed. In "Shrine at Cape Clear,"[13] a sense of a relentless divinity is articulated, an implacable enigma impenetrable by the mind of man. The cold, white statue in its shrine, normally a symbol of religious comfort, is portrayed as immovable and indifferent, a construction of stone, enigmatic even in indifference to the hopeful approaches of created things in worship. The sea brings its spray, the drowned their prayers, art its inspiration, the bay its silences, and the tributes are accepted indifferently. By contrast, the men faced with danger on the seas glimpse the truth of the enigma and know the risk of abandoning the false securities of the relation of God and Man embodied in the obeisance made to the statue.

In other poems, God appears as a God of pain. In the poem "Pisces,"[14] God is seen as the creator of pain, who made the trout to be eaten as bread by the pretty lady and her man. The cruelty implicit in the act of redemption is therefore held up for scrutiny, the innocent trout and the innocent Christ sacrificed for an unheeding world pose the question mark about God. In the poem "Echoes,"[15] the traditional image of the loving Father is shattered by the substituted image of the harsh, demanding, petulant God who demands sacrifice. Creation, however, is too feeble to respond, and God's second call for blood brings him the pale, meager shapes who obey his call. Both God's call to man and man's response are "echoes," feeble shadows not possessing the substance of contact. The poem reverses the traditional concept of sacrifice, and proclaims instead the sense of protest at the conditions that govern human existence in the demands of an Infinite God.

This awesome vision of the "dark" side of God is extended to a reading of God as Betrayer and vengeful Destroyer. The poem "The Island" is a terrible indictment of the Creator, and holds the Genesis myth in ironic juxtaposition with the narrative of the poem.

And God said. I will build a church here
And cause this people to worship me,
And afflict them with poverty and sickness
In return for centuries of hard work
And patience. And its walls shall be hard as
Their hearts, and its windows let in the light
Grudgingly, as their minds do, and the priest's words be drowned
By the wind's caterwauling. All this I will do,

Said God, and watch the bitterness in their eyes
Grow, and their lips suppurate with
Their prayers. And their women shall bring forth
On my altars, and I will choose the best
Of them to be thrown back into the sea.

And that was only on one island.[16]

The sense of absence, loss, and lack of certainty about God and the subsequent reading of the world as neutral and lacking in significance has led to a reflexive construction of God as basically malignant, a Destroyer, an Avenger. The success of these latter poems is partly in the shock they deliver to traditional religious expectations—a shock made possible through the deft employment of irony. The ironic twist to traditional religious symbols of service, church, God, and the traditional image of God as Creator, Love, Father, emphasize absence by counterpoint. The juxtaposition of traditional Christian symbols with their negation and the transgression of traditional insights about God that it affords, allows for a variety of alternative constructions, which in turn attempt to reconstruct "Reality." The displacements of the image of God make explicit man's inadequacy to know an Infinite God, since finite modes of knowing are by definition limited. Moreover, the explicit denials of spiritual significance to material presence, as for example in "Bats not angels appear in the high roof," pursue the limitations of the finite to their logical conclusion. The urbane, self-consciously, unillusioned manner of portrayal serves to emphasize the pose of disinterested observation of the "facts" as they are, or as the world will have them be. But the pose is deceptive, for this seemingly objective statement of the facts is reversed in the negative discount of the irony encapsulated in these poems. The negative element in irony is particularly appropriate in this context. The double layered nature of irony—at its simplest, its ability to say something in terms of what it is not—enables the poet to state and to cancel simultaneously any proposition. Language, consequently, parallels and dramatizes the basic presence/absence opposition that structures the religious framework, since statement and reversal of statement, the positive and the negative, appear simultaneously in irony. The movement into absence in the poems is therefore a maneuver, by which the poet first builds up the idea of a malignant God, and then by another maneuver subverts the acceptance of the initial proposition. The discount of irony forbids acceptance of any stated proposition as "Truth." But since the relation of God and Man is basically asymmetrical, no complete resolution is offered by irony. Only a continually anguished exposition of the impassed and contradictory nature of the relation is open to presentation, for God will remain unknown and the human seeker will always seek to know. The literal reading of these poems presents alternative perspectives of Reality, the ironic dissolves these perspectives. The property of "absolute infinite negativity" in Kierkegaard's phrase, and the dialectic of regress that characterizes the ironic mode, inhibits a positive point of arrival, forbids closure to language. The movement can be paralleled in the tension of the religious schema, in the grounding of the significance of the mutable, finite world, in the Immutable, Inaccessible truth of God. The quasi-positive status of the world and the estrangement from finite reality that such a relation brings about, construct the terms for the on-going dialectic of the religious quest. The grounding of language and knowledge about God in negativity—through irony and absence—keep the quest for meaning in motion.

Since God remains in excess of finite reality, the translation of the extra-symbolic reality into finite terms cannot be undertaken in terms of affirmation, since the positives of the natural world are unable to define a reality in excess of themselves. The approach to God is consequently conducted in negative terms, through an exploration of what God is "not." The reification of the negative, the making of nothing into "something," appears to be one way around the problem.

> Why no! I never thought other than
> That God is that great absence
> In our lives, the empty silence
> Within, the place where we go
> Seeking, not in hope to
> Arrive or find. He keeps the interstices
> In our knowledge, the darkness
> Between stars. His are the echoes
> We follow, the footprints he has just
> Left. We put our hands in
> His side hoping to find

It warm. We look at people
And places as though he had looked
At them, too; but miss the reflection.
                                    ("Via Negativa")[17]

Finite and infinite though separate orders of reality are linked into relation
by the acceptance of "not." God is "not" and therefore to know God is to
know the "nots" of his creation, as the negative propositions in the poem
make clear—the great absence, the empty silence, the gaps in our knowledge, etc. But there is a problem, for what can be the value or content of
"not," of God as absence, silence, etc.? Can "something" that implies
"nothing," can whatever implies its own denial, be true? The law of contradiction would appear to forbid it. By using the language of paradox, however, Thomas attempts to hold the two conflicting orders, the competing
value systems of the infinite and the finite, in mutual tension, without allowing the one to override the other. But the aspiration to unity is frustrated.
What we have here is a kind of failure of religious statement, the inability
to say positively, *God is.* The exploration of "not" consequently signals limitation, and the partiality of knowing, the impossibility of arriving are built
into the religious endeavor itself. Language equivocates—it tells and does
not tell "the Truth." Thus, language as goal, as a means of arriving at
meaning or Truth "in the end," is rendered futile. "In the end" is paradox,
self-contradiction, a blank becomes the sum total of knowledge. Every
movement of language, as a result, confirms inadequacy. The dark point of
the discourse has the effect of the rebounding of language on itself, and
poetry becomes a writing of limitation.

The idea that God is in some sense the negation of the created world
has had long currency in religion. It is a familiar teaching in mystical writings, both Christian and non-Christian alike. In a tradition in which the
Immanent-Transcendent relation was secure, the transcendence of God
was accepted as a sign of plenitude, and the use of the negative was a sign
of confirmation, of an acceptance of the unity that seemed to characterize
the relation of God with creatures. Thomas à Kempis, for instance, in his
Imitation of Christ, culminates his catalog of the glories of creation with a
joyful admission of transcendence through the employment of the negative.
"Above all that thou art not O my God!" Similarly, in "negative theology,"
God has been defined through the use of negative particles like Immortable,
Unbounded, Immutable, and the like. The acceptance of the paradox of the
transcendental God who could be interpreted as both dark and light can be
found as late as the seventeenth century, in for example, a poem by Lord

Herbert of Cherbury, to whom the darkness of God did not presuppose an absence of light.

> Black beauty, which above the common light,
>   Whose Power can no colours here renew
>   But those which darkness can again subdue,
> Dost still remain unvary'd to the sight.
> And like an object equal to the view,
>   Art neither chang'd with day, nor hid with night;
>   When all these colours which the world call bright,
> And which old Poetry doth so pursue,
>
> Are with the night so perished and gone,
>   That of their being there remains no mark,
> Thou still abidest so intirely one,
>   That we may know thy blackness is a spark
> Of light inaccessible, and alone
>   Our darkness which can make us think it dark.
>   ("The Sonnet of Black Beauty")[18]

Similarly, in a Blake or a Traherne, the Infinitude of God was a cause for celebration. To see a World in a Grain of Sand is after all to exult in the excess of available meaning. Within the modern context, however, anguished over the experience of a divinity that has departed from the world, the transcendence of God would appear to create unbridgeable distances between God and Man.[19] The breaking of the "circle" of correspondence between God and creatures which was available in earlier times, has rendered God remote, "beyond" knowing. If the function of language were to be regarded as mimetic, then language would aspire to unreadability—or silence. Thus, the problem of what constitutes intelligibility must needs be faced. The reading of transcendence in terms of the negative has opened up a dark space, and has made it problematic. The process of intelligibility is obliged to take full stock of the negative element. The antithetical nature of this process has been articulated by T. S. Eliot.

> In order to arrive there,
> To arrive where you are, to get from where you are not
>   You must go by a way wherein there is no ecstasy,
> In order to arrive at what you do not know
>   You must go by the way which is the way of ignorance.
> In order to possess what you do not possess
>   You must go by the way of dispossession.
> In order to arrive at what you are not

You must go through the way in which you are not.
And what you do not know is the only thing you know,
And what you own is what you do not own
And where you are is where you are not.[20]

Negative and positive are not seen in terms of mutual exclusion, that is, either A or not A is true, but in contiguous relation, the one clarifying the status of the other. Consequently, the space of not knowing governs knowing, the space of nonpossession governs possession, and so on. But the writing remains dark, and intelligibility of Reality—the hoped for light of understanding—must needs flicker, remain at risk.

Such an acceptance of the negative element, however, does not resolve the problem. As Freud has pointed out in his study of negation,[21] the appearance of the negative sign in speech permits the entry into consciousness of otherwise painful and repressed material in the guise of denial. Once the "pain" is no longer ignored, the thinking process enriches itself with the subject matter of the negation, by taking into account what is repressed, but such an accounting remains an intellectual acceptance, not a resolution. On the level of experience, acceptance of the darkness of the Divinity does little to relieve the anguish at the impasse of attempting to know the Dark Deity. Within this antithetical framework, God is Not-Absence, Not-Silence, Not-Pain, but experienced as Absence, Silence, Pain. To explore the "not" is, therefore, to explore anguish, and anguish is posited as the inescapable condition of Christian existence. The effect of the "excessive" God being one of pain, pain becomes the place that the religious subject must occupy in its address to God. The quality of this pain consequently occupies much of the attention of the poetry. The poem "Evans" portrays the impotence of the self within this relation, for the darkness of the truth renders futile the priest's ministrations to a sick man faced with the impending darkness of death.

It was not the dark filling my eyes
And mouth appalled me; not even the drip
Of rain like blood from the one tree
Weather-tortured. It was the dark
Silting the veins of that sick man
I left stranded upon the vast
And lonely shore of his bleak bed.[22]

The consciousness of extinction as also a form of darkness leaves the priest appalled and helpless, unable to lighten the lonely burden of a dying man. The variations on "dark," on the physical, intellectual, and spiritual levels of the poem, only intensify the feeling of helplessness. The poem "They"[23] looks at the problem from another perspective, from the point of view of parishioners who seek the old securities of an easily available God of love. Pain is read as an absence of joy. They are confused by their "worsting" at the hands of a dark God whom they cannot know and will not accept. Pain and joy are opposed, the one necessarily excluding the other, thus keeping the alienations in the poem in motion.

In other poems, a sense of man's abandonment predominates, crystallized in the poetry in the recurring image of the untenanted Cross. The unmitigated nature of man's helplessness in his entrapment in this seemingly one-way address is articulated in the poem "After the Lecture."

> I've read your books, had glimpses of a climate
> That is rigorous, though not too hard
> For the spirit. I may have grown
> Since reading them; there is no scale
> To judge by, neither is the soul
> Measurable. I know all the tropes
> Of religion, how God is not there
> To go to: how time is what we buy
> With his absence, and how we look
> Through the near end of the binocular at pain,
> Evil, deformity. I have tried
> Bandaging my sharp eyes
> With humility, but still the hearing
> Of the ear holds; from as far off as Tibet
> The cries come.
>   From one not to be penned
> In a concept, and differing in kind
> From the human; whose attributes are the negations
> Of thought; who holds us at bay with
> His symbols, the opposed emblems
> Of hawk and dove, what can my prayers win
> For the kindred, souls brought to the bone
> To be tortured, and burning, burning
> Through history with their own strange light?[24]

The lecture has been given, but the attempt to make sense of it is frustrated. The stance of tired self-defeat that characterizes the opening lines of the poem points to the fact that the meaning of the text—the paradox of God, signified in the oppositional symbols of hawk and dove—has been explored before, but remains elusive. The implacable nature of the impasse is seen as universal—the cries from Tibet and the tortured souls burning through history signify the same condition of meaninglessness. The attempt to understand is defeated. The reversed binocular and the damaged eye make explicit the limitations of the eye that attempts to read the text and signal also the effect of limitation as one of pain, in the insistence of the "not" in the discourse. The necessity for and inevitability of the negative intensifies the sense of helplessness.

One way out of the impasse would be to accept the unacceptable, think the unthinkable, to make the negative nihilistic. The poem "Look" portrays the debate between two differing modes of religious belief—the one, a gentle mode fostered by hope and art, the other, the effect of pain, which nullifies the former, and which is posed as a possible "ultimate" level of truth. Man and the world faced with the darkness of the impasse read themselves as diseased, and speak their corruption. Hence the conclusion:

> We must dip belief
> Not in dew nor in the cool fountain
> Of beech buds, but in seas
> Of manure through which they squelch
> To the bleakness of their assignations.[25]

The other resolution would be to negate the necessity for the gap itself by turning to the positive world for truth, by accepting the God of Science and Technology, and killing the mystery with chemicals. The machine is given uncompromisingly unflattering treatment in Thomas's poetry. Opposed to the response of inarticulation, silence, muteness, in the face of a Dark God, is the insistent noise of the machine filling time and space with its own certainties.

> The tins marched to the music
> Of the conveyer belt. A billion
> Mouths opened. Production,
> Production, the wheels
> Whistled . . .[26]

The "I," appropriating the possibilities for self-assertion that scientific knowledge provides, knows itself secure in its investment of faith in the instant, unequivocal, positive truths of science.

> But the chemicals in
> My mind were not
> Ready, so I let
> Him go on, dissolving
> The word on my

Tongue. Friend, I had said,
Life is too short for
Religion; it takes time
To prepare a sacrifice
For the God. Give yourself
To science that reveals
All, asking no pay
For it. Knowledge is power . . .
("No Answer")[27]

The attempt to embody an Ultimate Reality in language has in fact resulted in the exploration of the terrain of the absence of that Reality. The various responses of frustration, protest, anguish, that are constructed in the poems are the various effects of that absence, given the oppositional structure of the framework. The self trapped in the asymmetrical relation with God lacks confirmation, and seems inevitably condemned to not knowing. Should the language of religious poetry, then, be declared fundamentally agnostic?

The alternative to this is available within the logic of the "gap" in the religious schema which has been so stringently probed in the verse. The recovery of religious meaning must be undertaken in such a way so as to preserve the function of the negative and the discourse to which it has given rise, namely, the rhetoric of not knowing, of anguish at absence, that characterizes the poetry. This Thomas does, but it is not an explicit or obvious maneuver in the poetry. Thomas maintains the mystery, the "gap," the space of not knowing, and seeks resolution within the moment of negation itself which has so heavily problematized the poetry. He points to Crucifixion, to the instant in the religious schema when the transcendental God is available, not in excess of majesty or plenitude, but in poverty, on a Cross, in negation. In man's denial of full selfhood and God's denial of Infinite Godhead, in negative exchange, the dialogue between man and God is transacted. The erstwhile anguish at absence in all its variegated forms becomes redemptive, since anguish, the negative, is the mark, the trace of the Infinite in the finite, the God-made-man of Christ in Crucifixion. In the poem, "The Musician," the parallel between the musician and Christ reveals the intimate co-presence of God and Man in anguish, and the cry of pain is reread as the music of redemption—the transformation itself being effected through the moment of negation.

I could see, too, the twitching of the fingers,
Caught temporarily in art's neurosis,
As we sat there or warmly applauded

This player who so beautifully suffered
For each of us upon his instrument.
So it must have been at Calvary
In the fiercer light of the thorns' halo,
The men standing by that one figure,
The hands bleeding, the mind bruised but calm,
And no one daring to interrupt
Because it was himself that he played,
And closer than all of them the God listened.[28]

The process of redemption signified in the Christian framework by Crucifixion presupposes the suffering, fragmented self continually acknowledging its need for God. The stripping down of man to a point of need, the signifying of man as "in lack," has been accomplished as the effect of the "gap," of the unknowable and infinite God. The self, by expressing its lack, its anguish, expresses simultaneously itself in lack and God as Infinite. Since the self is in lack at every point of its encounter with the God-of-excess, redemption is ever present. Moments of negativity, therefore, form the links in a redemptive chain that traces the discourse. But the asymmetrical nature of the relation will ensure that although God has redeemed man, [man] will continue "not-to-know," in a full sense, the meaning. The troubled anguish at the disjunction in which man's consciousness of meaning is constituted in the split of knowing and not knowing, will continue to put into question the very notion of his fullness of being. The structure of this disjunction can be traced in a poem like "Pietà," in which the organization of meaning is conducted in the passage through the "gap," which is itself constructed by the elliptical, spiral, unjoined movement of the poem, which keeps the structure in motion.

Always the same hills
Crowd the horizon,
Remote witnesses
Of the still scene.

And in the foreground
The tall Cross,
Sombre, untenanted,
Aches for the Body
That is back in the cradle
Of a maid's arms.[29]

In the foreground of the poem stands the untenanted Cross, and as man gazes in anguish at the stark mystery of his abandonment, somewhere, unseen, unknown, the absent Christ is born again, but out of focus to the gaze in the poem, thereby creating the disjunction. The moment of unknowing, however, permits itself to be read as also the moment of meaning.

For the priest, the long exploration has been a form of patient waiting for the God to speak. And the worship is in the waiting, in the acceptance of the delay and the deferment as the acceptance of God. God's silence in the poems becomes a form of speech declaring man's lack. Since man's experience of "lack" is his point of contact with the God-of-excess, the language of need, of not knowing, that characterizes the poems, becomes the language of address. The exploration ends where it began in a silent church, the absence, the silence, the muteness, summed up in the image of waiting.

> Moments of great calm,
> Kneeling before an altar
> Of wood in a stone church
> In summer, waiting for the God
> To speak;
>
>   • • •
>
>   Prompt me, God;
> But not yet. When I speak,
> Though it be you who speak
> Through me, something is lost.
> The meaning is in the waiting.
>   ("Kneeling")[30]

The significance of this image of waiting for the God to speak has been made clear by Thomas himself in an interview with John Ormond in 1972.

> God, reality, whatever it is, is not going to be forced, it's not going to be put to the question, it works in its own time. I suppose one projected this image of oneself kneeling, either entering a moorland, a lonely bare moorland, or entering the village church, and waiting, just waiting. And out of this, of course, comes the feeling that perhaps this is all that one is required to do. It's the Milton idea isn't it, that they also serve who only stand and wait?[31]

The "negative moment" in the poetry is consequently a split moment and functions in its duality and is productive of rhetorical insecurities that affect the reading. It signifies both absence and presence, a forgetting and a remembering, an effacement and an inscription. Language, in this discourse, loses its serenity, its confidence of presentation. The dual nature of the sign ensures that any postulated, organic, relation between sign and meaning must needs be subverted. In any one instance, there are alternatives, as the ironic, metaphorical, paradoxical moments in the poems make clear, alternatives that enter into the organization of the meaning in the poems by exceeding, transforming, defeating, contradicting, any "primary" or "literal" level of meaning. Language, if it asserts anything at all, asserts the priority of the "non-literal," as the mark of its subversion, in its encounter with excess, and its accommodation of the negative.

Such a resolution does not cancel the negative, however, but animates it and makes it productive and dynamic. It permits the production of meaning in relational terms, in the play of "differences"[32] that the negative establishes—in the construction of *what is* only in relation to *what is not*. The nature of Christian identity, for instance, is constructed in terms of risk. The construction of Christian subjectivity within negativity entails the breaking of the self, its destabilization, and its release into the drift of language and experience. The self "in lack" bearing the mark of the negative is deprived of security, and self-knowledge, and this displaced "I" in search of identity constantly repeating its predicament is the religious self in the making. The substance of selfhood changes with every encounter with God—its content being redefined according to the changing terms of the relation. The probing "I," the suffering "I," the "I" balked by silence or purged by pain, or protesting in frustration, are propositions of the religious framework, and are realized within and as the negative-positive tension that structures it. The productive, dynamic movement that such a relation engenders can be seen in the poem "Emerging," in the changing status of the self as it grapples with the mystery of God. Eschewing passivity, the self undertakes its drive for unity, for completion, for full status *in* God, for the abolishing of the negative. But the drive cannot produce completion, cannot erase the disjunction, cannot close the "gap." It can only realize the possibilities for "exchange" in negation that the "gap" makes available. The circular movement does not lead "back" to a point of origin, but "onward" to a greater realization of the myriad meanings that are possible within the unequal relation. Within this disjuncted movement, the meaning of subjectivity is produced, and prayer becomes the animation of the negative, in the emergence in language of different possibilities of the relation, not only in anguish, but in nostalgia, and hope.

> Hear my prayer, Lord, hear
> my prayer. As though you were deaf, myriads
> of mortals have kept up their shrill
> cry, explaining your silence by
> their unfitness.

               It begins to appear
this is not what prayer is about.
It is the annihilation of difference,
the consciousness of myself in you,
of you in me; the emerging
from the adolescence of nature
into the adult geometry
of the mind. I begin to recognize
you anew, God of form and number.
There are questions we are the solution
to, others whose echoes we must expand
to contain. Circular as our way
is, it leads not back to that snake-haunted
garden, but onward to the tall city
of glass that is the laboratory of the spirit.[33]

The insights gained from poem after poem are offered not as the full essence of the truth, but as partially produced forms of knowledge, as unstable moments of existence, the nature of the "truth" being what it is. The search for Christian identity, for wholeness, will consequently remain continually in motion, even against the knowledge of its own impossibility, and within its separation and distance from that which it is not. The poem "This to Do" affirms the nature of the quest and of its hard demands, in the continual engagement with the "not," the pre-condition of identity.

I have this that I must do
One day: overdraw on my balance
Of air, and breaking the surface
Of water go down into the green
Darkness in search for the door
To myself in dumbness and blindness
And uproar of scared blood
At the eardrums. There are no signposts
There but bones of the dead
Conger, no light but the pale
Phosphorous, where the slow corpses
Swag. I must go down with the poor
Purse of my body and buy courage,
Paying for it with the coins of my breath.[34]

The placing of the action of the poem in the future emphasizes the fact that such an exploration and engagement will always remain, yet to be done.

The object too is displaced. The plurality of perspectives on God points to the provisional nature of all forms of knowledge. In the poem

"Mediations," a variety of images of God are presented, and many ways of knowing him, but the withholding of privilege to any one image or mode of knowledge fragments any "ultimate" meaning of the term, and preserves the "gap."

And to one God says: Come
to me by numbers and
figures; see my beauty
in the angles between
stars, in the equations
of my kingdom. Bring
your lenses to the worship
of my dimensions: far
out and far in, there
is always more of me
in proportion. And to another:
I am the bush burning
at the centre of
your existence; you must put
your knowledge off and come
to me with your mind
bare. And to this one
he says: Because of
your high stomach, the bleakness
of your emotions, I
will come to you in the simplest
things, in the body
of a man hung on a tall
tree you have converted to
timber and you shall not know me.[35]

Consequently, there is no autonomous, unified level of reality that is offered as "Truth." The plurality of constituted forms of knowledge points also to the gaps in knowledge, the excess that cannot be known. The many approaches to God are attempts to construct meaning engendered by the basic mystery of the Unknowable God and in fact enrich the content of the poetry. The preservation of the mystery ensures the filling of the space between God and Man with the dissecting and diversifying and thus inter-rogating what might otherwise be a silent or an empty space. Thus the obscurity of excess generates the many attempts at meaning, the repeated beginnings. The refusal of monocular perspective, or one mode of address, or a single interpretation keeps in motion the infinity of perspectives and attempts to exhaust the problematic space between Man and God, in an effort to construct the very meaning of the terms. Consequently, the play of voices is volatile in the poems. The "I" argues with itself, or ruminates, or protests, in order to be heard or overheard, and thus disputes and debates the mystery. This is increasingly so, as the voice of God, when it is available, is available not as One but as Many, at different pitches, of many timbres, and often only by repute, at one remove. The use of the impersonal form generally to signify Reality ("It will always win . . . ," etc.) with the sense of anonymity that it creates inhibits the attribution of a specific meaning to it. The resulting indeterminacy in the poetry with regard to a unified and positive reading of Man and God need not necessarily be seen in terms of a threat to the understanding. The many attempts to reconstruct and to reread the value of the negative, which refuses ultimate specificity, have made available the many contents of subjectivity and the nature of the Godhead in terms of their mutual interrelations: of self in relation to an indeterminate Other, of Other in relation to an indeterminate self, which in turn makes available for us readings of religious poetry in terms of its tentativeness, its anguish, and its hope.

Notes

1. H. G. Wells, *Babes in the Darkling Wood* (New York: Alliance Book Corporation, 1940), 50.

2. R. S. Thomas, *H'm* (London: Macmillan, 1972), 33.

3. R. S. Thomas, ed., *The Penguin Book of Religious Verse* (Harmondsworth: Penguin, 1963), 9.

4. *Ibid.*, 8.

5. *Ibid.*, 9.

6. R. S. Thomas, *Song at the Year's Turning: Poems 1942–1954* (London: Rupert Hart-Davis, 1965), 114.

7. R. S. Thomas, *Pietà* (London: Rupert Hart-Davis, 1966), 44.

8. *Ibid.*, 36.

9. *Ibid.*, 15.

10. *H'm*, 12.

11. R. S. Thomas, *Not That He Brought Flowers* (London: Rupert Hart-Davis, 1968), 44.

12. *Pietà*, 8.

13. *Not That He Brought Flowers*, 18.

14. *Song at the Year's Turning*, 110.

15. *H'm*, 4.

16. *Ibid.*, 20.

17. *Ibid.*, 16.

18. Helen Gardner, ed., *The Metaphysical Poets* (Harmondsworth: Penguin, 1957), 93–94.

19. See for instance, J. Hillis Miller, *The Disappearance of God* (Cambridge: Harvard University Press, 1963), for an analysis of this problem.

20. T. S. Eliot, "East Coker," *Four Quartets* (London: Faber & Faber, 1959), 29.

21. S. Freud, "Negation," *The International Journal of Psychoanalysis*, 4:4 (October 1925): 367–71.

22. R. S. Thomas, *Poetry for Supper* (London: Rupert Hart-Davis, 1958), 15.

23. *Not That He Brought Flowers*, 39.

24. *Ibid.*, 22.

25. *Ibid.*, 36.

26. *H'm*, 22.

27. *Ibid.*, 7.

28. R. S. Thomas, *Tares* (London: Rupert Hart-Davis, 1961), 19.

29. *Pietà*, 14.

30. *Not That He Brought Flowers*, 32.

31. "R. S. Thomas: Priest and Poet, A transcript of John Ormond's film for B.B.C. Television broadcast on April 2nd 1972," *Poetry Wales*, 7:4 (1972): 51.

32. A systematic account of the concepts of "difference" / "differance" is to be found in the works of Jacques Derrida, especially *Speech and Phenomena* (Evanston: Northwestern University Press, 1973), and *Of Grammatology* (Baltimore: The Johns Hopkins University Press, 1976).

33. R. S. Thomas, *Laboratories of the Spirit* (London: Macmillan, 1975), 1.

34. *Pietà*, 12.

35. *Laboratories of the Spirit*, 17.

The Gap in the Hedge

R. S. Thomas's Emblem Poetry

Belinda Humfrey

Reprinted from the Anglo-Welsh Review, *26 (1977): 49–57.*

In searching R. S. Thomas's poems for natural description, for description of his country landscape ("The two things that appeal most strongly to my imagination are Wales and nature, especially as the latter manifests itself as a background to a way of life.") perhaps the fullest example we can find is "The Welsh Hill Country" of 1952.

> Too far for you to see
> The fluke and the foot-rot and the fat maggot
> Gnawing the skin from the small bones,
> The sheep are grazing at Bwlch-y-Fedwen,
> Arranged romantically in the usual manner
> On a bleak background of bald stone.
>
> Too far for you to see
> The moss and the mould on the cold chimneys,
> The nettles growing through the cracked doors,
> The houses stand empty at Nant-yr-Eira,
> There are holes in the roofs that are thatched with sunlight
> And the fields are reverting to the bare moor.
>
> Too far, too far to see
> The set of his eyes and the slow phthisis
> Wasting his frame under the ripped coat,
> There's a man still farming at Ty'n-y-Fawnog,
> Contributing grimly to the accepted pattern,
> The embryo music dead in his throat.

The "you" of the poem is the distant reader who looks from afar at a picturesque hillside, the sheep, the houses, and the laboring man, and is unaware of their ruin, decay, and pain. The poet, who is not mentioned, is presumably close to this suffering. The poem states things as they are. One cannot tell whether the phrases "the usual manner" and "the accepted pattern" in the first and last stanzas are a critique of our acceptance or of the laborer's acceptance. The binding tension of the poem's structure of imagery comes from the play between distance and close up in seeing. Although the poem in its three stanzas, dealing first with sheep on the hills, second with ruined cottages, third with the one man, appears to narrow our focus, it ends in a distancing, a withdrawal from the landscape with its reference to the nameless, representative Welshman, "There's a man still farming at Ty'n-y-Fawnog," and the poet is distanced by his declaration that the man's own poetry is still and not born, that the man is spiritually dead, "The embryo music dead in his throat." Here we are presented with nature as a background to a way of life with a vengeance.

There are poems where R. S. Thomas puts *himself* in a landscape, but the landscape is only there by inference, as in the poem "The Moor," which begins, "It was like a church to me," where the blessed quiet of the poet is all, and the only landscape reference is to "wind over grass." In "The Welsh Hill Country" the poet sees the dying landscape, the fields reverting to bare moor, but he does not set himself within the landscape. In this he is anti-Romantic. The lines,

> The sheep are grazing at Bwlch-y-Fedwen,
> Arranged romantically in the usual manner
> On a bleak background of bald stone,

appear to be a shorthand reference to landscape descriptions by some of the English Romantic poets. The lines also, in their poverty of detail, are a rejection of such landscape descriptions, full even when generalized by distance, such as Coleridge's

> The bare bleak mountain speckled thin with sheep;
> Grey clouds, that shadowing spot the sunny fields;
> And river, now with bushy rocks o'er-browed,
> Now winding bright and full, with naked banks;

in "Reflections on Having Left a Place of Retirement" (1776) where the landscape around the poet is interpreted for musings upon Life and his own way of life.

The concentrated focus in "The Welsh Hill Country" is typical of R. S. Thomas. He is not being especially realistic here, in his pointing to rot, cracks, and maggots; for him landscape is epitomized in men and their houses and their acre of land. His interest is in figures in a landscape, not landscape for itself. Like his hill farmers' minds, the poems are usually bound by a hedge's circumference.

If we pursue the suggestion that R. S. Thomas is deliberately anti-Romantic in his depiction of country people, it is easy to contrast them with Wordsworth's, even though both poets, especially in their early work, study human suffering. Wordsworth's shepherds are very differently conceived from R. S. Thomas's, although both put them before us as exemplary, primitive, or essential man. We may contrast, for example, Wordsworth's self-identification with the herdsman Wanderer of *The Excursion,* that noble, mute poet and sage philosopher, with R. S. Thomas's persona-poet, Iago Prytherch, as he is described in that much-discussed poem, "A Peasant," of 1946. The difference is that Wordsworth conceives his herdsman or shepherd to be in emotional and spiritual "communion" with the universe, even "the communion . . . of fear." (See especially Book I of *The Excursion.*) Thomas sees the farmer as having some earthy contact, but battling *against* the elements. Prytherch has more in common with Wordsworth's stoically enduring Leech-gatherer of "Resolution and Independence" (remote from the poet, though exemplary) than with the Wanderer or Michael. To grasp Thomas's divergence from Wordsworth's mode of seeing, one need only read the first seventy-seven lines of "Michael," which reveal Wordsworth's careful guidance of his readers into a clearly delineated scenery and into a sense of the shepherd himself and of his physical and emotional collaboration with the natural universe. Though the winds make him work, Michael knows "the pleasure that is in life itself." Michael is ruined by his determination to hold on to the entirety of his land, but he is certainly not brutalized by his surroundings.

However, the most interesting difference between the two poets' conception of the shepherd is seen not by looking at those lines in "A Peasant" which have caused so much comment on their presumptuous insult,

> And then at night see him fixed in his chair
> Motionless, except when he leans to gob in the fire.
> There is something frightening in the vacancy of his mind,

but by juxtaposing Wordsworth's introductory lines on Michael,

> he had been alone
> Amid the heart of many thousand mists,

with Thomas's first lines on his "Peasant" Iago,

Just an ordinary man of the bald Welsh hills
Who pens a few sheep in a gap of cloud.

Both poets may be unrealistic in their different presentations of our "prototype"; apart from this, the juxtaposition of lines clarifies the differences
in the two poets' quality of feeling and way of seeing essential man.

Another quite early poem, "The Gap in the Hedge" (1952), makes
Thomas's way of seeing clearer.

That man, Prytherch, with the torn cap,
I saw him often, framed in the gap
Between two hazels with his sharp eyes,
Bright as thorns, watching the sunrise
Filling the valley with its pale yellow
Light, where the sheep and the lambs went haloed
With grey mist lifting from the dew.
Or was it a likeness that the twigs drew
With bold pencilling upon that bare
Piece of the sky? For he's still there
At early morning, when the light is right
And I look up suddenly at a bird's flight.

Thomas writes in the Yeatsian tradition of variations on a theme and we
cannot pin him down in his view of Prytherch. A straight rejection of the
Wordsworthian thesis of the beneficial influence of the natural world is
stated clearly in poems like "No Through Road" and "Autumn on the
Land," the latter poem ending, after a description of the darkness within
a field farmer,

You must reverse
Your bland philosophy of nature, earth
Has of itself no power to make men wise.

But "The Gap in the Hedge" holds images of hope, aspiration, and ascent,
suggesting revelation. The poem also suggests that, in Wordsworth's phrase,
what the poet sees is "a prospect in the mind," not a temporary exterior or
"real" vision, but a possibly permanent sketch of mental vision, to be seen
"when the light is right."

In this poem, and in the two lines from "A Peasant," we are faced with
a sharply, if lightly, sketched diagram—"bold pencilling." As a poet, R. S.
Thomas uses a diagrammatic method; this is present in his earliest volumes
but has become clearer in his latest volumes. We can find occasional parallels to this method in Wordsworth's writings, especially when Wordsworth

is at his loftiest as poet-preacher, such as in his presentation of a cruciform apparition of an idealized shepherd ("him have I descried in distant sky, A solitary object and sublime . . . like an aerial cross"), or his emblematic vision of "Eternity" derived from the scenery as he descended after crossing the Alps (*The Prelude* [1850] VIII, 264–75; VI, 621–40).

However, the less forced, less doctrinal, landscape figure, or prospect in the mind, Wordsworth's Leech-gatherer, representing endurance, is a more appropriate forerunner of Thomas's country figures for us to remember in an attempt to define our contemporary poet's methods:

> In my mind's eye
> I seemed to see him pace
> About the weary moors continually
> Wandering about alone and silently.

This very inclination of R. S. Thomas's toward mental fictions, such as is highlighted by comparison with Wordsworth's depiction of country people, shows that it is more appropriate for us to look for affinities between Thomas and earlier Welsh-Anglican poet-priests, especially those three seventeenth-century Welsh poets whose imagery has real affinity with the popular pictorial emblem books of their time. (Although she does not mention Traherne, Rosemary Freeman in her *English Emblem Books* (1967) devotes an illuminating chapter to the poems of Herbert and Vaughan.) Vaughan, especially, is remarkable for his transformation of Welsh scenery into emblems of his religious aspirations, a practice which takes him beyond the stylized emblem-making of Quarles and his followers. My own observation is that there is a natural tendency to emblematic seeing in Welsh poets, old and new.

In "Iago Prytherch" (*Poetry for Supper*, 1958), referring back to the early poem "The Peasant" (1949), R. S. Thomas declares,

> I passed and saw you
> Labouring there, your dark figure
> Marring the simple geometry
> Of the square fields with its gaunt question.
> My poems were made in its long shadow
> Falling coldly across the page.

The peasant is a figure in the diagrammatic sense, a question mark. Prytherch, the hill farmer, is Thomas's meditative emblem of all his confrontations of life and its meaning. In this poem the diagrammatic emblem is especially striking with its mirror image of the question-mark man in a square field reflected as a square page containing a question-mark poem. In

The Bread of Truth (1963), in a short poem called "Alone" we are presented with the same notion of a lonely watcher looking at a single figure in a bare landscape and able to project all meaning onto the figure:

> To the watcher at the window
> Life could have had all
> Its meaning crammed into one
> Vertical figure, one shape that stood up
> From the bare landscape and walked on
> With a mind monstrous as you will.

In "The Face" (*Pietà*, 1966) the figure in the landscape is described entirely as a prospect in the mind:

> When I close my eyes, I can see it,
> That bare hill with the man ploughing. . . .
>
> He is never absent, but like a slave
> Answers to the mind's bidding,
> Endlessly ploughing. . . .
>
> . . . I can see his eye
> That expects nothing. . . .
>
> He will go on; that much is certain.
> Beneath him tenancies of the fields
> Will change; machinery turn
> All to noise. But on the walls
> Of the mind's gallery that face
> With the hills framing it will hang
> Unglorified, but stern like the soil.

The Welsh hills are unrealistically always bare because they are emblematic of a spiritual condition. The poet sees without what he has within. The landscapes are of the mind's eye, the mind's gallery (and the real Wales is forgotten). A distant figure in a landscape becomes a portrait in a frame. Wordsworth on the Leech-gatherer, while preaching endurance and independence against the ills of transient life, is also exploring the disparity between reality and vision. Although he writes of an actual man plowing as an emblem of endurance, R. S. Thomas is concerned only with vision.

The emblematic poems focusing on a figure framed upon a space or void showed Thomas's sympathy with the first existentialist theologian, Kierkegaard. In the 1970s Thomas's poems have been predominantly concerned with faith, and the "gap of clouds," "the gap in the hedge," has become more valuable in itself (as opposed to the penciled figures). That blessed state of "the mind's cession / Of its kingdom," described in "The Moor" (*Pietà*, 1966) has become of such importance as a mode of realizing God, that even the "frightening . . . vacancy of [the] mind" of "The Peasant" of thirty years ago might be seen as an anticipation of the "Via Negativa" defined in *H'm* (1972):

> Why no! I never thought other than
> That God is that great absence
> In our lives, the empty silence
> Within, the place where we go
> Seeking, not in hope to
> Arrive or find.

The emblematic celebrations of absence or gap are numerous within recent volumes. Perhaps thirty years of conditioning are necessary before the ironic presentation of a hole as a positive pictured revelation or vision can be acceptable.

H'm marked the beginning of this ironic emblem poetry. This title is open to a variety of interpretations, but it is certainly an emblem of a gap, a gap in which the "I" or "i" of "I AM" can certainly be known by its absence, its very invitation to speculative seeking. Yet the title poem of the volume is simply about the absence of God, or love, in a materialistic world. Whereas *Laboratories of the Spirit* (1975) is full of celebrations of mysterious "emptiness"; and "emptiness" is an often repeated word in that volume. Here Thomas's perennial tendency to meditate on an "untenanted cross," as a lonely priest testing his faith on absence, becomes heightened and we find him preaching clearly about glimpses of eternity. (See, for examples, two poems with emblematic diagrams of illumination, "The Bright Field" and "Hill Christmas.") The word "H'm" itself suggests the high point of absence so vital to the Christian religion, that fact that God sent no rescuing angels at the crucial time. But emblems of the vital spaces (or "interstices") in our knowledge lie at the very centers of his most remarkable recent poems about the nature of God in *Laboratories of the Spirit*.

"Selah" (a Hebrew word for a pause or gap in music) celebrates "skies that have the emptiness / of our affirmations" and "the chastity of the unthinking / body . . . violated by the spirit." And the concept of the body as a vacant cavity for the spirit, or God, is explained with a clear preaching of the Incarnation in "The Prisoner":

> *Deus absconditus!*
> We ransack the heavens,
> the distance between

stars; the last place we look
is in prison, his hideout
in flesh and bone.

And if the "great poem" will always be a hole, or gulf, or gap, or a challenge of endless potentiality, because the poet cannot get beyond its "frontier" to find in language his nameless, silent elusive God ("The Combat"),
the beautiful poem, "Sea-Watching," reveals that Thomas does not complain. "Sea-Watching" shows R. S. Thomas's consciously idiosyncratic use
of a diagrammatic emblem (an original use, I think, even were we to
search extravagantly for partial inspirations, such as Herbert's poems in
shapes, or the devices of *Tristram Shandy* and e.e. cummings!). The poem
describes prayer in the analogy and metaphor of watching for a rare bird.
The emblem here comes not from described images (like the question mark
falling from field to page in "Iago Prytherch") but through a repeated gap
in the flow of the poem's verses. At first, perhaps, the pauses or gaps suggest the poet's scanning the sea for the "rare bird," but in the final para-
graph the device of emptiness becomes clearly pregnant:

> There were days,
> so beautiful the emptiness
> it might have filled,
> its absence
> was as its presence.

A passing gap, a fleeting absence of words, pictorially visible within the
poem, conveys the poet's glimpse of eternity through mere supposition,
through "it might have."

Of course R. S. Thomas's emblem poems are a select few, but they
reveal severely and definitively this poet's temperamental mode of seeing
and the nature of his priestly craftsmanship. In the simple poem "Poetry
for Supper" (1967) he makes an old poet say, while valuing sudden illumination,

> Sunlight's a thing that needs a window
> Before it enters a dark room.
> Windows don't happen.

R. S. Thomas and the Vanishing God of Form and Number

Julian Gitzen

Reprinted from Contemporary Poetry: A Journal of Criticism, 5:2 (1983): 1–16.

> . . . I begin to recognize
> you anew, God of form and number.
> There are questions we are the solution
> to, others whose echoes we must expand
> to contain. Circular as our way
> is, it leads not back to that snake-haunted
> garden, but onward to the tall city
> of glass that is the laboratory of the spirit.
>
>   ("Emerging")

It is understandable that R. S. Thomas should complain of "critics' compulsive hurry / to place a poet," for the pattern of his own career might serve as a cautionary example. Until 1972 critics would have believed themselves justified in regarding Thomas as the somewhat dour celebrant of coastal Wales and its inhabitants, a priest, certainly, and distressed by the minimum of spirituality among his congregation, but predominantly a regional and nature poet. The publication in 1972 of *H'm* signaled a major change of theme as Thomas suddenly shifted the bulk of his effort to the pursuit of an absent and silent God, a chase which has now occupied him for a decade and which has revealed him as an intense religious spirit, but by no means an orthodox Christian. When a poet of Thomas's stature undertakes such a marked change in mid-career, that change deserves critical attention. It will be useful, therefore, to trace Thomas's efforts to verify God's existence (and to establish his character). He has been tireless in seeking empirical evidence of the Lord's presence in the world and concern about its affairs. In the years since 1972 the poet has grown more confident about certain divine attributes, but he remains as troubled and perplexed by God's persistent absence as he was in the 1966 poem "In Church," which features a solitary worshiper "testing his faith / On emptiness, nailing his questions / One by one to an untenanted cross." While his restless and unsatisfied yearning to see God face to face does credit to the poet, it threatens to exhaust his faithful readers.

Although Thomas evidently takes it for granted that he is addressing the Christian God, the divinity which he portrays possesses characteristics quite unlike those of the biblical Jehovah. Furthermore, it is significant that the poet's thematic emphasis falls far more heavily upon a creative God than upon a redemptive Christ. He requires a God chiefly to account for and give meaning and purpose to creation; in consequence, he remains more fascinated by the implications of Genesis than those of the Crucifixion. His predominantly metaphysical rather than ethical concerns may also explain the resignation with which he accepts that nature is indifferent to human pains and pleasures, and that God provides not only beauty, goodness, and health, but also ugliness, sickness, and the human degradation which the poet has observed as a country priest. Though he is painfully conscious of human weakness and evil, he is far less preoccupied with them than were such fellow believers as Auden and Lowell.

An empiricist, Thomas can draw no comfort from the alternative of mysticism. To be conceivable to him, the Almighty must assume some tangible form. While his anguished honesty has forced the poet to "abandon / my theories, the easier certainties / of belief," he has never surrendered his intuitive faith in material existence. It is natural to assume that a God whose works consist of three-dimensional and substantial forms, many of them capable of uttering sounds, will himself possess similar qualities. Thomas's poems frequently picture him kneeling in prayer, and these prayers are not intended as monologues. The supreme aim of his prayers is to evoke an audible divine reply, yet the prevailing response is silence. The less arduous of believers may find it difficult to continue with prayers which are received in total silence. For his part the poet strives to interpret "the language / of silence," but must number himself among "the deaf men," evidently destined never to hear a divine message palpable enough to supply the proof he yearns for. Will God answer one who calls him by name? His repeated failure to do so has afflicted the poet with doubt:

> Young
> I pronounced you. Older
> I still do, but seldomer
> now, leaning far out
> over an immense depth, letting
> your name go and waiting,
> somewhere between faith and doubt,
> for the echoes of its arrival.
>
> ("Waiting")

By loosing his imagination, the writer can summon the God he desires, and the God of Thomas's fanciful verse-fables is positively garrulous, yet the God of one's fancy is no substitute for a revealed deity, as Thomas is sadly aware. Indeed, the Lord's persistent silence appears to have become the most bedeviling problem of the poet's old age, judging from the frequency with which he returns to the subject in the recent (1981) volume, *Between Here and Now*. God's failure to answer words with words at length evokes the despairing query, "Has he his own / media of communication?" Years of quizzical interpretation of Heaven's silence may have produced some gains, for the poet claims to have heard, countering the song of the linnet, "another / voice, far out in space, / whose persuasiveness is the distance / from which it speaks." Although his prayers continue to meet with the silence which "Some take . . . for refusal," Thomas senses in it a mysterious and elusive "power" which impels him to continue questioning: "Is it consciousness trying to get through? / Am I under regard?"

God's silence is as vexing as his absence, the persistence of which leads Thomas to assert that he has never known God "as anything / but an absence," and to exclaim, "Why no! I never thought other than / That God is that great absence / In our lives." This absence drives the poet to seek traces of the Almighty in his handiwork, in the materials and processes of creation. God is "An unseen / power, whose sphere is the cell / and the electron." He is the master of "nodes and molecules," imagined as having "the face of a clock," and preoccupied with "abstruse / geometry." He delights in "figures / that beget more figures." That is, he deals in applied mathematics, presiding over natural laws which may be codified in numerical formulas. Above all, he reveals himself as mind in action, and divine radiance is the glow engendered by his powers of thought. "Night Sky" alludes fancifully to the shining of the stars as "a reflection of their intelligence" and explains:

> . . . Godhead
> is the colonisation by mind
>
> of untenanted space. It is its own
> light, a statement beyond language
> of conceptual truth.

If God is mind, then he must be at least partially recognizable to us, particularly if our prayers serve to expose elements of divinity within ourselves. If successful, the poet believes that our prayers may allow us to emerge "from the adolescence of nature / into the adult geometry of mind," becoming closer in character to divinity. Any hopes which he cherishes for the future of humanity are centered upon such a possibility.

While a clock-faced God busy with form and number may inspire awe and reverence, he is not a suitable auditor for the recital of human woe. An impulse to endow God with human attributes induces Thomas to portray a divinity who, while his human physiognomy may remain in doubt, does carry on recognizably human thought while betraying several appealingly ungodlike limitations. These characteristics emerge in numerous poems cast as miniature fables, at least a dozen of them variations upon a creation myth. The fables serve as a forceful reminder that Thomas's God functions primarily as a creator, although he is understandably concerned about the progress made by his creatures. While the miniature mythical fable or fantasy differs strikingly in character from Thomas's early pieces of regional realism, it serves his current needs by permitting him to escape constraints of time and space, the better to conceptualize his supernatural subject. The element of fancy allows for the portrayal of God's characteristics and conduct in much less restrictive terms than those applied to his customary empirical pursuit of the deity.

The fables reveal diverse qualities, some of them opposing, though not inconsistent with, the attributes of major deities. For instance, God's benevolence in "Making" is countered by malevolence in "The Island." "Cain" pictures him as self-sacrificing, while in "Soliloquy" he meditates worldwide destruction. Certainly these opposing features of temperament have long been attributed to the Christian God, but Thomas's deity differs from Jehovah in appearing not to have foreseen the consequences of his actions and to be surprised by some of the results of his own creative urge. Not only has he evidently not anticipated just what will appear at his command, but he finds it necessary to modify his work in the interest of balance and continuity. In "Rough," for instance, newly created human beings so easily and so ruthlessly dominate other animal life that God sees fit to introduce "a handful of germs" to inhibit human progress. In "Dialogue" God admits to being "under constraint" to the extent that he did not create from nothing. Matter, he confesses, "was always here." His work consisted of "refinement," but he concedes that humanity was ill-conceived, "my waste / of breath, the casualty / of my imagination."

While such admissions do little to glorify humanity, they also identify Thomas's God as the unwitting agent not only of good but also of evil. Like Hughes's divinity in *Crow*, he is capable of unintentionally creating a monster which he then proves powerless to eliminate. No sooner has "The Hand" appeared than God realizes that it will serve as an instrument both of construction and destruction, but when he is "tempted to undo the joints / of the fingers," the hand resists, and God recognizes that destiny requires its survival. Similarly, in a misguided effort to alleviate human misery, God supplies mankind with "The Tool," and thereafter accepts the blame for the suffering caused by a multitude of tools. "God's Story" reveals that the knowledge supplied by "the green tree" once extracted from the Lord's side produced "the cold touch of the machine" which has left a bewildered deity "seeking himself among / the dumb cogs and tireless camshafts."

From a practical standpoint it makes little difference whether the machine was deliberately introduced as an agent of mischief by a jealous God who was then unable to destroy it ("Other") or emerged as the logical outgrowth of human thought. What matters is that Thomas and his God agree in condemning the machine as an evil, a viewpoint all the more remarkable since Thomas's God is a mathematician to whom the design of machines must be second nature. Although impatient readers might be tempted to refute this evidently simplistic condemnation of machines, it is not the erroneousness of but rather the implications of this view which should concern us here. In at least one notable respect Thomas has maintained consistency throughout his poetic career: he has remained from the first an enemy of "progress" insofar as progress is identified with increased mechanization, the relentless expansion of gadgets, the triumph of materialism, and the crumbling of regional customs and values in the face of televised internationalism. Looking ruefully back to our prelapsarian ancestors, Thomas finds a "perfection" in the work of the Magdalenian cave-painters which is beyond the reach of their descendants who have "climbed up into the tree / of knowledge." While it is not surprising that Thomas should regret the passing of Edenic innocence, it is less immediately evident why he should so resolutely oppose the changes which have recently occurred in Wales. As a young man he found unrealistic the museum-like atmosphere there and complained, "You cannot live in the present / At least not in Wales," a land with neither present nor future,

> only the past,
> Brittle with relics,
> Wind-bitten towers and castles
> With sham ghosts;
> Mouldering quarries and mines;
> And an impotent people,
> Sick with inbreeding,
> Worrying the carcase of an old song.
>   ("Welsh Landscape")

Admittedly, the lament was softened by an ironic tone, and the poet offered no evidence that the trappings of the present would be preferable to those of the past. On the contrary, the invasion of rural Wales by dissatisfied English seeking relief from "the smell of petrol" only increased his uneasiness. But when satire sharpened his pen, as it did in *The Minister,* he perceived little enough spirituality among the tough hill farmers. Even when he looked sympathetically upon the weary laborer toiling in his fields, the poet found him an unlikely candidate for salvation:

> . . . on his meagre hearth
> The thin, shy soul has not begun its reign
> Over the darkness. Beauty, love and mirth
> And joy are strangers there.
>   You must revise
> Your bland philosophy of nature, earth
> Has of itself no power to make men wise.
>   ("Autumn on the Land")

If his judgments were harsh, there was never any doubt about Thomas's devotion to Wales and her people. But if conditions in Wales were deplorable, at least the country afforded a chance still for men like Twm of "The Airy Tomb" and Iago Prytherch to live with dignity and carry on their work "Unglorified, but stern like the soil." While the youthful poet may have regarded Wales as a relic of the past, the changes which have since brought it into the late twentieth century have left him in no doubt that however bad were the bad old days, they far surpassed an age devoid of both traditions and landmarks, with "hedges / uprooted, walls gone, a mobile people / hurrying to and fro on their fast / tractors." The springs of this ultraconservatism probably lie in Thomas's spiritual outlook and [his] need to reach God through his handiwork. Since the mathematician-God performs his wonders through nature, the out-of-doors is the proper setting for the worshipful person. To the extent that the machine represents a threat to nature, it becomes clear why Thomas and his God agree in denouncing it. Although it may lessen the spirit-stunning physical labors endured by previous generations, machinery draws attention and energy to itself and away from nature. Whatever the degree of divine participation, however, it is man not God who builds both machines and their logical extension, the cities which serve the profane interests of commerce and materialism. "The town / is malignant," growing and feeding upon the minerals and produce of the countryside, the land's bounty. On "Fair Day," the author hears "the noise of those / buying and selling and mortgaging / their consciences" under the sorrowing eyes of a stone Christ. An assault on nature is an affront to God, and any diminution in the out-of-doors means a corresponding reduction in the potential for human spirituality. The young of each generation need "The Moor," which they can enter "on soft foot, / Breath held like a cap in the hand" to sense the presence of God in "clean colours" and the "movement of wind over grass." Those up-to-date hill farmers who seek to model themselves upon the images "projected on their smooth screens" are in danger of forgetting the spiritual hunger which "only / bare ground, black thorns and the sky's / emptiness" can satisfy.

Nature may be awesome and beautiful, but the poet is soberly aware that neither it nor the God who created it is benign. Thomas's God remorselessly fashioned "the tooth that bruises" and ordained that the trout should die to supply "food for a man / And his pretty lady." He created "the wolf that watched the jackrabbit / cropping the grass," thereby establishing "a perfect, a self-regulating machine / of blood and faeces." The stunning scale of his gifts is dramatized each spring as he "join[s] together leaf / by leaf . . . the stanzas of / an immense poem," but his dread powers are not to be domesticated to human purposes; he confronts us instead with "the rioting / viruses under our lens." In brief, he is the God of death as well as of life, and as such Thomas persistently refers to him as a drinker of blood. Pain and evil have their place in this system, and we must learn to witness "virtue's / Defeat" and see "the young born / Fair, knowing the cancer / Awaits them."

It is a bleak outlook, born of the experiences of one in whose homeland the rigors of life are uncompromising. While supremacy must be granted to the Creator of fang and claw, what evidence can be cited by

Christians who claim for him also a boundless love? Though he wears a priest's garments, Thomas cannot in good conscience preach a doctrine which nature seems to refute and which will prove difficult for his weather-beaten parishioners to accept:

> 'Beloved, let us love one another,' the words are blown
> To pieces by the unchristened wind
> In the chapel rafters, and love's text
> Is riddled by the inhuman cry
> Of buzzards circling above the moor.
>
> (*The Minister*)

In traveling beyond Wales, Thomas has found little evidence to alter his view. In Spain, for example, he has encountered a climate as harsh and impoverishing as the cold, wet winds of Wales. The land surrounding Burgos is "parched" and the fields there are "bitter with sage / And this-tle." Men reap dried grass for forage, while "In the air an eagle / Circle[s], shadowless as the God / Who made that country and drinks its blood." Although he reads in "the book" that "God is love," the honest man can only report, "lifting my head / I do not find it so."

These are uncomfortable views for a Christian, regardless how unorthodox, and it is not surprising that Thomas eventually adopts the more satisfactory concept of creation itself as a massive act of love. The vast-ness of the galaxies is overwhelming; their formation poses a "mystery / terrifying enough to be named love." The splendor and precision of earthly life are tributes to the "Workmanship" of the Creator. The gift of life is of incalculable value, and though God may remain concealed, his creatures everywhere testify to his devotion. Even the silence which he so resolutely maintains may be part of "the metabolism / of the being of love." While nothing more dramatically bespeaks Thomas's inherent Christian premises than his conviction despite evidence to the contrary that God is love, it is noteworthy that his proof rests primarily upon the sacrificial act of creation and only secondarily upon the Passion of Christ.

Colin Meir correctly identified Thomas's central poetic concern when he asserted, "It is the subject matter which counts with R. S. Thomas; it is what the poems draw attention to: not the poet nor the poetry" (in Peter Jones and Michael Schmidt, eds., *British Poetry Since 1970: A Critical Survey* [Manchester: Carcanet, 1980], 1). Thomas's recent work is transparently poetry of direct statement in which descriptive images and metaphors take a subsidiary part. As is customary with poetry of ideas, these pieces often are patterned upon simple contrast, statement balanced by counterstatement, or abbreviated dialectic, usually moving from a negative to a modestly positive outlook. Despite consistent sincerity of tone, one detects an occasional convenient rhetorical gesture as the poet's ideas turn a sudden corner. "The Moon in Llŷn," for instance, paints a gloomy picture of the decay of faith, but no sooner have we been assured that "Religion is over" than a timely disclaimer is heard: "But a voice sounds / in my ear: Why so fast, / mortal?" Similarly, "In Context" opens with a recital of the poet's youthful views concerning his own self-importance and participation in "a larger pattern." It is a mild and unexceptionable brand of romanticism, yet without having dropped any hint that these have been merely fond hopes, the poem suddenly shifts ground: "Impossible dreamer! . . . It was not / I who lived, but life rather / that lived me." Proofs are not offered; the pattern is purely one of statement followed swiftly by counterstatement.

Thomas's personal anxiety and commitment usually deter him from distancing himself ironically from his subject, but though irony plays no very prominent part in his pursuit of the vanishing God, paradox abounds. The poet is compelled by "this great absence / that is like a presence." He grapples with "the uncertainties / of the imperatives of science." He must "learn to distrust the distrust / of feeling" and "yield to an unfelt pressure" which, though "irresistible," is capable of "everything / but coercion." The recognized perils of the quest lead him to define himself somewhat despairingly as

> . . . a seeker
> in time for that which is
> beyond time, that is everywhere
> and nowhere; no more before
> than after, yet always
> about to be; whose duration is
> of the mind, but free as
> Bergson would say of the mind's
> degradation of the eternal.
>   ("Abercuawg")

If Thomas's attraction to paradox is reminiscent of the Metaphysicals, the resemblance increases as rhetorical questions crowd into his lines. Questions are entirely appropriate in poems contemplating vast and intangible subjects, but there is a danger that glib and unanswerable questions may be posed solely to allow the author an easy escape from a labyrinth. Readers are justified in responding suspiciously to poems which end like "Perhaps" in a flurry of paradoxical, mind-twisting questions:

To suffer himself to be persuaded
of intentions in being other than the crossing
of a receding boundary which did not exist?
To yield to an unfelt pressure that, irresistible
in itself, had the character of everything
but coercion? To believe, looking up
into invisible eyes shielded against love's
glare, in the ubiquity of a vast concern?

As he ages, Thomas is evidently growing even more quizzical. At least the
percentage of his poems containing one or more questions is on the increase,
as reflected in three recent volumes. Of the sixty poems in *Laboratories of the
Spirit* (1975), twenty-nine, or 48 percent, contain questions. Of the forty-
two poems in *Frequencies* (1978), twenty-two, or 52 percent, raise questions.
Of the sixty-three poems in *Between Here and Now* (1981), thirty-seven, or
58 percent ask questions. Among this multitude are a number of genuine
posers, including: "What does it mean / life? . . . Is there a place / here for
the spirit? . . . How far is it to God? . . . What is time?" and "What is a
galaxy's meaning?"

The chief objection to such stupendous and unanswerable queries is
that they leave the topic approximately where they found it, as the poem's
thought circles back upon itself. Where such questions hold sway, an
atmosphere of bewilderment must arise, a problem intensified by Thomas's
frustrating tendency to forget or ignore gains made in previous inquiries
and to commence fresh poems on the assumption that he remains as far as
ever from his elusive quarry. However honest its findings, the reader can
hardly welcome yet another sally into the great unknown which spins yet
again around the edge of the same immense vacancy to return with the
forlorn conclusion, "we die, we die / with the knowledge that your resistance / is endless at the frontier of the great poem."

Not surprisingly, repetition of thought in Thomas is mirrored in
nearly identical form. The poet's characteristic expression is spare and direct.
(As an adjunct, note his increasing adoption of laconic one- or two-word
titles, in contrast to the more expansive titles of the youthful pieces.) The
great majority of his poems are in unrhymed lines and occupy a single page
each; a piece of forty lines is by his standards extremely long. The search
for the absent God proceeds by short steps of approximately equal length,
the uniformity of which in time grows monotonous.

Through varying his images a poet can of course lend freshness to
repeated ideas, a point strikingly exemplified by "The White Tiger," which
Thomas describes as "beautiful as God / must be beautiful" but trapped

inside its cage as God is trapped "within the confines / of our definition of him." This likening of God to a rare tiger has its counterpart in a briefer analogy between worshiper and artifact:

> . . . there is a stillness
> about certain Ming vases which in itself
> is a form of prayer, though to what god
> is not known.
>
> ("Scenes")

But just as Thomas will not desert either his chosen subject or form, so too he cherishes and frequently repeats a favorite image, that of the mirror or window. He dreads beholding "the emptiness of the interior / of the mirror that life holds up / to itself" but finds that the invisible deity is no more easily apprehended in the "clear mirror" of the intellect which merely reflects "the emptiness" where "God / should have been." As Freudians know, the mirror remains chiefly an instrument for self-examination, and it is in this capacity that Thomas most frequently evokes it, just as it is usually the poet himself who is represented as staring out of the window of consciousness. While it would be a misnomer to speak of Thomas as a confessional, considerable self-examination does occur during his ardent quest for the Almighty, for he must listen for the Lord's voice within as well as without: "The best journey to make / is inward. It is the interior / that calls." The poet brings to his introspection the same rigorous honesty with which he explores the external world. His estimate of himself and his accomplishments is not inflated. "Self-Portrait," for instance, laments

> All that skill,
> life, on the carving
> of the curved nostril and to no end
> but disgust.

In "The Calling" he recalls bitterly the disappointments which have attended his vocation. He has watched powerlessly "the soul's selling / of itself for a corner / by the body's fire." His frustrated hopes of encouraging spirituality among the Welsh hill farmers have taught him

> . . . the thinness
> of the window that is
> between you and life, and how
> the mind cuts itself if it goes through.

It is a commendable integrity, one which concedes that wisdom comes too little and too late, and that "At sixty there are still fables / to outgrow." Although he "had looked forward / to old age as a time of quietness," he must contend instead with

> . . . the void
> over my head and the distance
> within that the tireless signals
> come from.
> ("The New Mariner")

Though not the old man's frenzy which Yeats prayed for, this too suffices in its way to spur the aged poet into song. If even his most fervent admirers must find something to censure in Thomas's thematic and formal repetitiousness, he has recently given fresh proof that he remains a self-conscious artist seeking to extend and vary his subjects. Thus, *Between Here and Now* (1981) supplies individual verse "impressions" or commentaries to accompany thirty-three impressionist and postimpressionist paintings. While an occasional landscape among them offers a momentary glimpse of a setting reminiscent of the Wales of his youth ("It would be good to live / in this village with time / stationary"), he has found in these paintings a temporary respite from the besetting concerns of Wales and its absent God. Yet he can rightfully take pride in the plangent songs inspired by those subjects which have long tormented him, poems aptly described by their maker as "explosions timed / to go off in the blandness of time's face."

"On the Screen of Eternity"

Some Aspects of R. S. Thomas's Prose

Tony Brown

*Reprinted, as revised by the author, from The Powys Review, 6:1 (1987–1988): 5–15.

Writing in his autobiography, *Neb*, of his arrival in 1967 at Aberdaron, R. S. Thomas says that he had come to "the end of his own personal pilgrimage."[1] Geographically, he had come almost full circle: from Holyhead, where he spent his childhood; then (after university at Bangor and theological college in Cardiff) to posts as curate in the 1930s at Chirk and Hanmer (Maelor Saesneg) on the English border; and later westward, to livings at Manafon in Montgomeryshire, Eglwysfach near Aberystwyth and finally Aberdaron, with Holyhead visible on a clear day across the sea to the north. But more importantly, R. S. Thomas's pilgrimage, his search for "the real Wales of my imagination,"[2] begun as he gazed westward toward Wales from his exile at Hanmer, has been a spiritual and imaginative journey, one that has taken him across the boundary between two cultures.

It has not been an easy journey. The major obstacle on R. S. Thomas's pilgrimage, of course, was the fact that his had been an English-speaking upbringing. As he emphasized in an essay in 1958, "without the key of the Welsh language one and all must needs pass by the door that opens on the real Wales"; without the language, he says, one remains "a *dyn dieithr*, a stranger."[3] It is perhaps easy today, when opportunities for learning Welsh are so numerous, to underestimate Thomas's determined struggle, through the early years of the war, to master the Welsh language. One has to admire the sheer stubbornness which kept him traveling every week from Hanmer all the way to Llangollen to have his Welsh lesson (*Neb*, 40). Remarkably, by 1945 Thomas was sufficiently fluent to publish his first pieces of prose in Welsh, some short essays on the birds of the Welsh countryside, published in the Church in Wales weekly, *Y Llan* [*The Church*].[4] Other essays followed over the next seven years in the same journal and in *Y Fflam* [*The Flame*], the latter under the editorship of Euros Bowen.

Perhaps more significant than these early essays were some of the letters, in Welsh, which R. S. Thomas wrote to *Y Llan* in the immediate postwar years, letters which indicate another area of difficulty on his journey: his consciousness that the Church in which he served was failing to provide moral and spiritual leadership to Wales as a nation at an important point in her history. His nationalism and his pacifism come together in his criticism of the Church in Wales's continued acquiescence in the face of contemporary militarism, an acquiescence which he sees as typifying the Church in Wales's servile attitude toward England and its traditions:

> . . . One can expect to have leadership and inspiration from the Church, of course, but after all the un-Welsh attitude of the Church in Wales is only a reflection of the extensive anglicisation which has infiltrated the whole nation. And although the trouble in Dolgellau is very unpleasant,[5] we ought to welcome this opportunity for the Church to give a positive lead in matters of importance like these.
>
> Nobody can deny that our nation is caught in two minds at a fateful time in her history. Despite the two ugly wars which have gone by, there is continuous talk of another war, and considerable preparation in that direction. In the face of all this there are some preaching pacifism, some others demanding Welsh regiments, while the majority of our young people will be quietly joining the British army. Is the Church in Wales giving any consistent guidance in these circumstances? It isn't. It is accepting things as they are, as it did before and during the last war. How did it behave on that occasion? How many of its leaders, how many of its priests stood for peace and justice? Didn't they follow England servilely, praying for victory and singing the English national anthem on every occasion, while more than one of its priests joined the "Home Guard."
>
> I was more or less silent at that time. It was a very difficult time. But now, despite the trouble and the threats, there's some kind of peace in the world, and everybody has a duty to consolidate this peace. Wales is, as was said above, caught in two minds, but she has, as a small nation, an inclination toward pacifism and friendship. If the Church were ready to do its duty as the Church of Christ, it ought to take advantage of the situation, and give every support to that inclination.

But, alas, it prefers to leave things as they are. And things as they are smell of Englishness and Englishness is under suspicion now, because it has a bad reputation, not only in Wales, but in the world.

The purpose of this letter is not merely to denounce the English, although no small fault lies with them, because there are many of them in the Church in Wales, and they have a strong voice in church matters. And the majority of them are contemptuous of the Welsh nation. In this they are discourteous, if not un-Christian. Why is it necessary to have a bilingual church in an area which is wholly Welsh, just because there's a rich English person living there? If he wants to worship in the local church, let him learn its language. But it's necessary to remember that some of the fault is ours also. If we don't respect ourselves, if we don't have enough backbone to with-stand the English tide, we can't expect anything else but scorn.[6]

The attitudes toward war and toward England are ones with which we are familiar in R. S. Thomas's work, but until *Neb,* written some years after his retirement, we hear little in Thomas's prose about his attitudes toward the Church and its role in Welsh life. But the misgivings expressed here clearly continued to exist.

To date, R. S. Thomas has published over thirty essays, reviews and lectures in Welsh—not counting letters to the press—as well as his autobi-ography. But, as he says in an essay entitled *"Pe medrwn yr iaith . . ."* [*If I knew the language,* 1980],[7] for him prose is ultimately secondary; it is in poetry that he responds most fully to life "in all its variety and its com-plexity"—and yet R. S. Thomas has published only one poem in Welsh, "Y Gwladwr" ["The Countryman"] in *Y Fflam* in 1950. ("The last two lines were praised by Gwenallt," he told an interviewer in 1973, "but one swallow doesn't make a summer.")[8] Here is a third difficulty which Thomas has had to confront on his long pilgrimage. He explains in "If I knew the language . . ." and "Hunanladdiad y Llenor" ["The Creative Writer's Suicide," 1977] that he feels he lacks the intuitive sensitivity to the intrica-cies and nuances of the language which the native Welsh speaker has and, therefore, he lacks the confidence to make the critical discriminations which are a fundamental part of the process of poetic composition. The distress, the sense of inner division, which this situation must have caused Thomas over the years—the feeling that he cannot give full expression to his most profound thoughts and feelings *in* the language which represents so much to him and in which he now lives his life—would seem to have grown more acute as his view of the role of the Anglo-Welsh poet, the Welsh poet who writes in English, has changed.

As a young man Thomas felt that there were "signs . . . that the mantle of writers like T. Gwynn Jones and W. J. Gruffydd" was falling on those young writers, like himself, writing not in Welsh but in English ("Some Contemporary Scottish Writing," 1946) and that if they studied the work of the Welsh-language writers of the past these Anglo-Welsh poets might create in English a poetry which was distinctively Welsh, rooted in a tradition which was nonurban, nonindustrial. As Ned Thomas has pointed out, however, even by 1952 Thomas had shifted his ground considerably[9] and by 1977 ("The Creative Writer's Suicide") his anguish is clearly to be heard. In writing of the Welshman who has learned Welsh and who is then tempted to write in Welsh "in order to prove to himself and to the public that he is a true Welshman," Thomas is clearly writing out of a personal dilemma: "He will never become as good a writer in that language as he could be in English." R. S. Thomas is thus, poignantly, the victim of his own unrelenting idealism: for him the ultimate duty of the writer is to strive to create a masterpiece, to realize in words his vision of the truth.[10] For a Welsh poet such a masterpiece will be in Welsh "a work so Welsh as to defy every attempt to translate it successfully into another language, especially English" ("If I knew the language . . ."), but such expertise Thomas feels to be beyond him and so, in his own eyes, he is unworthy of the title *Welsh* writer. "Who has suffered, if I have not suffered? For I bear in my body the marks of this conflict" ("The Creative Writer's Suicide").

When one looks at R. S. Thomas's earliest prose in Welsh, the essays in *Y Llan* and *Y Fflam,* it is clear that he himself had been doing what he was urging other young Anglo-Welsh poets to do, namely studying poetry in Welsh. One is struck by his knowledge, even in the early 1940s, of the work of, for example, Ellis Wynne, Gwili, and Williams-Parry, as well as his knowledge of the Bible in Welsh. One notices, too, that the central themes of Thomas's writing are already being sounded: his deep love of the Welsh countryside, a place where one may be imaginatively alive and spiritually whole; his awareness at the same time of the vulnerability of this way of life, the need for Wales to resist the deadening effects of materialism, industrialism, and militarism, which he identifies from the outset, as we have seen, with the influence of England. The intense idealism and patriotism are already there in the young man in his early thirties. One notices, too, the rather curious chronological pattern of Thomas's Welsh writing. After these early pieces in Welsh, most of his prose in the 1950s and 1960s is in English, critical essays, reviews, and introductions to his own selections of English poets, including Herbert, Wordsworth, and Edward Thomas. This is also the period, of course, in which R. S. Thomas was establishing himself as a major poet in English. With the move to Aberdaron in 1967, the subject matter of his poetry changed; thereafter, his poetry concerns itself less with the cultural and political plight of Wales than with issues both more universal and more private: with man's essential loneliness and his search for God. Thomas's concern for Wales and her future has not, of course, decreased; if anything it has become more urgent. But, feeling that he has come home to "the real Wales" for which he had long searched, able now in Llŷn to live his life almost wholly in Welsh, he seems to have chosen to voice that concern not in English but in Welsh and not, therefore, in poetry but in prose. Since 1972 and, significantly perhaps, his account in "Y Llwybrau Gynt" of his early life and his first steps on the road to becoming a true Welshman, he has published very little prose in English, speaking instead directly and passionately to the Welsh-speaking Welsh themselves, through essays, letters to the press, public lectures, and, indeed, from the platform of the National Eisteddfod itself, urging them to be true to their traditions, on their guard in defense of their culture: "Awake, awake; put on your strength."[11]

Aware of the central role which the poet once had in Welsh society, giving voice to its essential values and aspirations, R. S. Thomas has always perceived the poet's function to be an essentially public one; in other words, as he has argued on a number of occasions, he sees his two callings, as priest and poet, to be inextricably linked. The poet, like the priest, should give moral and spiritual leadership; it is a far more idealistic notion of the poet's role and influence than has been the usual case in postwar English poetry. ("Poetry makes nothing happen," wrote W. H. Auden.)[12] As Ned Thomas and Tony Conran in particular have pointed out, R. S. Thomas's view of the poet's social role is rooted in the idealism of the Romantic poets, to whom he frequently alludes in his essays.[13] In the interview which he gave to John Ormond in 1972 he emphasizes the fact that the word "imagination" has for him the meaning which Coleridge gave to it: "The highest means known to the human psyche of getting into contact with the ultimate reality . . . The ultimate reality is what we call God."[14] The poet, therefore, the person of particular imaginative power and creative gifts, is possessed of special spiritual insight and as such is equipped to be, as Shelley saw him, society's "unacknowledged legislator." Thomas refers to Shelley's description of the poet in his essay "Some Contemporary Scottish Writing" (1946) and goes on to argue that only by expressing the highest ideals and aspirations in poetry is it possible to "at long last change the people and lead them to their essential dignity." This idealistic vision of the poet as spiritual guide, "winnowing and purifying . . . the people," is especially strong in R. S. Thomas's early writing. The poet should be a healer, rigorously purging the spiritual sickness of the age:

> Consider, you,
> Whose rough hands manipulate
> The fine bones of a sick culture,
> What areas of that infirm body
> Depend solely on a poet's cure.
> ("The Cure," *Poetry for Supper,* 1958)

It is a stance Thomas himself has taken from the beginning, in his prose as well as in his poetry, urging, warning:

> Degeneration is to be seen in every part of our national life. As long as there are food and drink, greyhounds and cinemas, the majority of our people don't care what government is in power. The churches and the chapels will be empty soon because of [these attitudes], and the fine arts are almost dead already.

In the essay quoted here, "Arian a Swydd" ("Money and Position," 1946),[15] R. S. Thomas compares the situation in Wales with that in Ireland, where he feels materialism has all but destroyed the idealism and optimism which gave birth to her independence. The comparison of Wales with her Celtic neighbours is a recurring one in his early writing. (We learn from *Neb* that he visited Scotland and Ireland in the 1930s, and a number of his early poems were published first in Dublin.) In "Some Contemporary Scottish Writing," he looks back to the power of Raftery in Ireland and Twm o'r Nant in Wales to attack the unprincipled and mean in the past. But in the 1940s, among contemporary writers he sees the Scottish poet, Hugh MacDiarmid, as providing a model of what, for Thomas, the poet should be: a figure of lonely integrity, speaking out against the uniformity, materialism, and bureaucracy of modern life, which stifle the imaginative and spiritual freedom of the individual. While Thomas, like MacDiarmid, sees these destructive influences as having their origins in English commercialism and English government, both writers reserve their fiercest scorn for those of their own people who fail to see the dangers, whose eyes are fixed on material advancement. In the 1980s Thomas sees the threat to be all the greater and the necessity for the Welsh writer to sound a warning to his society to be, consequently, even more urgent. In "If I knew the language . . . ," for example, he wishes his Welsh were as powerful and as flexible as that of Ellis Wynne, author of *Gweledigaetheu y Bardd Cwsc:*

If he had the language / To Isaiah the language — cf. Isaiah; then shall the go there instead

I would use it to reveal the hypocrisy, the idleness and the servility of the nation today, and scourge them until my readers would blush from top to toe, and take a solemn oath to regain through discipline and self-sacrifice the integrity and dignity which belonged to their ancestors.

The other side of the poet's role, of course, is to raise the eyes of the people to a higher ideal, to make them aware that even the things of their ordinary, everyday lives have significance. The task of the poet, Thomas told Bedwyr Lewis Jones in an interview in 1969, is

> to show the true glory of life. I don't believe in poets who over-analyse and belittle man. The rôle of the poet is to elevate man also, and life, and the earth.[16]

He goes on to say that however dirty and humble the farm worker may seem in his little field, "yet the sun shines on his field suddenly and without warning and there's some glory there too." As so often in R. S. Thomas's work, the laborer on the Welsh hill is an emblem which has more universal significance: whoever the individual is, however prosaic his or her life may seem, it can be transformed if seen in the light of its spiritual reality. ("If the doors of perception were cleansed every thing would appear to man as it is, infinite," wrote Blake, another Romantic poet to whom Thomas refers on several occasions in his essays.) By the expression of his vision in his poetry, the poet, Thomas argues, can begin to bring about a change of awareness, can revitalize the imagination of his readers, bringing them to a fuller awareness of their spiritual reality and, ultimately, of God: "The nearest we approach to God . . . is as creative beings," he says in his introduction to *The Penguin Book of Religious Verse*, 1963. The harsher tones with which we are familiar in R. S. Thomas's writing are, manifestly, an expression of his disappointment at society's falling short, and a measure of his idealism:

> I want to see the splendour of people and things, and their shadows which appear greater than they because of the light which throws their shadows on the screen of eternity.
>
> ("If I knew the language . . .")

The state of being which Thomas holds up as a condition toward which men should aspire is frequently expressed in terms of cleanness, simplicity, plainness, and clarity, in contrast to the gray, impersonal complexity of our modern world:

> . . . earth
> That is strong here and clean
> And plain in its meaning . . .
> ("Those Others," *Tares,* 1961)

※ Poetry teaches how to feel !

What God was there made himself felt,
Not listened to, in clean colours,
    . . . I walked on,
Simple and poor . . .
                    ("The Moor," *Pietà,* 1966)

                    Occasions
on which a clean air entered our nostrils
off swept seas were instances
we sought to recapture.
            ("That Place," *Laboratories of the Spirit,* 1975)

Only through being alert and honest and brave will we succeed in
doing our duty and deliver a clean Wales [Cymru lân] to the future.
                    ("O'm Cwmpas" ["Around Us," 1977])[17]

It is a nexus of ideas which has its origins, evidently, in Thomas's own temperament. We notice, for example, in "Y Llwybrau Gynt" his fond recol-
lection of the close of summer days in the sun and sea air of the countryside
around Holyhead: ". . . a glass of cold water before going to bed tasted mar-
vellous, and the white sheets were smooth and refreshing." His autobiographical writing—"Y Llwybrau Gynt," *Neb,* "Dylanwadau," ["Influences,"
1986][18]—makes clear how potent an influence on the growing poet were
those boyhood days in the countryside of Anglesey; in *Neb* especially he
emphasizes the sense of longing for the landscape of his youth which he
felt as his career took him elsewhere, "a longing which would be an
influence on him throughout the years which followed" (*Neb,* 29), and we
notice, too, how he is able to identify with "the anguish and the yearning"
for his home in Anglesey felt by the exiled Goronwy Owen.[19]

As R. S. Thomas stood in the 1930s on the "flat uninteresting land"
around Hanmer, gazing at the mountains away to the west, the longing he
felt "to get back to the real Wales of my imagination" was, in other words,
intimately connected to his longing for the simple, spontaneous pleasure,
the sense of imaginative freedom and vitality which he associated with the
countryside around Holyhead, now seemingly lost forever. When, still in
the 1930s, his reading of Yeats and "Fiona Macleod" (the pen name of
William Sharp, 1855–1905) suggested to him that among the peasantry of
Galway and the Western Isles of Scotland it was still possible to find
"exactly the life he would like to live among the peat and the heather and
the shores of the west" (*Neb,* 33), Thomas journeyed to those distant areas.
But although the sound of the country people's Gaelic "and the smell of
peat in his nostrils raised his spirits and filled his heart with new hope"

(*Neb*, 36), he found that the rural way of life described by Yeats and MacLeod had almost completely disappeared. The way of life he was searching for *was*, in Thomas's view, once to be found in Wales itself, in the high summer pasture, the life of the *hafod*, a life he sees as having been free and clean and imaginatively rich:

> There is Eden's garden, its gate open, fresh as it has always been, unsmudged by the world. The larks sing high in the sky. No foot-prints have bruised the dew . . . This is the world they went up into on May Day with their flocks from *yr hendre*, the winter house, to *yr hafod*, the shieling. They spent long days here, swapping *englynion* over the peat cutting.

Even as he evokes this romantic vision in "The Mountains" (1968), one is again perhaps aware of the depth of personal association for a writer whose boyhood was spent within sight of the mountains of Snowdonia: ". . . to live near mountains is to be in touch with Eden, with lost childhood" ("The Mountains"). But the life of the *hafod*, too, has long gone, swept away by more modern patterns of agricultural life; in the hills of Montgomeryshire he finds only emptiness and the ruins of the *hafotai*:

> The wind is licking their bones. The old people died, and the world drew their children closer to itself, leaving the area—desolate [yn anghyfannedd]. Yes, the word hurts the mind. When I am there, I hear the curlew mourning the people who have passed away, and I dream of the days that were, the days of *Calan Mai* and the *hafoty*; days when the Welsh went to the high pastures to live for a season at least "At the bright hem of God, / In the heather, in the heather".
>
> ("Maldwyn," 1951)[20]

But in R. S. Thomas's writing, the search for a place where people may attain their essential freedom and dignity, where they may gain inti-mations of the eternal, has continued, that place "we . . . would spend / the rest of our lives looking for" ("That Place," *Laboratories of the Spirit*).[21] It is a country place, clean and bright, usually with trees, a place where the silence is broken only by the song of birds and the sound of clear-running streams:

> A bird chimes
>   from a green tree
> the hour that is no hour
>   you know.
>   ("Arrival," *Later Poems*, 1983)

Such scenes, such moments at the "intersection of the timeless / With time,"[22] run like an elusive thread through Thomas's writing:

> For one hour
> I have known Eden, the still place
> We hunger for.
>   ("Again," *Not That He Brought Flowers*, 1968)

> For one brief hour the summer came
> To the tree's branches and we heard
> In the green shade Rhiannon's birds
> Singing tirelessly as the streams
> That pluck glad tunes from the grey stones
> Of Powys of the broken hills.
>   ("The Tree," *An Acre of Land*, 1952)

This last example evokes the brief period of communal harmony and free-dom achieved by Owain Glyndŵr, inspired we notice by the songs of his poet; for the state of being indicated by this recurring set of images is one which R. S. Thomas repeatedly associates specifically with Wales and with the tranquillity of the Welsh countryside. The connection is made most explicitly, of course, in "Abercuawg," the remarkable lecture which R. S. Thomas gave at the National Eisteddfod in 1976: "Wherever Abercuawg may be, it is a place of trees and fields and flowers and bright unpolluted streams, where the cuckoos continue to sing." It is essentially a vision of a transfigured Wales, in which it would be possible to live a life of calm sim-plicity and spiritual awareness, a place for which, Thomas says, he is "ready to make sacrifices, maybe even to die."

But even as the social, and indeed political, implications of the recur-ring motif, the elusive place, receive their fullest expression, it is made clear that the place is not a geographical location but a spiritual ideal. The true value is in the aspiration *toward* the ideal; Abercuawg will never be reached,

> but through striving to see it, through longing for it, through refus-ing to accept that it belongs to the past and has fallen into oblivion; through refusing to accept something second-hand in its place [man] will succeed in preserving it as an eternal possibility.

It is an ideal of continual imaginative aspiration, a refusal of the blunted responses and imaginative inertia of a commercial age—"No, this is not it." It is by means of the power of the imagination—"The highest means known to the human psyche of getting into contact with the ultimate reality"—that the individual searches "within time, for something which is above time, and yet, which is ever on the verge of being." The search for Abercuawg, in other words, is a search for spiritual awareness, for intimations of the eternal, of God: "May it not be that alongside us, made invisible by the thinnest of veils, is the heaven we seek?" ("Where do we go from here?" 1974). The search is a constant striving to keep clean "the doors of perception." It is a struggle which recalls those images of lonely aspiration in "The Mountains":

> There is the huge tug of gravity, the desire of the bone for the ground, with the dogged spirit hauling the flesh upward. Rare flowers tremble, waver, just out of reach.

It is an image of the individual's struggle to realize himself/herself fully, in the face of all those forces in modern life which seek to deny that individuality.

The search for Abercuawg is above all for R. S. Thomas an image of the lonely struggle of the writer to keep his/her own creative channels open, with the added burden of having to provide a signpost for others. As we have seen, early in his career Thomas found a model of the stance the writer should take in the work of Hugh MacDiarmid, admiring his determined resistance to "the all-pervading twentieth-century rationalism that goes hand in hand with western democracy and industrial development" ("Some Contemporary Scottish Writing"). But in Wales, in the writing of Saunders Lewis, Thomas found a figure whose stance was in many ways similar and even more sympathetic. Points of comparison between the writing of R. S. Thomas and that of Saunders Lewis have been mentioned by several critics,[23] but the relationship of the two writers' work has still to be fully explored. One does, however, note that in *Neb* Thomas tells of visiting Saunders Lewis in 1945. He had been so stirred by an essay which Saunders Lewis had published in *Y Faner*[24] that he went, without invitation, to visit the author at Llanfarian:

> [R. S. Thomas] was received kindly and began to talk in English about his ideals and his plans, but before long he was encouraged by Saunders to go on in his clumsy Welsh.
>
> (*Neb*, 45)

This was a potent force with which to come into contact for a young writer just beginning to find his voice, and a young man setting out on his search for the "real Wales." Thomas does not mention reading more of Saunders Lewis's work, but it seems more than likely that he did (we remember that *Canlyn Arthur* had been published in 1938), and he refers to Saunders Lewis admiringly in "Some Contemporary Scottish Writing" as a writer who had set aside his own career as a poet in order to dedicate himself to the nationalist cause in Wales. In Saunders Lewis's writing Thomas would have found many attitudes toward which he would have been sympathetic in the 1930s and 1940s, to judge from the opinions which he himself expresses in his early essays. He would have found, as in MacDiarmid, an antipathy to the (English) centralized democratic state whose social and economic systems Saunders Lewis saw as taking away the independence of the individual: "It is not the job of the government of a country to create a complete system and an economic machinery for the people of the country to accept and conform to."[25] In Saunders Lewis, too, he would have found a vision of a society based not on the impersonal city, the creation of capitalism and industrialism, but on small, mainly rural, communities, communities living and working in the Welsh country-side—and speaking Welsh. The language not only provided a living link with the traditions of the past but was fundamental to the maintenance of Welsh identity and unity in the face of those forces which sought to deny it: "To create a Welsh-speaking Wales [Cymru uniaith] is the surest way to build up a country in which the oppression of international capitalism cannot live."[26] As we have seen, not only has R. S. Thomas from the beginning associated all that he considers most valuable in life with a vision of rural communities living a life which is simple but imaginatively alive, but that the survival of the "real Wales" is inseparable from the survival of the Welsh language is a view which he holds even more passionately today than in the 1940s:

> I do not see any other way towards unity in Wales but through the Welsh language . . . If anyone believes he can experience the Welshness of Wales without the language, he's fooling himself. Every mountain and stream, every farm and little lane announces to the world that landscape is not mere landscape in Wales.
>
> ("Undod" ["Unity," 1985])[27]

By way of a brief aside, we might note that the vision of a society in which wealth is not held by a few capitalists or controlled by government but by a large number of small groups, communities, or individuals, a society in which the individual can work his/her own land, live his/her own life, free of the centralized state, Saunders Lewis found in, among other places, the "distributism" of Hilaire Belloc and G. K. Chesterton.[28] Their criticism of a centralized system of government run by (and in the interests of) international capitalism was expressed in a number of books published just before the First World War, notably Chesterton's *What's Wrong with the World* (1910) and Belloc's *The Servile State* (1912). What was wrong with the world, they argued, was that capitalist wealth had become concentrated in the hands of a small group of plutocrats who controlled not only the economic structure of Britain but also the Parliamentary parties and, in order to further their own ends, Britain's foreign policies. Moreover, the plutocratic state was becoming as mechanized and as indifferent to the individual as the vast factories which financed it. Chesterton and Belloc essentially anticipated E. F. Schumacher and his view that "small is beautiful." They advocated the break-up of the centralized state and a reversion to smaller, independent economic units, with industry existing in small, predominantly rural communities, a vision which formed the basis of the "Distributist" movement in which Chesterton and Belloc were involved in the 1920s and 1930s.[29] Whether R. S. Thomas had any knowledge of the work of these writers is uncertain, though he would have found many of their ideas to his taste. It is worth noting that Belloc's vision of a "Peasant State," emphasizing political freedom, an attachment to a locality or region, and a concern with the produce of the land, was based on an idealized vision of French peasant life; he saw the life of the rural community as preserving a respect for tradition, a sense of rootedness and a strong religious sense, all of which was in sharp contrast to the rootlessness and materialism of modern industrial society. There is something, too, of the same nostalgia for a preindustrial past of which R. S. Thomas has been accused. At the heart of this social vision is the figure of the peasant, sturdy and independent.

R. S. Thomas's ideal of rural community—derived from Wordsworth, from Yeats and MacLeod, and perhaps from these other sources—met reality at Manafon in the 1940s and his early poetry is, manifestly, an effort to wrestle with the discrepancy, as well as with his own sense of his incapacity to minister to the community as its priest. It is a community which, even as Thomas watches, is gradually being invaded by the values of the modern commercial world. Iago Prytherch, having been absent from Thomas's poetry for some years, is finally laid to rest in "Gone?" (*Frequencies*, 1978); by now the countryside is a place of tractors and televisions, the trees replaced by "a forest of aerials." The Wales Thomas surveys, far from being that tranquil place of birdsong, trees, and streams, is increasingly seen to be in actuality a spiritual and imaginative wasteland,[30] whose outer form is

> street after street of modern characterless houses, each one with its garage and its television aerial; a place from which the trees and the birds and the flowers have fled before the yearly extension of

concrete and tarmacadam; where people do the same kind of soul-
less, monotonous work to support more and more of their kind.

("Abercuawg")

It is the place of Blake's "dark Satanic mills," where "the doors of perception" are clogged and the life of the spirit cannot survive:

> . . . the dust spreads
> Its carpet. Over the creeds
> And masterpieces our wheels go.
> ("No Answer," *H'm,* 1972)

And the language is lost, too:

> In the drab streets
> That never knew
> The cold stream's sibilants
> Our tongues are coated with
> A dustier speech.
> ("Expatriates," *Poetry for Supper,* 1958)

This sense of desolation is poignantly caught in "Unity" when Thomas
speaks of one year when, because of the weather, the migratory birds—
those birds that represent so much in R. S. Thomas's life and in his
writing—did not come to Aberdaron:

> It was a sad experience to wander Mynydd Mawr in the dawn, and
> walk the lanes and hollows, without seeing anything. It was like a
> museum. I said to everyone: "I remember how it was once, the sky
> and the lanes full." It is a symbol of Pen Llŷn without the Welsh
> language, the deathliness which would be there.

Moreover, these images of desolation which are associated with Wales are
linked in a very direct way in Thomas's mind with images of a more
universal desolation. If it is man's desire to better himself in material things,
in the goods of the modern world, which is ultimately responsible for
destroying the life of the *hafotai,* "leaving the area—desolate," Thomas now
sees the same values, on a national and international level, as threatening
the future of the whole earth: "Man's cupidity, to use a medieval term, has
placed in his hands the ability to make the world desolate" ("Nadolig
Niwcliar," ["A Nuclear Christmas," 1982]).[31] The threat of nuclear warfare, and especially the absurd claims of some political leaders that it is possible to fight a nuclear war and win, has caused Thomas, whose pacifism
was being sounded loud and clear in the 1940s, to speak out, not only in

his writing but on public platforms, on behalf of the campaign against nuclear weapons. They represent the ultimate threat of the age of the machine, the complete negation of Abercuawg: "The earth smoked, no birds sang" ("Once," *H'm*).

As people far beyond the borders of Wales have awoken to the threat to the earth's survival from nuclear weapons, from industrial pollution and from overexploitation of natural resources, the themes R. S. Thomas has been sounding for many years in a specifically Welsh context have taken on even more clearly a more universal significance.[32] But while others are also now arguing that "small is beautiful," the struggle, both in Wales and beyond, has become more urgent and his tones have become more bleak, at times even despairing, especially when he looks at Wales itself: "The end of the nation is plain . . . Its people don't think like Welsh people nor act like Welsh people. There are only the relics of a nation left on their lips."[33] Even after his long pilgrimage back to Welsh-speaking Wales, the sense of being an exile, "an exile in my own land"[34] is still present: a fervent supporter of the Welsh language in a Wales in which the language struggles for survival, an advocate of the simple life of the countryside in a land echoing with the sound of machinery, a man concerned with the things of the imagination and the spirit in a society devoted to quite different values. "A displaced person" Wynn Thomas has called him;[35] it is a very different picture from the earlier idealistic vision of the poet as imaginative leader of his society, "winnowing and purifying" the people. A recurring motif in the later poetry has been one of loneliness, of the poets and men of vision as isolated, their words unheard or ignored:

> Among the forests
> Of metal the one human
> Sound was the lament of
> The poets for deciduous language.
> > ("Postscript," *H'm*)

> It was a time when wise men
> Were not silent, but stifled
> By vast noise.
> > ("Period," *H'm*)

> I see the wise man
> with his mouth open shouting
> inaudibly on this side of the abyss.
> > ("Eheu! Fugaces," *The Way of It,* 1977)

At times one is reminded of the Old Testament prophets whose words R. S. Thomas echoes on several occasions. He continues to speak out to the Welsh people from his cottage at the tip of the Llŷn peninsula, warning, criticizing, urging higher ideals. His geographical journey may have come to its end, but his late poetry, with its recurring images of traveling, of pilgrimage and exploration, shows that the spiritual journey goes on, the inner search for glimpses of the "ultimate reality," signs of God's presence. Despite the dust of the wasteland, R. S. Thomas clearly still holds to his vision of man's spiritual existence, the shadow man casts on the screen of eternity:

> Man is the dream of a shadow. But when the
>   god-given brightness comes
> A bright light is among men, and an age that is
>   gentle comes to birth.[36]

Notes

1.   R. S. Thomas, *Neb* [*Nobody*] (Caernarfon: Gwasg Gwynedd, 1985), 85.

2.   "Y Llwybrau Gynt" ["The Paths Gone By"] in *R. S. Thomas: Selected Prose,* ed. Sandra Anstey (Bridgend: Poetry Wales Press, 1983), 138. Where a translation of an essay originally published in Welsh appears in this selection, I have used that text in quotations. Otherwise the translations are my own and the original Welsh source is given. I am grateful for the assistance and advice of Mrs. Megan Tomos of the University of Wales, Bangor, Translation Unit, in matters of translation. In the case of essays originally published in English, unless another source is cited, the text is to be found in *Selected Prose.*

3.   "The Welsh Parlour," *Listener,* 16 January 1958, 119.

4.   See "Adar y Plwyfi" ["Birds of the Parishes"], *Y Llan,* 28 September 1945, 5; "Adar y Gaeaf" ["Birds of the Winter"], *Y Llan,* 28 December 1945, 8.

5.   During the week of the National Eisteddfod at Dolgellau in 1949 the Union Jack had been flown from the tower of the parish church, only to be pulled down by nationalists. The incident gave rise to a discussion in the columns of *Y Llan* as to the relationship between the Church and Wales of which the present letter formed a part.

6.   *Y Llan,* 2 September 1949, 5. See also R. S. Thomas's letters to the same journal on 7 March 1947, 6, and 3 February 1950, 8.

7.   *Y Faner,* 11 January 1980, 4.

8.   "Gwilym Rees Hughes yn holi R. S. Thomas," *Barn,* 129 (1973), 386.

9. See Ned Thomas's discussion of R. S. Thomas's shift in attitude to the role of the Anglo-Welsh writer, in the introduction to *Selected Prose,* 13–15.

10. See "The Creative Writer's Suicide," *Selected Prose,* 170, and "Pe medrwn yr iaith. . . ."

11. *Isaiah,* 52:1. R. S. Thomas quotes the verse at the conclusion of the letter to *Y Llan,* quoted above.

12. W. H. Auden, "In Memory of W. B. Yeats."

13. See Ned Thomas's introduction to *Selected Prose* and Anthony Conran, *The Cost of Strangeness: Essays on the English Poets of Wales* (Llandysul: Gomer, 1982), 220–28.

14. John Ormond, "R. S. Thomas: Priest and Poet," *Poetry Wales,* 7:4 (1972): 54.

15. *Y Fflam,* 1 (1946), 29–30.

16. Bedwyr Lewis Jones, "R. S. Thomas," *Barn,* 76 (1969), n.p. The interview is in the supplement, "O'r Stiwdio."

17. *Y Faner,* 4 March 1977, 9.

18. *Y Faner,* 7 November 1986, 12–13.

19. In R. S. Thomas's speech as President of the Day at the National Eisteddfod at Llangefni, 3 August 1983. See *Y Glorian Ddyddiol* ('Steddfod,' 1983), 6 August 1983, 2, and *Llawlyfr Eisteddfod Genedlaethol Cymru,* 1983, 105–7. The speech is reprinted in *Pe Medrwn yr Iaith.*

20. *Y Llan,* 9 March 1951, 7–8. On the verse quoted at the end of the passage, see *Selected Prose,* 25.

21. On this motif and its significance, see also Simon Barker's review of *Selected Prose, Poetry Wales,* 20:1 (1984): 72–79.

22. T. S. Eliot, "The Dry Salvages."

23. See, for example, Dafydd Elis Thomas, "The Image of Wales in R. S. Thomas's Poetry," *Poetry Wales,* 7:4 (1972): 63, 65–66, and Randal Jenkins, "The Occasional Prose of R. S. Thomas" in the same issue, 101.

24. S[aunders] L[ewis], "Cwrs y Byd" ["The Way of the World"], *Baner ac Amserau Cymru,* 27 June 1945, 1.

25. Saunders Lewis, "Deg Pwynt Polisi," *Canlyn Arthur* ["Ten Points of Policy," *In the Steps of Arthur*] (Aberystwyth: Gwasg Aberystwyth, 1938), 11.

26. "Un Iaith i Cymru" ["One Language for Wales"], *Canlyn Arthur,* 60.

27. The J. R. Jones Memorial Lecture, University College, Swansea, 9 December 1985. The full text is in *Pe Medrwn yr Iaith* and a translation in *Planet,* 70 (August/September 1988): 29–42.

28. See, for example, Dafydd Glyn Jones's essay on Saunders Lewis's political thought in *Presenting Saunders Lewis,* ed. Alun R. Jones and Gwyn Thomas (Cardiff: University of Wales Press, 1972), p. 36.

29. The fullest recent account of Chesterton and Belloc's political writing and of the Distributist movement is Jay P. Corrin, *G. K. Chesterton and Hilaire Belloc: The Battle Against Modernity* (London: Ohio University Press, 1981).

30. "Border Blues" (*Poetry for Supper*, 1958) would seem at times consciously to echo some of T. S. Eliot's techniques in *The Waste Land*.

31. *Barn*, 251/2 (December 1983/January 1984): 420–21.

32. See R. S. Thomas's comments in "R. S. Thomas Talks to J. B. Lethbridge," *Anglo-Welsh Review*, 74 (1983): 42.

33. Interview with Rhys Owen, *Pais* (September 1983): 9.

34. Eisteddfod speech, 1983. See note 19.

35. Lecture to The Welsh Academy, Aberystwyth, October 1985. See "Agweddau ar farddoniaeth y chwedegau" ["Aspects of the Poetry of the Sixties"] in M. Wynn Thomas, ed., *R. S. Thomas: Y Cawr Awenydd* [roughly, *R. S. Thomas: Giant Literary Talent*] (Llandysul: Gomer, 1990), 39.

36. Pindar's Eighth *Pythian Ode,* in a translation by E. M. Forster. R. S. Thomas paraphrased the ode in *Neb,* 87.

The Unmanageable Bone

Language in R. S. Thomas's Poetry

Patrick Deane

Reprinted from Renascence: Essays on Values in Literature, *XLII:4 (Summer 1990): 213–36.*

There is much to be said for the view, widely held by R. S. Thomas's critics and evidently endorsed by the poet himself and his publisher, that his career so far can be divided into two relatively distinct parts. The first, summarized by the *Selected Poems 1946–1968,* is overwhelmingly concerned with matters Welsh: Thomas's archetypal peasant, Iago Prytherch, is the creation of this period and comes before us, "Just an ordinary man of the bald Welsh hills" (*Selected Poems,* 3), in poem after poem. Prytherch provides Thomas with a focus for his sustained and rigorously unsentimental interrogation of the Welsh identity, his nationalistic themes, and his concern at the decay of the rural structure in Wales. The poems of this period are, by Thomas's own description, propaganda: in 1963 he told an audience at the University College of Swansea that "there is always lurking in the back of my poetry a kind of moralistic or propagandist intention" (*Selected Prose,* 83). In 1968, however, he published *Not That He Brought Flowers,* a volume in which some radical changes are evident. And in the same year he confessed to having become tired of his old themes, of "strutting and beating my chest and saying 'I am Welsh'" (*Selected Prose,* 110).

  H'm, published in 1972, made an even more dramatic departure from Thomas's earlier work. Wales had disappeared completely as an explicit— or even an implicit—subject, and so had Iago Prytherch; in place of the somewhat prosaic style of the late sixties there was something new, a deliberately primitive language with its origins in ritual and chant; and there was a direct confrontation with problems such as man's relation to his God, human suffering, and futility, all of which had been dealt with obliquely, if at all, in the earlier poems. The volume was characterized overall by a boldly mythopoeic thrust and a pervading pessimism that has led Peter Abbs to compare it with Ted Hughes's *Crow,* published in the same year. Although Thomas's poetry since *H'm* seems to have regained its composure somewhat, it has remained largely with that volume's subject matter, and what A. M. Allchin (119) characterized as "a certain hardening of the [Thomas] style" in *H'm* has not entirely let up. The main trends of this second phase of R. S. Thomas's career have been summarized by the publication of the *Later Poems 1972–1982,* which appeared in 1983. As we shall see, certain of the new poems contained in that volume and those which make up Thomas's latest collection, *Experimenting with an Amen* (1986),[1] indicate that the consolidation effected by *Later Poems 1972–1982* was prelude to a significant shift, if not in subject matter, in poetic attitude.

Anxiety about language and its relation to truth has been generally regarded as something new to R. S. Thomas in his second or "later" phase. Certainly, in all the poems of the fifties and early sixties there is little sense of a linguistic crisis to match crises of other kinds—the depopulation of the Welsh hill country and the spread of urbanization, for example. The poet is worried about many things, but not greatly about his ability to discuss them meaningfully. With *H'm,* however, Thomas's subject has become the impotence, caprice, or absence of the Word, a crisis from which the verbal body of the poem cannot be isolated. In the volume's title piece, language is painfully spare. The lines are written in the teeth of silence:

> and one said
> speak to us of love
> and the preacher opened
> his mouth and the word God
> fell out so they tried
> again speak to us
> of God then but the preacher
> was silent reaching
> his arms out but the little
> children the ones with
> big bellies and bow
> legs that were like

a razor shell
were too weak to come
(*H'm*, 33)

If the poem's title is pre-verbal—a grunt which R. S. Thomas has implied could be either "a sceptical question . . . [or] a purr of contentment" (Wilson, 67), or both—then the lines themselves are barely verbal. One is struck by the overwhelming number of monosyllabic and even monomor-phemic words, the rudimentary syntax ("and . . . and . . . and . . . but . . . but"), and the absence of punctuation and capital letters, those refiners of the brute utterance. Furthermore, pervasive use of enjambment produces in the reader a growing anxiety about the poem's continuation: each line end-ing raises the possibility that the statement begun may trail off into silence. And of course Thomas's refusal to punctuate the end of the last line denies closure to the whole. Speech has not come to anything.

Though all the poems of *H'm* seem to be implicated in the same sort of linguistic crisis, language itself is never explicitly mentioned in the vol-ume—with one important exception, to which I shall return. But in Thomas's next major collection, *Laboratories of the Spirit* (1975), all the struggles which occupied him in the pages of *H'm*—between God and man, indifference and passion, meaning and futility—become focused on the matter of language. The real battle, as it emerges in Thomas's second phase, is the individual's struggle to open communication with his God. But God's resistance to appropriation by human language is absolute. If we suspected that "H'm" was a version of "Him," and that the apostrophe was a concession to the unnameability of God, this is confirmed in a poem that is central to all of Thomas's work:

THE COMBAT

You have no name.
We have wrestled with you all
day, and now night approaches,
the darkness from which we emerged
seeking; and anonymous
you withdraw, leaving us nursing
our bruises, our dislocations.

For the failure of language
there is no redress. The physicists
tell us your size, the chemists

the ingredients of your
thinking. But who you are
does not appear, nor why
on the innocent marches
of vocabulary you should choose
to engage us, belabouring us
with your silence. We die, we die
with the knowledge that your resistance
is endless at the frontier of the great poem.

(*Laboratories*, 43)

Those bleak last lines proclaim that what one might call the poem of immanence, in which words have an intrinsic connection to the Word, will be eternally denied us. There is the poem we are reading and the "great poem," and the frontier between them is uncrossable. One would think that such a realization would compel the poet to silence, but for Thomas God's intractibility is double-edged. In a later volume, *Between Here and Now* (1981), he wonders if what is here called the "great poem" is, in fact, "a sentence without words" (97), and in that phrase we have a suggestion not only of how the poem of immanence defies our normal linguistic categories, but also of how we are bound by it and to it: silence is a "sentence" in that we are held by it, unable to escape. God's refusal to join in communication with man is a silent judgment pronounced upon him, one that commits the writer to work continually for re-admission to linguistic plenitude. As John Mole (134) has noticed, Thomas makes a similar play on the word "sentence" in "Shadows," a poem from *Frequencies* (1978). There the poet reiterates his view that the world's abject darkness implies God's presence—"Surely there exists somewhere," he pleaded in *Laboratories of the Spirit* (46), ". . . the one light that can cast such shadows"—and he resigns himself to listen for God's word in the "language / of silence, the sentence / without an end" (25). Thus, in "The Combat" Thomas finds himself belabored by silence, "engaged" in a way that will not allow him to give up the struggle. Even though "we die / with the knowledge that your resistance / is endless," we are committed to strive endlessly at the frontier between words and the Word. So, in a later poem, "Pluperfect,"

It was because there was nothing to do
that I did it; because silence was golden
I broke it.

(*Between*, 89)

• • •

In Thomas's later poems, the speaker is in a bind, quite literally enthralled by contradiction. He is painfully aware of his deprivation and dispossession, and yet quite unable to relinquish his vision of plenitude. Thomas has taken Keats's statement on negative capability as a motto for all poets, especially religious ones (*Selected Prose*, 66), but in his own work one senses that being in uncertainties, mysteries, and doubts is an—albeit fruitful—affliction. What energizes Thomas's poems is precisely a kind of "irritable reaching" after truth, what one poem calls "the verbal hunger / for the thing in itself" (*Frequencies*, 7). Even in *H'm*, where nourishment for the soul seems almost hopelessly scarce, the hunger never quite becomes despondency. Thomas's desire to enter what later poems will visualize as God's garden, his aspiration to a language which will make real connection with "the thing in itself," never wholly disappears.

Despite the assertion in "Via Negativa," a keynote poem for *H'm*, that the speaker has never accepted immanence as a real possibility—"Why no! I never thought other than / That God is that great absence / In our lives" (16)—we find that in another poem in the volume, "Postscript," the poets of the modern age are said to sing a lament "for deciduous language" (22). That last is a perplexing phrase, meaning perhaps that the poets express their regret at the fleeting or ephemeral nature of language. This interpretation is supported by the terms in which *Experimenting with an Amen* enjoins its reader to set store by immutable truths: "Navigate by such stars as are not / leaves falling from life's / deciduous tree" (45). But for R. S. Thomas the word "deciduous" suggests more than a broad ephemerality; its point is always sharpened by a powerful sense of dispossession, estrangement from the ideal. A useful gloss is to be found in the "Prayer" with which *Later Poems 1972–1982* ends:

> Baudelaire's grave
> not too far
> from the tree of science.
> Mine, too,
> since I sought and failed
> to steal from it,
> somewhere within sight
> of the tree of poetry
> that is eternity wearing
> the green leaves of time.
> (214)

That last definition of poetry is crucial, for it presents individual poems as manifestations in time of a timeless principle, leaves on the tree of eternity.

In Thomas the tree invariably recalls the cross of Christ, so we may carry the metaphor further and say that according to this definition poetry is something nourished by, and impossible without, real connection with God.

What afflicts the poets in "Postscript," and R. S. Thomas in *H'm* as a whole, is a dreadful sense that real connection of this sort is temporary, and invariably a thing of the past. While poems may be leaves on the tree of eternity, the curse is that the tree is not evergreen, but deciduous. By this analogy language is out of touch more than it is in touch with God. It is this state of linguistic dispossession that is mourned in "Postscript" and its reference to a "deciduous language"—the one explicit mention of language, incidentally, in the whole of *H'm*.

The point has to be made, however, that the phrase is in effect ambivalent. Placed in the context of Thomas's recurring metaphors, it becomes clearly negative, but taken at face value and in the context of "Postscript" alone, "deciduous language" can seem positive:

> As life improved, their poems
> Grew sadder and sadder. Was there oil
> For the machine? It was
> The vinegar in the poets' cup.
>
> The tins marched to the music
> Of the conveyor belt. A billion
> Mouths opened. Production,
> Production, the wheels
>
> Whistled. Among the forests
> Of metal the one human
> Sound was the lament of
> The poets for deciduous language.
>
> (22)

Language is here implicated in a dialectic which opposes a pre-industrial, Edenic world to our contemporary industrialized one, and the word "deciduous" proclaims its alliance with the former. What the poets lament is a type of language profoundly allied with the forces of nature. By this interpretation, therefore, "deciduous" appears to imply exactly the opposite of what was suggested earlier; in this context, it indicates integration rather than dispossession, an ideal rather than a fallen condition, and some intrinsic connection between language and "the thing in itself."

These observations, coupled with the thought that what is lamented is usually something lost, or something that existed in the past, must surely cast us back to Eden, to the garden, and to the world which, in R. S. Thomas's poetry, is frequently (though not unequivocally) considered in these terms: rural Wales. The poets' lament for a "deciduous language" returns us to Thomas's earlier phase, usually considered so distinct from this one, where we may be surprised to find in his deliberations on the predicament of the Welsh peasantry an ongoing—if buried—concern with language and its relation to "the thing in itself." His immanentist aspirations do not appear out of nowhere in *H'm* and the later poems; they are simply uncovered for us and subjected to rigorous development. In fact, the pessimism of *H'm* grows out of a dismissal or at least a reevaluation of past ideas, of an earlier belief in the possibilities for communion with God in a life lived on the land and close to its simplest inhabitants. As early as *Song at the Year's Turning* (1955), Thomas was skeptical of what he called "the old lie / Of green places" and of the ideal of "man united with the earth" (*Song*, 115). Those phrases come from the volume's final poem, aptly titled "No Through Road," but despite his skepticism, he was to remain drawn to the road of rural idealism for almost twenty years. Even in *H'm*, when the possibility of following that route was almost entirely gone, we have seen that the Wordsworthian ideal of a language rooted in the earth still attracted him. Thomas's later obsession with a language of immanence must be seen in the context of this earlier preoccupation, and it is to this that I will now turn.

● ● ●

Though Thomas's earlier books focus almost exclusively on the rural world, they lack the kind of contented passivity that would make them bucolic. Instead, they record a restless search for the pastoral that is summarized in this "Song" from *An Acre of Land*, first published by a small Welsh press in 1952:

> Wandering, wandering, hoping to find
> The ring of mushrooms with the wet rind,
> Cold to the touch, but bright with dew,
> A green asylum from time's range.
>
> And finding instead the harsh ways
> Of the ruinous wind and the clawed rain;
> The storm's hysteria in the bush;
> The wild creatures and their pain.
>
> (*Song*, 62)

The speaker hopes for "A green asylum from time's range": what could this be other than Eden? The phrase is of particular interest because of the word "green," which throughout Thomas's work is used with almost talismanic significance to suggest integration and wholeness. When those two things are thought to be unattainable, of course, he proclaims greenness an illusion—as in "the old lie / Of green places"—but the color never loses its association with a prelapsarian state of oneness. The word is used three times in fifteen lines in a nationalistic poem called "The Tree," where Wales under Owain Glyn Dŵr is presented as a version of Eden: whole, healthy, and strong. Glyn Dŵr, raised by the music of his bard to an awareness of his countrymen's dispossession "under the barbed string / Of English law, starving among / The sleek woods no longer theirs," goes on to regain a kind of paradise:

> . . . something in his song
> Stopped me, held me; the bright harp
> Was strung with fire, the music burned
> All but the one green thought away.
> The thought grew to a great tree
> In the full spring of the year;
> The far tribes rallied to its green
> Banner waving in the wind;
> Its roots were nourished with their blood.
> And days were fair under those boughs;
> The dawn foray, the dusk carouse
> Bred the stout limb and blither heart
> That marked us of Llewelyn's brood.
> It was with us as with the great;
> For one brief hour the summer came
> To the tree's branches and we heard
> In the green shade Rhiannon's birds
> Singing tirelessly as the streams
> That pluck glad tunes from the grey stones
> Of Powys of the broken hills.
>
> (*Song,* 56–57)

In this early poem, the search for a nationalistic paradise, for a free Wales, is couched in terms that will recur constantly in Thomas's work as the poet continues to search, his goal undergoing gradual metamorphosis. In other poems, Eden will shed its Welsh character and become more generalized as "a green asylum from time's range"; in later poems, it will become a metaphor for a certain linguistic climate, in which words' dispossession from "the thing in itself" will be ended. Accordingly, the ideal poem is conceived as a "green" leaf on the tree of eternity. The tree of the Welsh nation will become the tree of the cross, by which Paradise is regained, and ultimately the tree of poetry. The garden and the tree are two of those figures in Thomas's work which, as Mole has pointed out, become "counters manipulated in a passionate game of definition" (136). The word "green" is another one, used continually as a counter signifying the integrated, the reconciled, the Edenic. Its extraordinary significance in "The Tree" is brought home to us by the curious way in which, recalling Marvell's "The Garden," it is applied to something as abstract and colorless as thought or to the absence of direct sunlight, as in the phrase "the green shade." Such usages suggest that green is not a color but a state, in both senses of the word: it is a oneness, a unity, and in this particular poem it is the Welsh nation.

• • •

It is in one of Thomas's Iago Prytherch poems that "green" is first applied to language. The poet is in dialogue with Prytherch and with his own past belief in the redeeming possibilities of a return to rural life:

> The temptation is to go back,
> To make tryst with the pale ghost
> Of an earlier self, to summon
> To the mind's hearth, as I would now,
> You, Prytherch, there to renew
> The lost poetry of our talk
> Over the embers of that world
> We built together. . . .

The question that dogs the poet is whether it is possible, despite intervening intellectual misgivings, to return to an earlier vision of rustic plenitude:

> And if I yield and you come
> As in the old days with nature's
> Lore green on your tongue,
> Your coat a sack, pinned at the corners
> With the rain's drops, could the talk begin
> Where it left off? Have I not been
> Too long away?

(*Poetry for Supper,* 14)

That "nature's / Lore," its body of tradition and knowledge, should be "green" on Prytherch's tongue suggests his close association with the land. Indeed it implies that he speaks the same language, that in his speech there is no dissociation of the word from the "thing in itself." The point is made by taking an adjective usually reserved for elements in the natural world and applying it to a human faculty; similarly, in other poems Thomas finds that faculty in nature. In *The Bread of Truth* (1963) for example, he remarks that he prefers listening to "The bare language of grass" than "To what the woods say" (17). The speech of Iago Prytherch, as Thomas imagines him, is at one with the discourse of nature.

In another poem from *The Bread of Truth,* the speaker meditates on an unnamed peasant (who might as well be Prytherch) who "was in the fields when I set out" and "in the fields when I came back." It is implied that the speaker has been drawn away from the rural world, figuratively as well as literally, and the peasant seems to address him on his return:

> You will return,
> He intimated; the heart's roots
> Are here under this black soil
> I labour at. A change of wind
> Can bring the smooth town to a stop;
> The grass whispers beneath the flags;
> Every right word on your tongue
> Has a green taste. It is the mind
> Calling you, eager to paint
> Its distances; but the truth's here,
> Closer than the world will confess,
> In this bare bone of life that I pick.
>
> (38)

The tension that animates this poem is the same one discernible in the dialogue with Prytherch, discussed before: the poet is ambivalent about the rustic world and about whether immersion in it is the way to "truth." The question is kept open, the possibility of plenitude devastatingly deprived of fulsomeness or sentimentality (the peasant picks a "bare bone of life"), and the point is made that it is not the mind, but the senses and instincts that might take purchase on "truth." Thus "green" may also suggest naïveté in what are surely the poem's most telling lines: "Every right word on your tongue / Has a green taste." Though the speaker keeps his distance from the peasant and all he represents, the arguments he attributes to the latter are strongly felt—all the more powerfully, in fact, for their austerity and primitive simplicity. The suggestion that language is "right" when inseparable from the natural world is informed by a remarkable conviction; for the speaker, it is very possibly correct.

Prytherch's complete alliance with the "Green Categories" of nature is sympathetically treated in a poem by that title in *Poetry for Supper* (1958). There, in the first line, the speaker sets up a distinction between life lived with the mind and by natural instinct: "You never heard of Kant, did you,

Prytherch?" The "green" life of integration is movingly evoked in the middle stanza:

> Here all is sure;
> Things exist rooted in the flesh,
> Stone, tree and flower. Even while you sleep
> In your low room, the dark moor exerts
> Its pressure on the timbers. Space and time
> Are not the mathematics that your will
> Imposes, but a green calendar
> Your heart observes; how else could you
> Find your way home or know when to die
> With the slow patience of the men who raised
> This landmark to the moor's deep tides?
>
> (19)

From here the poem moves to a complicated conclusion in which Kant and Prytherch are imagined reconciled at night together in the latter's small garden, "fenced from the wild moor's / Constant aggression" and sharing their faith "over a star's blue fire." Perhaps this means that both men were seeking the same thing, but again—and typically—Thomas is noncommital: we are only told this "could" have happened. At any rate, this is the poem in which Prytherch's "greenness" is most explicitly described, and it explains why, when he speaks, nature's lore is "green" on his tongue: all things, including language, are rooted "in the flesh, / Stone, tree and flower."

This, presumably, is the kind of linguistic climate which Thomas wishes to evoke when, in the dark and dispossessed world of *H'm,* his poets lament a "deciduous language." But as we have seen, the ideal of a language inseparable from "the thing in itself" is never felt to be more than a possibility—even in those very early poems of Thomas in which the rustic life presents itself most strongly as the way to "truth." What one poem views positively as Prytherch's "green" speech—eloquently inarticulate—another reads as a sign of the "frightening . . . vacancy of his mind" (*Song,* 21). That is to say, the "bare bone" of life lived close to nature may, to the intellectual outsider, promise a higher kind of nourishment, but it may as easily deliver starvation. Thomas passionately wants to believe in the attainability of linguistic plenitude, in the possibility that there may be some kind of "language not to be betrayed"—to use his namesake Edward Thomas's phrase (100)—but his intellect and experience prompt him otherwise. Thus the poems concerned with Prytherch and the life he represents are frequently cast as postscripts, valedictions, and temptations.

• • •

These earlier poems to some extent explain the tormenting sense of loss which afflicts almost all of Thomas's work in the seventies. The sort[s] of ideals which, though always to some extent remote were felt as relatively immediate in the fifties and sixties, have receded beyond the bounds of contemplation to become something almost mythical which it is the duty of the bards to recall and lament. In *H'm* it is the sense of dispossession that predominates, while in subsequent volumes Thomas's acknowledgment that an evergreen language is a thing of the past—if it ever existed—leads him to search for new avenues of communication with the absolute. He attempts, to use his own metaphor from the "Prayer" which sums up his later phase, to seek out and steal from the tree of science. His poems come to resemble those of the English metaphysicals in the deliberateness with which contemporary science and technology are yoked in the service of theological speculation. The new physics, space travel, and even film become sources of metaphor. Thus, in *Frequencies,* a volume which takes its title from physics, there is a poem called "The Film of God," in which the audience finds itself confronted with nothing but the "natural background" of God's picture: we see a bare landscape and hear only its natural sounds. A shadow falls across this image "as though / of an unseen writer bending over / his work," and as the spool turns we wait "for the figure that cast it / to come into view for us to / identify it." It does not do so, and as the film ends, "we are still waiting" (47).

The conceit here is new, though the theme is not. We are still in the world according to *H'm.* But in other poems from *Laboratories of the Spirit* and *Frequencies,* there is a real sense that with Thomas's new language, his rejection of primitivistic ideals of "greenness" and his acceptance of science, there is a fundamental change in attitude. The first poem in *Laboratories of the Spirit* is significantly entitled "Emerging":

> Not as in the old days I pray,
> God. My life is not what it was.
> Yours, too, accepts the presence of
> the machine? Once I would have asked
> healing. I go now to be doctored,
> to drink sinlessly of the blood
> of my brother, to lend my flesh
> as manuscript of the great poem
> of the scalpel. I would have knelt
> long, wrestling with you, wearing
> you down. Hear my prayer, Lord, hear
> my prayer. As though you were deaf, myriads
> of mortals have kept up their shrill

cry, explaining your silence by
their unfitness.

It begins to appear
this is not what prayer is about.
It is the annihilation of difference,
the consciousness of myself in you,
of you in me; the emerging
from the adolescence of nature
into the adult geometry
of the mind. I begin to recognize
you anew, God of form and number.
There are questions we are the solution
to, others whose echoes we must expand
to contain. Circular as our way
is, it leads not back to that snake-haunted
garden, but onward to the tall city
of glass that is the laboratory of the spirit.

(1)

This poem accomplishes a radical revision of Thomas's earlier views on language and the problem of communicating with God. Eden, that "snake-haunted garden," is abandoned as an ideal, and "nature," hitherto always viewed as the locus of fulfillment, is somewhat stigmatized by connection with the word "adolescence." Attempts to break through God's silence, to attain a language of plenitude, are dismissed as "not what prayer is about," and the perennially tormenting problem of dispossession is removed at a stroke: prayer, instead of arising from a consciousness of difference, must be based on the annihilation of difference. The loss of Eden and of a language able to take purchase on "the thing in itself" becomes far less troubling if, in fact, paradise is within. Thus Thomas writes that proper prayer is "the consciousness of myself in you, / of you in me."

This shift in perspective bypasses the whole question of God's intractibility to ordinary language by postulating first that the Word is "in" the speaker as he speaks, and second that true communication with the deity is not, in any case, verbal and outwardly directed, but silent and contemplative. Significantly, this poem which was placed so portentously on the first page of *Laboratories of the Spirit,* is omitted altogether from the *Later Poems 1972–1982,* perhaps because Thomas realized that it fudged what had always been the central question of his writings. In the later volume, *Between Here and Now,* there is a poem called "One Way," which affirms that, for this poet at least, there is no escaping the commitment to speech:

There was a frontier
I crossed whose passport
was human speech. Looking back
was to silence, to that
wood of hands fumbling
for the unseen thing. I
named it and it was
here. I held out words
to them and they smelled
them. Space gave, time was
eroded. There was one being
would not reply. God,
I whispered, refining
my technique, signalling
to him on the frequencies
I commanded. But always
amid the air's garrulousness
there was the one station
that remained closed.
                    Was
there an alternative
medium? There were some claimed
to be able to call him
down to drink insatiably
at the dark sumps of blood.

                    (95)

  • • •

Though in a number of Thomas's later poems scientific analogies do seem
to be forcing the speaker to redefine and reconceive the poet's central preoccupation—how to make God "give" to human speech—for the most
part, as in this example, they simply provide a fresh set of metaphors for its
expression. This poem asks whether the problem could be solved by the discovery of an "alternative medium" of communication, and the point is that
the language of science has proved to be no less deciduous, no less out of
touch with the deity, than the "green" language of Iago Prytherch. Indeed,
in many of Thomas's new poems, a confidence in the ability of science to
take hold of the infinite is presented as mortally dangerous:

    The scientists breach
    themselves with their Caesarian
    births, and we blame them for it.
    What shall we do

with the knowledge growing
into a tree that to shelter
under is to be lightning struck?
(*Later Poems,* 182)

In those last lines we have the image of the tree of science which, as Thomas tells us in his "prayer," he "sought and failed / to steal from." A sense of failure is there in Thomas's poems even from his first attempts to break with rustic idealism and march with science to the door of heaven, but it is articulated with resonant finality in these lines from "The Absence," one of the last poems in *Frequencies:*

I modernise the anachronism

of my language, but he is no more here
than before. Genes and molecules
have no more power to call
him up than the incense of the Hebrews

at their altars. My equations fail
as my words do. What resource have I
other than the emptiness without him of my whole
being, a vacuum he may not abhor?

(48)

This poem marks an important transition in Thomas's work, a reasoned abatement of that verbal hunger "for the thing in itself," and it points toward some of the new poems included in *Later Poems 1972– 1982,* where the poet seems content to wait upon his God. "Content" is perhaps not the best word, since the waiting is frequently a strenuous business, but there are a number of poems in which for the first time Thomas seems keen to accept the little his God gives him and to see it as plenitude. The irritable reaching after a language of immanence that has always marked Thomas's work is sometimes suppressed in these poems, and the point is made that communication with God occurs in His own time, cannot be forced, and makes use of unexpected channels. Thus, what is surely Thomas's most positive poem to date, "Suddenly":

Suddenly after long silence
he has become voluble.
He addresses me from a myriad
directions with the fluency
of water, the articulateness
of green leaves; and in the genes,
too, the components

of my existence. The rock,
so long speechless, is the library
of his poetry. He sings to me
in the chain-saw, writes
with the surgeon's hand
on the skin's parchment messages
of healing. The weather
is his mind's turbine
driving the earth's bulk round
and around on its remedial
journey. I have no need
to despair; as at
some second Pentecost
of a Gentile, I listen to the things
round me: weeds, stones, instruments,
the machine itself, all
speaking to me in the vernacular
of the purposes of One who is.

(Later Poems, 201)

"I have no need to despair" keeps despair a real possibility, despite the gathering mood of affirmation; this is not quite the rapture of a Hopkins, but it tends in that direction. While it would be misleading to suggest that this sort of poem is common in Thomas's work of the early eighties, the few such examples are striking because they have no precedents in almost thirty years of his published poetry. The sort of acceptance upon which they are based—that it is "our destiny / . . . to be outside" of God's communing with himself (*Later Poems*, 206), and that we must simply "Wait" (193)—is however, returned to again and again in the poems of that period. This commitment to time replaces the earlier poems' impatient search for "A green asylum from time's range," and it also provides Thomas with a solution to his specifically linguistic problem: what relation, if any, can there be between God and the words with which we attempt to describe him?

How this is so is made clear in one of Thomas's prose pieces from just after *Laboratories of the Spirit*. Originally an address given in Welsh at the National Eisteddfod in 1976, it incidentally reveals the quite remarkable extent to which his concern with language and immanence is bound up with the nationalistic concerns usually thought abandoned after 1972. His topic, he tells us, is "the whole problem of names, and words, and things, and the connection between them"—no minor matter, as he himself acknowledges in full awareness of trends in contemporary linguistics. But as is typical of Thomas, there follows no rebuttal or recapitulation of

Saussure. Instead, the discussion focuses on a single word from a Welsh poem by the bardic poet Llywarch Hen—"Abercuawg," a "town or village where the cuckoos sing" (*Selected Prose,* 155). Thomas tells us of his several failed attempts to find and visit the place to which the word refers: he manages to locate the historical site—where two rivers meeting were called *Cuog*—but he confesses that though it is "a very fine place," it is not what is signified to him by Llywarch Hen's Abercuawg.

• • •

After a brief and selective survey of linguistic theories, he moves from the "primitive" notion that "words are able to cast a spell on things and keep hold of them" (157) to the observation that "sometimes language succeeds too well": great writers, he says, sometimes create figures which "are more real than reality itself, as it were" (159). Hamlet is that sort of creation— "more alive than the various Robert Williamses or John Smiths of whose existence I have certain and unambiguous proof"—and so also, Thomas tentatively suggests, might be his own Iago Prytherch. If Abercuawg is in the same category, the question arises of what sort of existence the place can be said to have. Obviously, the world of fact—or "things," to use Thomas's own word—can supply nothing to go with the name, and for the poet this is an intolerable thought. "As a Welshman," he writes, "I see no meaning to my life if there is no such place as Abercuawg" (155). At first the essence of Welshness, Abercuawg gradually takes on Edenic significance, and by the end of the essay it is not only Thomas's cultural identity but also his Christian faith that depends on there being some satisfactory answer to the apparent truth that Abercuawg is nothing more than a name. Reading, we are witnesses to the drama of reason as Thomas forces his way through to a positive interpretation of what has always been for him an ineluctable and tormenting fact—that though we may have names for God and plenitude, that does not necessarily make them real.

The solution for him is to reject what the world of "fact" seems to tell us, to argue that searching for Abercuawg in the Welsh countryside is futile because what the word stands for is not real and static, but in a perpetual state of becoming. Paraphrasing Bergson, he suggests that "it is the function of the understanding to capture things as they are" (161), and points out that this makes the mind ill-equipped to grasp plenitude:

> And I am searching for the real Abercuawg, but I know, if I proceed along the wrong road, if I attempt to catch and comprehend it with the brain alone it will become ashes in my hand. In the words of that old Scottish verse:

I would not find,
For when I find, I know
I shall have clasped the wandering wind
and built a house of snow.

Is it then a matter of continuing the search? It seems so.

This, then, is Thomas's solution to the problem of whether—or in what
way—Abercuawg can be said to exist:

> . . . Abercuawg exists where the few become many, or the many few,
> that everlasting occasion which we can neither see nor comprehend,
> but which nevertheless compels our acceptance. We are searching,
> therefore, within time, for something which is above time, and yet
> which is ever on the verge of being.
>
> (163)

This acceptance of time has hopeful nationalistic implications—Wales need
not remain "brittle with relics" of its golden past, as Thomas described it
in 1952 (*Song,* 63), but may look to the future for fulfillment—and it also
has spiritual promise. "In accepting the process of becoming," Thomas
writes, "man realises that he is a created being":

> This is man's estate. He is always on the verge of comprehending
> God, but insomuch as he is a mortal creature, he never will. Nor will
> he ever see Abercuawg. . . .
>
> We come closer to discovering it . . . not through forming an image
> of it in our language, but through feeling it with our whole being.
>
> (*Selected Prose,* 164–65)

These sentences provide an answer, though not a solution, to the
three problems which have worried Thomas, and he has worried constantly,
since 1946: how God can be comprehended, His plenitude made accessi-
ble, and human language used so as to achieve both these ends. The message of the Abercuawg essay—that one should be consoled rather than
frustrated by the inability to grasp infinity by naming it—effectively proclaims Thomas's earlier combat with God "on the innocent marches / of
vocabulary" a futile exercise. But at the same time it is a vindication of that
struggle, since to receive consolation one must be constantly failing.

Conclusions of this sort must, to some extent, account for the
changed tone of those new poems in *Later Poems 1972–1982,* in which the
battle to forge a link between words and the Word is, if not over, carried
on rather conventionally. And the peace which prevails in certain of the
poems is inextricably bound up with the sense of defeat; it is an ascetic,

rather than a pleasurable contentment. The scars of battle are very much with Thomas in this work, where he has come to resemble the poet whose speculative portrait he painted in an early poem, "Llanrheadr Ym Mochnant":

> There is no portrait of him
> But in the gallery of
> The imagination: a brow
> With the air's feathers
> Spilled on it? A cheek
> Too hollow? rows of teeth
> Broken on the unmanageable bone
>
> Of language?
>
> (*Not*, 21)

• • •

A sense of past toil is strong in one of the last new pieces included in *Later Poems 1972–1982*, a poem significantly titled "Arrival." Here there is a lyrical, if chastened, simplicity, an openness to evocation surely derived from the suppression of that impatient verbal hunger for clear referentiality, the compulsion to make words apprehend things. And there is also the suggestion that what the earlier poems called a "green asylum from time's range" may be attained through an acceptance of time. A number of figures familiar from Thomas's verse before *H'm* reappear—the "green tree," notably—asking to be reexamined in this new climate of reconciliation. The poet's journey, it is revealed, has been a circular one, but with the adjustment in perspective represented by the Abercuawg essay, its continuation promises to be infinitely more rewarding. While in the earlier poems, plenitude was always to be irritably sought, here it discloses itself as a gift:

> Not conscious
>   that you have been seeking
>   suddenly
>   you come upon it
>
> the village in the Welsh hills
>   dust free
>   with no road out
> but the one you came in by.
>
>   A bird chimes
>   from a green tree

```
the hour that is no hour
    you know. The river dawdles
to hold a mirror for you
where you may see yourself
    as you are, a traveller
    with the moon's halo
above him, who has arrived
after long journeying where he
    began, catching this
one truth by surprise
that there is everything to look forward to.
                              (Later Poems, 203)
```

There is a risk of overestimating the potency of this conclusion. The title, "Arrival," suggests relief and finality, and the rhetorical currents which weave through the whole do carry you inexorably to a kind of crest in that final line. But the fact remains that the revelation of the end is explicitly an unexpected one; it is articulated in self-consciously banal terms ("there is everything to look forward to"); and these things together tend to prevent the revelation as it is described from quite eclipsing the protracted difficulties endured in achieving it. The ending of this poem—and the philosophical resolution which the work as a whole is attempting to realize—is in other words deeply problematic.

The difficulties which afflict Thomas's newly arrived-at consolation become the focus of the volume which has recently appeared, appropriately entitled *Experimenting with an Amen*. Here, the poet is frank about his dissatisfaction with the kind of revelation described in "Arrival" and "Suddenly": "God," he writes in "Cones," "it is not your reflections / we seek, wonderful as they are / in the live fibre" (*Experimenting*, 3). The "presence" of God is still what man really needs, and oblique revelation is at best a mild consolation, at worst a kind of teasing:

FOLK TALE

```
Prayers like gravel
    flung at the sky's
window, hoping to attract
            the loved one's
attention. But without
    visible plaits to let
down for the believer
            to climb up,
```

to what purpose open
    that far casement?
        I would
have refrained long since
    but that peering once
through my locked fingers
I thought that I detected
    the movement of a curtain.

(53)

What strikes one most about *Experimenting with an Amen* is Thomas's absolute refusal to accept as a conclusion what is, for him, painfully inconclusive. Movements in the curtain of creation, though for some sufficient to sustain a life of pious contentment, are for him tormenting, even in their pleasure. In those promising new poems from *Later Poems 1972–1982*, pleasure in God's "reflections . . . in the live fibre" fuels the rhetoric of affirmation. But as we have seen, an intellectual awareness of what must be endured for the sake of such rare insights exerts a powerfully dampening influence. In *Experimenting with an Amen*, the possibility of attaining a Hopkinsian rapture in the face of the universe is almost wholly discounted. The volume does seem to have arrived at certain conclusions founded upon a kind of acceptance, but it is an acceptance considerably less ingenuous and optimistic than that which characterizes poems like "Suddenly" and "Arrival." It can be traced back to the Abercuawg essay and to the implication there that a constantly failing struggle with the absolute is, if not the means to success, then as satisfactory a spiritual—and poetic—state as man can attain. The new poems of *Later Poems 1972–1982* flirted with the idea of ceasing the struggle in a gesture of faith and patience, which would paradoxically effect a reconciliation with the divine. In Thomas's most recent poems, that resolution has evidently been reconsidered. In "Revision," which is thematically the center of *Experimenting with an Amen*, the speaker carries on a dialogue with his catechist, asserting that man and God, language and the tree of eternity, are as far apart as ever:

". . . there are two beings
so that, when one is present, the other
is far off. There is no room
for them both."
        "Life's simpleton,
know this gulf you have created
can be crossed by prayer. Let me hear
if you can walk it."

"I have walked it.
It is called silence, and is a rope
                over an unfathomable
abyss, which goes on and on
never arriving."
                "So that your Amen
is unsaid. Know, friend, the arrival
is the grace given to maintain
your balance, the power which supplies
not the maggot of flame you desired,
that consumes the flesh, but the unseen
current between two points, coming
to song in the nerves, as in the telegraph
wires, the tighter that they are drawn."
                                    (22–23)

• • •

One is struck by that last image because its implications are so radically different from those attached to a related one in the poem "Suddenly." There God is said to "sing" to the speaker "in the chain saw." Here, however, the speaker is not a passive auditor, nor is the song remote; it is produced by the agitation of his own nerves, becoming more vibrant as they are stretched to the breaking point. The contrast sums up Thomas's movement from the early to the mid-eighties, a shift from a rather willed and potentially sentimental delight in the salutary beauty of God's dappled things, to a more rigorous valorization of doubt. In terms of Thomas's career as a whole, that movement represents a return (though not a regression) to past assumptions—particularly those of 1976 and the Abercuawg essay. Whereas "Arrival" and "Suddenly" seemed to embrace the principal message of that essay—man will never comprehend God—with an instant slackening of intellectual and emotional tension, *Experimenting with an Amen* revives it by a re-infusion of tension, an acknowledgment that the solution it represents is a sentence of further suffering.

The end of a life devoted to taking purchase on the infinite is shown to be a failure; indeed, "your Amen / is unsaid"—prayers and supplications cannot ever be concluded. Instead, the arrival, the ultimate attainment, is the ability (a God-given "grace") to survive in a state of doubt and dispossession. "Man's meaning," another poem hints, is

. . . in the keeping of himself
afloat over seventy thousand
fathoms, tacking against winds

coming from no direction,
going in no direction. . . .

(*Experimenting*, 32)

God manifests himself only in this kind of human struggle. "Revision" tells us that he is the "unseen current" generated by the combining in man of fleshly limitation and transcendent aspiration; he does not appear in "the maggot of flame . . . that consumes the flesh," "unmanning" man, to use Thomas's own word from "Testimonies" (*Experimenting*, 4).

This acceptance of the physicality (and hence the limitation) of human existence has ramifications throughout Thomas's latest volume. While earlier collections, particularly those before 1972, tended to denigrate a life of exclusive physicality—we remember the earthy peasant said to "pick a bare bone of life"—the body is here treated with pathos, and even sometimes as a repository for wisdom, a source of modest inspiration. Just as Thomas tended to use the word "green" as a token of integration, he focuses the notion of physicality on the word "bone." In the first poem of the collection, he imagines the soul "refrigerating / under the nuclear winter" "in its bone tent"; the body is protective of the spirit, and it appears all the more positive and sympathetic because what it is protecting the spirit against is the scientific "after- / birth of thought: $E=mc^2$" (*Experimenting*, 1). In other poems, the speaker is urged to put his trust in "the bone's wisdom" (14); ghosts are "boneless presences" (26); evolution is man's "ascent by a bone / ladder" (9); time is the "bone / on which all have beaten out / their message to the mind / that would soar" (28). The connection between "bone" and time is more elaborate in "Countering," where time and timelessness, the physical and the spiritual, are shown to be implicated in the sort of dialectic which "Revision" sees as man's ultimate "arrival":

Then take my hand that is
of the bone the island
is made of, and looking at
me say what time it is
on love's face, for we have
no business here other than
to disprove certainties the clock knows.

(33)

"Llanrheadr Ym Mochnant," we recall, described language as a bone, and from this perspective it is clear that that was intended to indicate much more than the mere hardness and intractibility of words. In Thomas's universe, "bone" betokens an absolute and inescapable connection with time and matter. A poet whose commitment is to "disprove" those non-spiritual "certainties" inherent in the medium, to take hold on the nature of his God, is bound to find the bone unmanageable. But the point made in Thomas's latest book is that he must keep on chewing. This painful act is in its own way sacramental.

Note

1. Since this article was written, Thomas has published *Welsh Airs,* a collection of his old and new poems on Welsh subjects. The volume, placed not with Macmillan (his usual publisher) but with Poetry Wales Press, draws together poems that are, however interesting, tangential to the present concerns of his poetry. In 1985 Poetry Wales Press brought out a similar volume, *Ingrowing Thoughts,* which showcased another of Thomas's interests, namely the relation between poetry and the visual arts.

Works Cited

Abbs, Peter. "The Revival of the Mythopoeic Imagination—A Study of R. S. Thomas and Ted Hughes," *Poetry Wales* 10:4 (1975). Rpt. Anstey 99–115.

Allchin, A. M. "Emerging: A Look at Some of R. S. Thomas's More Recent Poems," *Theology* 81:683 (1978). Rpt. Anstey 117–29.

Anstey, Sandra, ed. *Critical Writings on R. S. Thomas.* Bridgend: Poetry Wales Press, 1982.

Mole, John. "Signals from the Periphery," *TLS* 2 June 1978. Rpt. Anstey 131–36.

Thomas, Edward. *Collected Poems.* London: Faber and Faber, 1949.

Thomas, R. S. *Song at the Year's Turning.* London: Rupert Hart-Davis, 1955.

———. *Poetry for Supper.* London: Rupert Hart-Davis, 1958.

———. *The Bread of Truth.* London: Rupert Hart-Davis; Chester Springs: Dufour Editions, 1963.

———. *Not That He Brought Flowers.* London: Rupert Hart-Davis, 1968.

———. *H'm.* London: Macmillan, 1972.

———. *Selected Poems 1946–1968.* London: Hart-Davis, MacGibbon, 1973.

———. *Laboratories of the Spirit.* London: Macmillan, 1975.

———. *Frequencies.* London: Macmillan, 1978.

———. *Between Here and Now.* London: Macmillan, 1981.

————. *Later Poems 1972-1982*. London: Macmillan, 1983.

————. *Selected Prose*. Ed. Sandra Anstey. Bridgend: Poetry Wales Press, 1983.

————. *Ingrowing Thoughts*. Bridgend: Poetry Wales Press, 1985.

————. *Experimenting with an Amen*. London: Macmillan, 1986.

————. *Welsh Airs*. Bridgend: Poetry Wales Press, 1987.

Wilson, Timothy. "R. S. Thomas." *The Guardian* 15 September 1972. Rpt. Anstey 65–71.

"Pessimism and Its Counters"

Between Here and Now and **After**[1]

James A. Davies

R. S. Thomas was sixty-eight when he published *Between Here and Now.* That its main section, "Impressions," consisted of poems about paintings was not wholly unexpected. Thomas's wife is the painter Mildred E. Eldridge; he has always been interested in art. From *The Bread of Truth* (1963) onwards he has written poems about specific artistic creations: "Souillac: Le Sacrifice d'Abraham," for example, is a response to the carving around the main door of the abbey church at Souillac in the Dordogne. Poems about "Degas: Woman Combing" and "Veneziano: The Annunciation" are included in *Laboratories of the Spirit* (1975). What is remarkable is that R. S. Thomas should decide to write a sequence. For, of the thirteen volumes preceding *Between Here and Now* the only deviation from the individual poem is *What Is a Welshman?* (1974), Thomas's most unsuccessful volume, a slight series of sour attempts to answer the title's questions.

"Impressions" consists of thirty-three short lyric responses to French impressionist paintings; on each left-hand page is a black-and-white reproduction, on each right-hand page a poem.[2] Thomas's choice of paintings in itself has thematic significance. The first three are, in order, Monet's "Lady with a Parasol," Jongkind's "The Beach at Sainte-Adresse" and Monet's "The Bas-Bréau Road." In all three the central feature—the lady, a boat, the road—merges with its surroundings. This fosters a sense of the lady as one of a series of objects, a view supported by her lack of facial characterization, and highlights the slightly disturbing relationship between the human (and the manmade) and its environment, the latter tending to overwhelm the former. The effect, particularly of "Lady with a Parasol," is of oppressive loneliness, this last accentuated by the enforced viewing stance: the viewer does not identify with the lady or become involved in the scenes, but remains distanced, looking at or into the pictures.

This three-picture introduction is to a lonely world of caught moments. Rarely is there any sense of friendship or personal involvement. Members of groups, even of families, stare away from each other and out of the picture, as in Bazille's "Family Reunion" and Manet's "The Balcony." In Cézanne's "The Card Players" both concentrate on their cards. Even a professional relationship is hard to sustain: in Degas's "The Dancing Class," apart from one impassively staring ballerina, the pupils ignore the old ballet-master. In Toulouse-Lautrec's "Jane Avril Dancing" the dancer turns her back on her audience, a couple who stare sternly elsewhere. Only in Renoir's "The Bathers," the final picture of the sequence, is there personal contact beyond the obviously physical; to this last picture (and its poem) this essay will return.

Intensifying this sense of alienation are three recurring motifs: the ineffectual church, empty country places and small villages, peasants and their urban successors. In a number of pictures the church tends to merge with or be dominated by its surroundings; the country places convey a still-ness that is more disturbing than idyllic; peasants and successors are reminders of the harsh reality of a working-class life that is in stark con-trast to the style and beauty of the bourgeois scenes.

To the general sadness of the sequence, to its general sense of ossification, there are only six exceptions. Degas's "The Musicians in the Orchestra" conveys the brilliant energy of the ballet; a train puffs power-fully through "The Gare Saint-Lazare"; Arab dancers sway and swirl in Renoir's "Muslim Festival at Algiers"; Van Gogh's half-demented vision makes the church at Auvers tremble violently; Jane Avril pirouettes self-sufficiently; Cézanne, in "The Repentant Magdalen," offers a mysterious, ambiguous portrayal of what seems to be Mary Magdalen at the foot of the Cross, her body tense with anguish, her profiled face showing anguish softening into calm.

The three recurring motifs block off alternatives by exposing their inadequacies: religious faith cannot assert itself, life in nature can be far from idyllic, the life of simple toil produces weariness and can brutalize. The six exceptions comment powerfully on the world that remains. In such a world, energy and force find expression only in risqué entertainment, new technology, colorful alien ceremonies, deep religious feeling, and on the fringes of insanity. Technology and insanity apart—though these may well suggest social strain and stress—the exceptions involve physical and erotic pleasure. The repentant harlot, in particular, bears witness to submerged sexual need.

The paintings hint at a decadent society whose members, whatever their class, behind their facades so often desire sensual stimulation. It thus seems appropriate that the final paintings of the sequence begin to suggest a moral conclusion. In "Rouen Cathedral, Full Sunshine" bright light overwhelms the building; this picture is followed by Rousseau's "The Snake Charmer," Thomas's penultimate choice, in which a sinister piper plays in a strange tropical wilderness. Together, these two pictures appear to demonstrate a loveless, lonely world rejecting the spiritual and embracing dark depravity. But the final painting, Renoir's "The Bathers," suggests, as Bazin notes, "a state of pristine innocence," with the bathers "soaking in a kind of primordial mud. . . . The same glowing fluid circulates in their bodies as in those Eden-like meadows."[3] The uneasy merging of the sequence's first three pictures is replaced by harmony between the human and the natural, alienation by intimacy, the frozen by healthful vigor. The sequence ends, unexpectedly and powerfully, with a sudden glimpse of an ideal world.

• • •

Thomas's choice of paintings creates a disturbing vision of human society on which his poems comment and to which they respond. The essentials of that response can be discerned in the introductory poem, "Lady with a Parasol."

It consists of four stanzas each of four irregular lines. Each stanza is linked to the next through the continuation of a sentence that begins in the preceding stanza. The reader's awareness of the sentences—as distinct from the stanzas—is increased by the poem's lack of capital letters: the poem begins with a capital, each sentence begins with one, but the lines do not. The poem's argument proceeds from sentence to sentence and not from stanza to stanza. The stress on the sentence thus generates tension between it and the stanza, or, to put it another way, between the irregular entity and the formal unit. The former impels the poem toward fragmentation—the poem breaking up into a series of sentences—the latter struggles to impose order through stanzaic form.

The poem opens with a question followed by three categorical statements. Through the latter a certainty accumulates that continues into the final sentence:

> But that arm
> is sturdy, the carriage
> erect, the bust ample enough
> for a peasant to lay his
> head there, dreaming of harvest.

But in this sentence two heavily stressed clauses are followed by a final statement in which further emphasis is replaced by a lyricism that quickly fades into the feminine effects of "dreaming of harvest." The lack of a strong climax goes some way toward undermining that earlier confidence; the poem ends slightly tentatively, slightly uneasily.

We, too, must be uneasy because of that lack of stress and because of our sense of the poem's narrator. For the latter begins disturbingly:

> Why keep the sun
> from the head, when the grass
> is a fire about
> the feet?

The four definite articles are crucial in the reduction of the lady to an object. And though that lady begins out of doors and ends in bed with a man, the narrator's attitude does not change: the lady remains a number of bodily parts, a source of physical comfort for a "peasant" whose mind is elsewhere. The narrator is neither compassionate nor involved but cold, austere, cynical. His measured, formal, slightly-archaic language—"concocts," "sturdy," "carriage," "bust," "ample"—acts as a distancing barrier. He implies a reader whose opinion is not sought and who seems willing to be passive. The narrator asks the question and confidently—until the final wavering—asserts his own answer.

The clash between fragment and form, the final uneasiness, the awkward relationship between assertive narrator and intended reader, in themselves dramatize central themes. In the poem's very first sentence, already quoted, the grassy fire around the lady's feet points to human/natural opposition. That notion is underlined in the second sentence, in its concern with offense—"She wields her umbrella"—and defense, the umbrella becoming a "shield" against "summer's unreal missiles." The lady and her setting struggle one against the other. Rather than harmony the poem portrays division and break-up that are echoed in the poem's main structural clash.

Further, the poem is concerned with posturing, with suggestive/deceptive appearance. The lady's parasol is

> a borrowing
> from the mystery shadow
> concocts

and, as such, for the narrator, a pointer to the creative power of art. The parasol is also a pretense of effeminacy, a veneer of "fashion" behind which, the narrator suggests, may be a basic earthiness and compliant sexuality. Appearances may be deceptive and the poem's prosodic pattern—through which initial confidence declines into that final tentativeness—dramatizes the difficulty of knowing. And the narrator's uncertain relationship with his intended reader mirrors, and so underlines, the real reader's similar uncertainty about the lady. It becomes appropriate that this introductory poem does not celebrate successful human contacts.

• • •

"Lady with a Parasol" is followed by three poems that, together, enact a movement away from ordering form. "The Beach at Sainte-Adresse" preserves the four-line stanza but almost wholly subsumes the force of the stanza form within sentences that are, in comparison with "Lady with a Parasol," syntactically more complex and convoluted:

> However skilfully
> the blue surface mirrors
>
> the sky, to the boat it is
> the glass lid of a coffin
> within which by cold lips
> the wooden carcases are mumbled.

The stanza division is simply not apparent to the reader carefully negotiating the sentence's deepening structure. In "The Bas-Bréau Road" stanzas become paragraphs to accommodate the dominant sentence. In "Family Reunion," the fourth poem in the sequence, the sentence itself is threatened by short, staccato lines that highlight the clause and the phrase. "Portrait of a Young Woman," however, restores the power of the sentence. "Portrait of Madame Gaudibert" struggles to accommodate sentences within stanzas only for both to hover, momentarily and disconcertingly, on the brink of incoherence:

> Comforting
> to think how, for a moment
> at least, Monet on even

```
        keel paddled himself
        on with strokes not
                of an oar but
        of a fast-dipping brush.
```

The qualifying phrase, "for a moment / at least," the negative held in suspension by the line break and typographical arrangement, hinder progression and prevent the sentence [from] asserting its complete shape. The poem that follows, "Mademoiselle Dihau at the Piano," is a single verse-paragraph in which five sentences retain their forceful shape through shortening lines. It preceded the eighth poem, "Musicians in the Orchestra," which marks a return to the four-line stanzas of the first two poems. Such stanzas, here, contain with difficulty a single strong sentence.

Indeed, a sense of difficulty dominates these eight poems. Form is strained, order under pressure, the poems impelled toward the separation of their parts before regaining some measure of stanzaic control. That control—the ordering effect of the four-line stanza—is more strongly exerted in the twelve poems from "Musicians in the Orchestra" through "The Bridge at Maincy." All but two have the basic stanza form. The exceptions are "The Repentant Magdalen," in which the response to intense religious feeling is reflected in a staccato sequence of clauses and phrases, and "The Gare Saint-Lazare," where technological achievement at first finds appropriate style:

```
        The engines
            are ready to start,
        but why travel
            where they are aimed
        at?
```

The disjoined lines, the isolated word, subvert the sentence and insist on the fragment.

From "The Card Players" onwards—the final fourteen poems—only four poems are in four-line stanzas. In "The Card Players" sentences give way to phrases made strange and partly incoherent through intrusive typography:

```
        The pipe without
        smoke, the empty
        bottle, the light
        on the wall are the clock
        they go by.
            Only their minds
            lazily as flies
            drift
```

"Women Ironing" shows vividly the sequence's increasing concern to portray the disconnected:

> one hand
>   on cheek the other
> on the bottle
>   mouth open
> her neighbour
>   with hands clasped
> not in prayer . . .

The poem, deprived of punctuation, of all capitals, even, as here, of constant grammatical coherence, breaks into pieces.

"The Card Players" and "Women Ironing" are examples of the impulse toward formlessness that strengthens through these later poems and leads to the three poems that—like the final three paintings—combine into a conclusion. "Rouen Cathedral, Full Sunshine" generates tension between sentence and line: the short, quickening lines strive to detach themselves from the sentences that contain them. "The Snake Charmer" is an unexpected return to the four-line stanza, an ordered response to a prelapsarian world. That glimpse of order is quickly replaced by the collapsing structures of "The Bathers." In this, the closing poem, a first impression of tumbling, neo-Skeltonic lines gives way before the power of the glittering, suggestive fragment—"Here is flesh," "naked / for us to gaze / our fill on," or "This / is the mind's feast"—that defies line arrangement, resists sentence progression, and is the poem's basic unit. The final sentence provides a brilliantly appropriate conclusion to the poem and to the sequence:

> These bodies,
> smooth as bells
>   from art's stroking, toll
> an unheard music,
>   keep such firmness
> of line as never,
>   under the lapping
> of all this light
>   to become blurred or dim.

The sentence becomes phrases, the line arrangement creates incoherent moments, the stress pattern exposes, by slightly detaching, such individual words as, for example, "bells," "toll," "firmness," "lapping," "blurred." Here, as throughout the sequence of poems, the effect is intensely and fittingly visual. The reader's last and strongest impression is of insistent fragmentation.

And any lingering sense of formal order is further undermined by the sound of most endings, by fading cadences, uncertain emphases that deny climax and firm shaping. In this respect "Lady with a Parasol" is typical; few poems in this sequence have sharp, emphatic last lines. "The Beach at Sainte-Adresse," "Portrait of Dr. Gachet," "Rouen Cathedral, Full Sunshine," and "The Bathers" are among poems that end with words or phrases—"mumbled," "diagnosis," "flown," "blurred or dim"—that defy stressing. The ending of "The Bas-Bréau Road" is a good example of how Thomas can brilliantly use other technical devices to support the final faltering:

> It has the quietness of time
> before the first motor-car
> startled it, worrying it
> with such ideas as
> that there are destinations.

In this sequence the complex sentence winding its way through closing lines is a favorite Thomas usage. Here, as it winds, Thomas, as it were, "de-poetizes" it: the unpleasing sibilance of "ideas as," the syntactical and alliterative awkwardness of "as / that there," are two ways in which progression is hindered, lyricism resisted, and a crescendo prevented.

Such endings not only contribute to our sense of formlessness but also dramatize the narrator's persisting uncertainty and so deepen our awareness of his character. As the sequence proceeds we penetrate his apparent detachment. For example, the use, in most of the poems, of the first-person plural, is at first the voice of authority:

> We watch them. They watch
> what? The world passes,
> they remain, looking
> as they were meant to do
> at a spectacle
> beyond us.

Again and again this procedure is adopted: the narrator asks his question, provides his own answer, assumes the agreement, even collusion, of his reader. But authoritative confidence accumulates into over-insistence. Constant assertions in themselves become expressions of uncertainty, even before the endings.

Only two poems are in the first-person singular, and each affords direct insight into the narrator's character. "Portrait of a Young Woman" opens in mid-conversation:

I imagine he intended
other things: tonal
values, the light and shade
of her cheek.

           To me innocence
is its meaning.

The narrator opposes his moral concern to the implied aestheticism of his
reader. But that morality is essentially cynical: to the narrators the young
woman's innocence and youth make her a temptress who will inevitably
provoke and desire sexual violation.

"Kitchen Garden, Trees in Bloom," the second first-person singular
poem, begins a celebration of rural life that is quickly undermined in
stanza two:

I know the dry smell
    of sunlight in rooms
where the clock's insect
    aggravates the hour.

Rural beauty deceives; reality is arid and tedious. This the narrator knows,
whereas his reader, the poem implies, responds conventionally to the har-
monious and idyllic suggestiveness of orchards in springtime.

In these two poems the narrator's reader is essentially naive, invariably deceived by appearances. The narrator, however, here and throughout, is deeply suspicious of a world in which appearance and reality rarely
appear to coincide: The "Lady with a Parasol" makes a "pretence /
at effeminacy"; the "blue surface" of Jongkind's sea is really "the glass lid of
a coffin"; the confident masks of Bazille's bourgeois family "challenge /
us to find / where they failed"; "Madame Gaudibert" waits to play a part;
the "Young Woman Sewing" inhabits a "chrysalis"; "La Belle Angèle"
only seems demure; "Justine Dieuhl" may not be modest.

All surfaces are masks. Behind them, asserts the narrator in this poetic
response to the paintings' suggestions of religion in decline and consequent
decadence, is a fallen world. In three early poems this notion is given
explicit force and wider mythic power through reference to Eden. In
"Family Reunion" the rich bourgeois figures are

In groups
    under the tree,
none of them sorry
for having partaken
    of its knowledge.

In "Portrait of a Young Woman" the woman is herself a tree behind whose innocence "temptation can shelter." The seemingly unattainable Mademoiselle Dihau is a "mellow-fleshed, / sun-polished fruit."

The narrator's fallen world smoulders with sexual activity, either actual—Bazille's servants "out of sight / snatching a moment / to beget offspring"—or suggested through provocative gesture—Renoir's Muslim dancers like cockerels "rampant upon a background / of dung." Or, as so often, it is latent: the young woman awaiting arousal; the "Young Woman Sewing," who, in lines that include a startling play on "period," expects to leave her "chrysalis" and "spread her wings"; "La Belle Angèle," whose "other self" is "the cat-like image" that is sensual as well as violent.

The world, behind its facades, seems to quiver on the edge of sexual anarchy like the musicians in Degas's orchestra who retain self-control only by being forced to look away from

> the skirts' rising and falling
> that turns men to swine.

And as the sequence proceeds and sexual references accumulate—such as the woman in "Absinthe" waiting for inevitable intercourse, and Jane Avril's intimations of a sexual "heaven"—the narrator himself, despite his affected detachment, betrays his own involvement:

> The hands,
> large enough for encircling
> the waist's stem, are,
>   as ours should be, in
> perfect repose, not accessory
> to the plucking of her own flower.

Justine Dieuhl is reduced to a vulnerable flower-object that, through lingering, near-salacious rhythms, becomes the passive stimulator of the narrator's desire to violate.

Because the narrator ultimately lacks confidence in appearances and is disturbed, consciously and subconsciously, by the reality he discerns, we can understand his desperate glances at other possibilities. One such "glance" is "The Repentant Magdalen" poem that posits escape through repentance, through Christ's love that will "clear the flesh of / its offences" and deprive the sexual life of all importance. Another is "Landscape at Chaponval," which considers a more secular idyll:

> It would be good to live
> in this village with time

stationary and the clouds
going by.

Always there is "art," either in comforting opposition to newfan-
gledness, as when the figures in "The Edge of the Village" exchange

progress without a murmur
for the leisureliness of art,

or as "recuperation / from time" in "Kitchen Garden, Trees in Bloom."
Of "Women Ironing" the narrator feels able to write that

this is art
overcoming permanently
the temptation to answer
a yawn with a yawn.

Art is "a sacrament / in itself" and, in "The Alyscamps at Arles," more
inspiring and compelling than fading religion; it can offer a "diagnosis," as
it does of Dr. Gachet. It is at once a refuge, a consoling transformer of
reality, a source of immortality.

But the desperation in these glances at the religious life, rural bliss,
and the consolation of art, is only too apparent. The rejection of the sexual in "The Repentant Magdalen" is not only unconvincing beside the
erotic content of "Young Woman Sewing" and "Justine Dieuhl," but the
attempts at calm assertion—"She loved / much, so is free / of remorse," or
"What she repents of / is no matter"—are at odds with the formlessness
toward which the poem as a whole is impelled. The resulting tension dramatizes the possibility of break-up, of anarchic collapse, rather than a
notion of spiritual serenity. As for rural bliss: the Chaponval poem is, of
course, no more than wish fulfilment. As for art: the narrator turns *that* into
a cosy construct in which he struggles to believe. He writes, of the
anguished, repentant Magdalen, that

The painter
standing aside has shown
us eternity's rainbow
after the human storm.

An approach to experience that does not disturb, that does not penetrate,
is hardly art. The triteness of these lines and, in particular, of their central
"rainbow" image, is a clear demonstration that the narrator's desperate
glances are no more than attempts to evade a decadent and confusing world.

This evasion dominates the three-poem conclusion. As Monet's cathedral is overwhelmed by glaring sunlight and the poem, again, threatens structural collapse, the narrator tries to turn his poem into an expression of faith, and attempts to catch

> the excitement of migrants
> newly arrived from a tremendous
> presence.

The poem's closing decline into the flatly tentative wholly undermines his endeavors. To Rousseau's "The Snake Charmer" the narrator responds with an evocation of paradise and of the "innocence" of the piper's music that is at odds with the threatening, snake-filled world and bestial figure. Finally, the narrator attempts to celebrate the ideal world of Renoir's "The Bathers," only for the force of his moralistic assertions—for example, the bathers are "naked / for us to gaze / our fill on, but / without lust"—to be undermined not only by our sense of a disordered world implicit in the tumbling lines and fragmented form, but also by the narrator's continual and inadvertent revelation of his powerful sensuality:

> These bodies,
> smooth as bells
> from art's stroking, toll
> an unheard music.

In the face of such vicarious fondling the narrator's platonic posturing remains far from convincing.

• • •

Thomas's choice and arrangement of paintings speak bleakly of a decadent world. Their references to sexual need, to submerged sexuality, are developed, in the poems, into a powerful portrayal of the potentially anarchic sexual force, the surging impulse toward chaos, that lies close to the seemingly urbane and peaceful surfaces of a fallen world. The narrator's futile evasions demonstrate that, for him, it is impossible to escape the innate fleshly instinct.

Such intense pessimism is also found in *Ingrowing Thoughts,* Thomas's second sequence of poems about pictures, which he published in 1985, aged seventy-two. Here the pictures are modern, often surrealistic, typified by Picasso's "Guernica," Matisse's "Portrait of a Girl in a Yellow Dress," Chagall's "Lilac above the River," Magritte's "The Red Model" and Dali's "Drawing." As with "Impressions," the volume is an integrated sequence, generating meaning through juxtaposition and relationship, recurring motifs and developing themes.

This is not to say that no picture-and-poem can stand on its own; one that certainly does is "Lilac above the River":

> A vase large enough
> for the tree of life
> where Adam consoles
> Eve for her breasts' apples
>
> spherical as the moon over
> the river of knowledge
> he has built his house by.
> Their geometry was her ruin.

Here is much to praise, such as the artistry that allows the bleak finality of the closing line to undermine the rhythmic drive of that first long sentence, the familiar Thomas procedure of creating tension between sentence and stanza as the latter imposes momentary incoherence upon the former, plus the startling use of "geometry" that does much to reduce Chagall's disturbing but powerful romanticism to the sterility of lust.

But "Lilac above the River" gains greatly when read in context. It links, for example, with Thomas's use of the Eden myth in "L'Abbaye de Chartre" and "Drawing," this use reflecting his central concern, here as in "Impressions," with sexuality as a destructive, anarchic force. Further, the stanza-form of this poem, four unrhymed lines, together with its appearance on the page, is one instance of Thomas's continuing interest, throughout this later sequence, in poetry's visual meaning, in the effect—on, for example, line endings—of typographical arrangement. In "Impressions" poetic form fragments into glittering "impressions" that reinforce our sense of a disordered world; in *Ingrowing Thoughts* the constant regrouping and rearranging of words reflects and comments on the disturbing inconsequentiality of existence that is central to the surrealist vision.

Thomas thus re-explores earlier ideas; he does this again in his continuing ambiguous response to God and faith. The ineffectual church of "Impressions" recurs in *Ingrowing Thoughts,* when, for example, Thomas writes, in "Father and Son," that "Heaven is far off, back / of the bombed town," or, in "The Oracle," that

> life in the end
> is profane, our worshipping

done in the cemetery
of a blackboard.

Yet *Ingrowing Thoughts* differs from "Impressions" in stressing two additional themes. One begins "Guernica," and so opens the sequence:

The day before
    it was calm.
In the days after
    a new masterpiece
was born of imagination's wandering
    of the smashed city.

Sudden destruction, the increasingly tenuous relationship between the past and the present, the questioning of both synchronic and diachronic coherence, are not wholly new ideas in Thomas's work. They develop from his exploration of the importance and continuing effect of history and tradition in such early poems as, for example, "Welsh Landscape" and "A Welshman to Any Tourist." But these ideas have never before been expressed by Thomas with such pessimistic power or range of reference, as is evident, again, in his poem on John Selby Bigge's "Composition":

In the foreground the wreckage
    of the old world, tossed
spars, agitated waters,
                reefs, shoals—
    nobody to blame.

Secondly, the "smashed city" reference and the "Guernica" poem as a whole begin the sequence's preoccupation with the violence of modern war. This is the subject of one of its finest poems, that on Ben Shahn's "Father and Child," already quoted in part, in which old certainties are "displaced" by modern realities:

Times change:
no longer the virgin
ample-lapped; the child fallen
in it from an adjacent heaven.

Heaven is far off, back
of the bombed town.

The theme can be found, again, in, for example, the response to Magritte's "On the Threshold of Liberty" and in the final picture, Diana Brinton Lee's "Drawing by a Child," in which—a brilliant touch by the sequence selector—the explosive doodles recall the images and visual arrangement of Picasso's "Guernica."

The title of *Ingrowing Thoughts* reminds us of the extent to which the volume reflects nagging problems and troubles. Like its predecessor, "Impressions," the sequence invariably disturbs. Together, these two sets of poems about paintings represent Thomas at his grimmest, his most pessimistic and despairing. Yet his narrators, with all their futile evasions, are neither the real readers nor the poet. The distinctions are crucial. That *we* understand, that R. S. Thomas enables us to understand, the narrator's predicament, is a consoling indication that those worlds of paintings and poems may exist as salutary examples and not as the only ways of living.

This sense of possible alternatives to Thomas's blackness is a pointer to aspects of his later work. Throughout his seventies he has retained the capacity to surprise. Of course, old preoccupations persist: for example, he continues to agonize over the absence of God, over the fact that, as one commentator has written, "the times are out of touch with religion" and that Thomas's "problem in verse is to show that religion is not out of touch with the times."[4] Indeed, the problem is a great one and the poetic wrestlings of his old age are sometimes "terrible" in the manner of Hopkins. He finds his own "cliffs of fall"[5] in "Revision":

> "Life's simpleton,
> know this gulf you have created
> can be crossed by prayer. Let me hear
> if you can walk it."
>   "I have walked it.
> It is called silence, and is a rope
>   over an unfathomable
> abyss, which goes on and on
> never arriving."
>   (*EA*, 22)

Or, again, in "Strands":

> Is there a far side
> to an abyss, and can our wings
> take us there?
>   (*EA*, 32)

We are reminded of this "gulf" and of this "abyss," in "Song," when a survivor of the modern age is urged to "dance / at the grave's edge" (*EA*, 27) and we recognize both chasms as ways to death. Most disturbingly, dropping past "cliffs of fall" might be the only way to God or, even, what it means to be with God: "Father, I said . . . there are precipices / within you." (*C*, 53)

That said, in the later work of this old and austerely turbulent priest are powerfully positive assertions. Moss on a grave stone allows the idea of resurrection,

> of a dove daily
> returning from its journey
> over the dark waters
> with green in its bill.
>
> (*ERS*, 43)

"The Fly" ends perhaps more positively than any earlier poem, by referring to

> the dust they say
> man came from and to which,
> I say, he will not return.
>
> (*EA*, 8)

And in *Counterpoint* (1990), in a reference to those who outlive the machine culture of the present, Thomas balances Christian joy and suffering in a manner rarely found in his early work:

> They will return
> without moving to an innocence
> as in advance of their knowledge
> as the smile of the Christ child was of its cross.
>
> (*C*, 56)

Such a positive note can be detected in poems on country places. The beautiful "Arrival" describes a "village in the Welsh hills" on which the traveler stumbles "suddenly" to escape the bonds of time and experience and to realize "that there is everything to look forward to" (*LP*, 203). For quiet places are now prized: at "Sarn Rhiw" "the bay breaks / into a smile" (*EA*, 26), elsewhere "the woods were holier than a cathedral": "I need the tall woods, / so church-like" (*ERS*, 26–27).

As for his poetic art: his work was often "bitter" and as frequently disappointing:

> From meditation on a flower
> you think more flowers will be born
> of your mind? . . .

> . . . You know what flowers
> do best on.
>
> (*ERS*, 22–23)

Yet the inspirational sense is stronger: "Against the deciduousness of man there stand art, music, poetry" (*ERS*, 30) and "he defended himself with the fact that Jesus was a poet" (*ERS*, 88).

Thus Thomas's narrator responds positively to the consolations of religion, rural places, and the power of poetry. Above all, making a late but triumphant entry into his work is a celebration of married love. Four poems make the point.

"Seventieth Birthday" rejects scientific description and in its insistence on metaphor embraces poetry as the only means of apprehending love. The poem—and here we must surely equate Thomas with his narrator—is about his aging wife. It ends with love countering terror:

> You are drifting away from
> me on the whitening current of your hair.
> I lean far out from the bone's bough,
> knowing the hand I extend
> can save nothing of you but your love.
>
> (*BHN*, 94)

The terror is in a subtext that dramatizes physical decline and death's consequences; the text consoles by asserting, with a fine irony, the greater value of unchanging love.

"Strays" explores the same theme. The aging woman is in physical decline, a "scarecrow" with "loss of face." The man can offer little for physical horizons have contracted: "If I take her arm / there is nowhere to go." Yet, though the grave beckons—"under us the earth's fathoms waiting"—they are happy together:

> We are alone and strollers
> of a fine day
>
> (*LP*, 181)

The superb "strollers," combining the intimate and the carefree, summarizes all we need to know.

"He and She," included in *Experimenting with an Amen* (1986), is a poem about happiness through habitual communing that goes beyond words—"noiselessly / they conversed"—to "Thoughts mingling." "Time's wave" is overcome by the "mind's stream"; through love dangers are crossed:

There were fathoms in her,
too, and sometimes he crossed
them and landed and was not repulsed.

(*EA,* 7)

The final poem of *The Echoes Return Slow* again adopts sea symbolism in what is surely one of Thomas's most moving poems. His wife is both
in time, a

calendar
to time's passing, who is now open
at the last month,

and like the "timeless sea." And when he sees in his wife's smile the assertion that "'Over love's depths only the surface is wrinkled'" (*ERS,* 121) we
know that, for this poet, love is no longer simply a stay against the terrors
of life's sea but has appropriated that sea, and all else, to itself.

In such poems we are a long way from the bleak vision of "Impressions"
and *Ingrowing Thoughts.* Though Thomas has continued to write sequences,
they remain outnumbered by single lyrics. And even his most important
venture, the autobiographical *The Echoes Return Slow,* does not succeed in
subsuming all its sections. These four poems stand out from the body of
his work in their insistence on the positive force of human love. For in them
are no impulses toward fragmentation. In each, stanzaic form controls sentences, stressed endings exhibit confident conclusions.

In essence Thomas is saying that "love conquers all," which is a great
cliché and, as such, a reminder of a fine poet's ability to freshen even the most
hackneyed idea. This love is married, long-lasting, a function of the essential serenity of old age. Certainly it is very different from the anarchic sexuality of the earlier sequences, which it implicitly rejects. A cynic might say
that Thomas's flight from such anarchy is no more than an indication that
all passion is spent; but even the most cynical must be moved by the emotional force and persuasive artistry of these late celebrations.

Notes

1. Versions of parts of this essay were previously published as follows:
"Attempts to Evade: R. S. Thomas's 'Impressions,'" *The Anglo-Welsh Review,* 79
(1985): 70–83; "*Ingrowing Thoughts,* by R. S. Thomas," *The Anglo-Welsh Review,*
81 (1985): 112–14.

All references to Thomas's two sequences of poems about paintings are to:
Between Here and Now (London: Macmillan, 1981), 11–77.
Ingrowing Thoughts (Bridgend: Poetry Wales Press, 1985).

Other references to Thomas's poetry within this essay are abbreviated as follows:

BHN   *Between Here and Now* (London: Macmillan, 1981).
LP   *Later Poems: A Selection* (London: Macmillan, 1983).
EA   *Experimenting with an Amen* (London: Macmillan, 1986).
ERS   *The Echoes Return Slow* (London: Macmillan, 1988).
C   *Counterpoint* (Newcastle upon Tyne: Bloodaxe Books, 1990).

2. Though the reproductions are in black-and-white, several of the poems, to judge only from internal references, are responses to color, which might explain Thomas's note on the section's title page: "With acknowledgements to *Impressionist Paintings in the Louvre* by Germain Bazin (Thames and Hudson, 1958)." That Thomas paid careful attention to Bazin's commentary on the color plates is evident from echoes of the latter's text in the poems (see e.g., Bazin, 208, and the poem "Women Ironing").

Bazin's volume has a central sequence of 96 color plates followed by 261 small monochrome reproductions crammed onto 32 pages. All but one of Thomas's 33 paintings are taken from the sequence of color plates and follow its order, which is mainly chronological. The exception is Monet's "Lady with a Parasol," the first painting in Thomas's series, which Bazin includes as a tiny (4cm x 6cm) monochrome reproduction. Thomas's poem is a response to this monochrome print: his description of the lady as "brown already" does not apply to versions in color.

Two titles are changed: Cézanne's "The Bridge at Mennecy" becomes, in Thomas, "The Bridge at Maincy"; Pissarro's "Kitchen Garden. Trees in Blossom" is changed to "Kitchen Garden. Trees in Bloom." Modern works on Cézanne use Thomas's title. Both alternations effect a very slight strengthening of the lyrical.

One important correction is required to explain the puzzling poem on Pissarro's "The Louveciennes Road." Thomas's details—the season, the number of figures, the position in the road of the horse and cart—do not fit the painting. But they do fit "The Edge of the Village," which is the next Pissarro in Bazin's sequence. Future editions should correct this error.

3. Bazin, 270.

4. D. Z. Phillips, *R. S. Thomas: Poet of the Hidden God* (London, Macmillan, 1986), 158–59.

5. Gerard Manley Hopkins, "No worse, there is none."

Bibliography

Books by R. S. Thomas

POETRY

The Stones of the Field. Druid Press, 1946.
An Acre of Land. Montgomeryshire Printing Company, 1952.
The Minister. Montgomeryshire Printing Company, 1953.
Song at the Year's Turning: Poems 1942–1954. Rupert Hart-Davis, 1955.
Poetry for Supper. Rupert Hart-Davis, 1958.
Tares. Rupert Hart-Davis, 1961.
The Bread of Truth. Rupert Hart-Davis, 1963.
Pietà. Rupert Hart-Davis, 1966.
Not That He Brought Flowers. Rupert Hart-Davis, 1968.
Young and Old. Chatto and Windus, 1972.
H'm. Macmillan, 1972.
Selected Poems, 1946–1968. Hart-Davis/MacGibbon, 1973.
What Is a Welshman? Christopher Davies, 1974.
Laboratories of the Spirit. Macmillan, 1975.
The Way of It. Coelfrith Press, 1977.
Frequencies. Macmillan, 1978.
Between Here and Now. Macmillan, 1981.
Later Poems, 1972–1982. Macmillan, 1983.
Ingrowing Thoughts. Poetry Wales Press, 1985.
Destinations. Celandine Press, 1985.
Experimenting With an Amen. Macmillan, 1986.
Welsh Airs. Poetry Wales Press, 1987.
The Echoes Return Slow. Macmillan, 1988.
Counterpoint. Bloodaxe Books, 1990.

PROSE

Words and the Poet. W. D. Thomas Memorial Lecture. University of
  Wales Press, 1964.
Abercuawg. Y ddarlith lenyddol flynyddol, Eisteddfod Genedlaethol
  Cymru Aberteifi a'r Cylch, Gwasg Gomer, 1976—National
  Eisteddfod Annual Literary Lecture, Cardigan. Gomer Press, 1976.
R. S. Thomas: Selected Prose. Edited by Sandra Anstey. Poetry Wales
  Press, 1983.

EDITIONS

The Batsford Book of Country Verse. Batsford, 1961.
The Penguin Book of Religious Verse. Penguin, 1963.
Edward Thomas: Selected Poems. Faber & Faber, 1964.
A Choice of George Herbert's Verse. Faber & Faber, 1967.
A Choice of Wordsworth's Verse. Faber & Faber, 1971.

Books on Thomas

Anstey, Sandra, ed., *Critical Writings on R. S. Thomas*. Poetry Wales Press,
  1982.
Merchant, W. Moelwyn. *R. S. Thomas*. University of Wales Press, 1979;
  reprinted by The University of Arkansas Press, 1990.
Phillips, D. Z. *R. S. Thomas: Poet of the Hidden God*. Macmillan, 1986.
Volk, Sabine. *Grenzpfähle der Wirklichkeit: Approaches to the Poetry of R. S.
  Thomas*. Verlag Peter Lang, 1985.
Ward, J. P. *The Poetry of R. S. Thomas*. Poetry Wales Press, 1987.

Special Issues (Journals) devoted to Thomas

Stephens, Meic, ed., *Poetry Wales*. Spring 1972.
Ward, J. P, ed., *Poetry Wales*. Spring 1979.

Selected Essays on Thomas

* indicates an essay included in this collection

Ackerman, John. "Man and Nature in the Poetry of R. S. Thomas." *Poetry Wales* VII:4 (1972): 15–26.

Adkins, Joan F. "R. S. Thomas and 'A Little Point.'" *The Little Review* 13/14 (1980): 15–19.

Allchin, A. M. "The Poetry of R. S. Thomas: An Introduction." *Theology* LXXIII:605 (1970): 488–95.

Allchin, A. M. "Emerging: A Look at Some of R. S. Thomas' More Recent Poems." *Theology* LXXXI:683 (1978): 352–61.

Bedient, Calvin. "On R. S. Thomas." *Critical Quarterly* XIV:3 (1972): 253–68.

Bianchi, Tony. "R. S. Thomas and His Readers," in Tony Curtis, ed., *Wales: The Imagined Nation: Studies in Cultural and National Identity* (Poetry Wales Press, 1988): 71–95.

Brown, Tony. "Language, Poetry and Silence: Some Themes in the Poetry of R. S. Thomas," in William Tydeman, *The Welsh Connection* (Gomer Press, 1986): 159–85.

* Brown, Tony. "'On the Screen of Eternity': Some Aspects of R. S. Thomas's Prose." *The Powys Review* 6:1 (1987–88): 5–15.

Castay, Marie-Thérèse. "R. S. Thomas." *Apex* 3 (1978): 8–27.

Conran, Anthony. "R. S. Thomas as a Mystical Poet." *Poetry Wales* XIV:4 (1979): 11–25.

Conran, Anthony. "Aspects of R. S. Thomas," in *The Cost of Strangeness: Essays on the English Poets of Wales* (Gomer Press, 1982): 220–62.

* Davie, Donald. "R. S. Thomas's Poetry of the Church of Wales." *Religion & Literature* 19:2 (Summer 1987): 35–47.

Davies, James A. "Participating Readers: Three Poems by R. S. Thomas." *Poetry Wales* 18 (1983): 72–83.

Davies, James A. "Attempts to Evade: R. S. Thomas's 'Impressions.' " *The Anglo-Welsh Review* 79 (1985): 70–83.

Davies, Walford. "R. S. Thomas: The Poem's Harsher Condition." *The New Welsh Review* 3 (1990): 15–26.

* Davis, William V. "R. S. Thomas: Poet-Priest of the Apocalyptic Mode." *South Central Review* 4:4 (Winter 1987): 92–106.

* Deane, Patrick. "The Unmanageable Bone: Language in R. S. Thomas's Poetry." *Renascence* VLII:4 (Summer 1990): 213–36.

Dyson, A. E. "The Poetry of R. S. Thomas." *Critical Quarterly* XX:2 (1978): 5–31.

Dyson, A. E. *Yeats, Eliot and R. S. Thomas: Riding the Echo.* (Macmillan, 1981): 285–326.

★ Gitzen, Julian. "R. S. Thomas and the Vanishing God of Form and Number." *Contemporary Poetry: A Journal of Criticism* 5:2 (1983): 1–16.

Gordon, I. R. F. "'The Adult Geometry of the Mind': The Recent Poetry of R. S. Thomas." *The Little Review* 13/14 (1980): 12–14.

Gruffydd, Peter. "The Poetry of R. S. Thomas." *Poetry Wales,* II:1(1966): 13–17.

★ Herman, Vimala. "Negativity and Language in the Religious Poetry of R. S. Thomas." *ELH* 45:4 (Winter 1978): 710–31.

★ Humfrey, Belinda. "The Gap in the Hedge: R. S. Thomas's Emblem Poetry." *The Anglo-Welsh Review* XXVI:58 (1977): 49–57.

Jenkins, Randal. "R. S. Thomas: Occasional Prose." *Poetry Wales* VII:4 (1972): 93–108.

Keith, W. J. "R. S. Thomas," in *Dictionary of Literary Biography.* Vol. 27 (Gale Research, 1984): 346–56.

Knapp, J. F. "The Poetry of R. S. Thomas." *Twentieth Century Literature* 17 (1971): 1–9.

Lewis, H. D. "The Later Poetry of R. S. Thomas." *Poetry Wales* XIV:4 (1979) 26–30.

Mathias, Roland. "Philosophy and Religion in the Poetry of R. S. Thomas." *Poetry Wales* VII:4 (1972): 27–45.

Matthews, Laurella. "The Poetry of R. S. Thomas." *Province* XI:4 (1960): 132–40.

Meir, Colin. *British Poetry since 1970: A Critical Survey,* ed. Peter Jones and Michael Schmidt (Carcanet, 1980): 1–13.

Merchant, W. Moelwyn. "R. S. Thomas." *Critical Quarterly* II:4 (1960): 341–51.

Mole, John. "The Recent Poetry of R. S. Thomas." *New Poetry* 43 (1978): 6–11.

Morris, Brian. "Mr. Thomas's Present Concerns." *Poetry Wales* XIV:4 (1979): 31–42.

★ Morris, Brian. "The Topography of R. S. Thomas." *The Little Review* 13/14 (1980): 5–11.

Morris, John S. "'The Hail of Love'—Self-Recognition in R. S. Thomas." *The Little Review* 13/14 (1980): 30–36.

* Nisbet, Robert. "R. S. Thomas: The Landscape of Near-Despair."
Planet 35 (1976): 26–30.

Ormond, John. "R. S. Thomas: Priest and Poet." *Poetry Wales* VII:4
(1972): 42–57.

Peach, Linden. "R. S. Thomas: Dylan's Successor?" in *The Prose
Writings of Dylan Thomas* (Barnes and Noble, 1988): 106–29.

Price, Cecil. "The Poetry of R. S. Thomas." *The Welsh Anvil* IV
(1952): 82–86.

Savill, H. J. "The Iago Pytherch Poems of R. S. Thomas." *The Anglo-
Welsh Review* XX:45 (1971): 143–54.

Shivpuri, Jagdish. "Two Contemporary Poets in English: Jon Silkin and
R. S. Thomas." *Siddha* 10 (1975): 1–25.

Thomas, Dafydd Elis. "The Image of Wales in R. S. Thomas's Poetry."
Poetry Wales, VII:4 (1972): 59–66.

Thomas, R. George. "The Poetry of R. S. Thomas." *A Review of
English Literature* III:4 (1962): 85–89.

Thomas, R. George. *Andrew Young and R. S. Thomas.* (Longman,
1964): 27–41.

* Thomas, R. George. *"Humanus Sum:* A Second Look at R. S.
Thomas." *The Anglo-Welsh Review* XVIII:42 (1970): 55–62.

* Vicary, J. D. *"Via Negativa:* Absence and Presence in the Recent Poetry
of R. S. Thomas." *Critical Quarterly* 27:3 (Autumn 1985): 41–51.

Waterman, Andrew. "Closing the Shutters: *Frequencies* and the Poetry
of R. S. Thomas." *Poetry Wales* XIV:4 (1979): 90–103.